2

Alan McSeveny Rachel McSeveny Diane McSeveny-Foster

Pearson Australia
(a division of Pearson Australia Group Pty Ltd)
459–471 Church St, Level 1, Building B, Richmond, Victoria, 3121
PO Box 23360, Melbourne, Victoria 8012
www.pearson.com.au

First published 2024 by Pearson Australia
2028 2027 2026 2025
10 9 8 7 6 5 4 3 2 1

Publishers: Sophie Matta and Kerry Nagle
Project Manager: Michelle Thomas
Production Editor: Laura Rentsch
Development Editor: Rachel Elliott
Designer: Anne Donald
Proofreader: Laura Rentsch
Rights & Permissions Editor: Alice McBroom
Cover Design: Jennifer Johnston
Cover Art: Michael Barter
Illustrator: Michael Barter
Desktop Operator: Jit-Pin Chong, David Doyle
Printed in Malaysia by Vivar

ISBN 978 0 6557 0876 6
Pearson Australia Group Pty Ltd ABN 40 004 245 943

Attributions
We would like to thank the following for permission to reproduce copyright material.

Acknowledgement of Country
Pearson respects and honours Aboriginal and Torres Strait Islander Elders past, present and future. We acknowledge the stories, traditions and living cultures of the Traditional Custodians of the lands on which our company is located and where we conduct our business. Pearson is committed to honouring Australian Aboriginal and Torres Strait Islander peoples' unique cultural and spiritual relationships to the land, waters and seas and their rich contribution to society.

Aboriginal and Torres Strait Islander peoples are advised that this text may contain images, voices and names of deceased persons.

What is Australian Signpost Maths?

Australian Signpost Maths is a mathematics program providing direction and support for teaching and learning. The series covers the content and skills presented in the Australian Curriculum (v9) Mathematics F–6.

A Student Book and an online Teacher Resource are provided for Foundation.

For Years 1 to 6, a Student Book, an online Teacher Resource and a Mentals Book are provided for each year level. The online Teacher Resources provide a wealth of support for teachers.

The content has been carefully sequenced within each year level and across the F–6 series to take into account students' expected mathematical development. However, from the rich and varied material provided, teachers can develop individual learning programs to meet the needs of each student.

The Student Books are designed to support explicit teaching methods. Many group activities are provided in Activity, Investigation and Fun spots within the Student Books and the online Teacher Resource.

To maximise the benefits of the program, the Student Book, the online Teacher Resource and the Mentals Book should be used together.

Student Books

Mentals Books

Teacher Resource

Structure of Australian Signpost Maths

In the F–2 books, the worksheet pages cover all three elements: Number sense and algebra, Measurement and geometry, and Statistics and probability. These are presented in a recommended order. Each unit of 4 pages usually begins with Number or Algebra. The Contents cross-reference allows teachers to quickly find the pages where each concept has been covered.

Within the program, explicit teaching, critical and creative thinking, language development and identification and treatment of weaknesses are given high priority.

Identification and addressing areas of need

Five progress tests are designed to identify each student's areas of need, and the follow-up program after each of the tests is designed to address these needs. A reference to the relevant worksheet page is given for each test question. A remediation record page is used to track the student's progress.

These testing resources can be found in the online Teacher Resource.

Parallel progress retests are provided for further testing after remediation has taken place. See pages 142 and 143 of this book for more information.

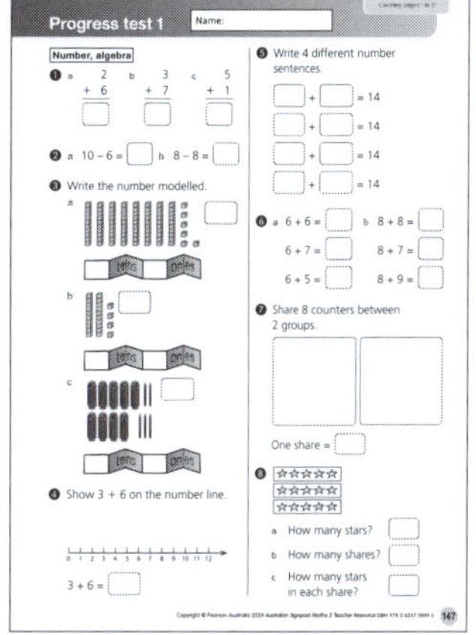

Progress test 1 Name:

Number, algebra

1 a 2 + 6 = ☐ b 3 + 7 = ☐ c 5 + 1 = ☐

2 a 10 − 6 = ☐ b 8 − 8 = ☐

3 Write the number modelled.
a ☐ tens ☐ ones
b ☐ tens ☐ ones
c ☐ tens ☐ ones

4 Show 3 + 6 on the number line.
3 + 6 = ☐

5 Write 4 different number sentences.
☐ + ☐ = 14
☐ + ☐ = 14
☐ + ☐ = 14
☐ + ☐ = 14

6 a 6 + 6 = ☐ 6 + 7 = ☐ 6 + 5 = ☐
b 8 + 8 = ☐ 8 + 7 = ☐ 8 + 9 = ☐

7 Share 8 counters between 2 groups.
One share = ☐

8
a How many stars? ☐
b How many shares? ☐
c How many stars in each share? ☐

147

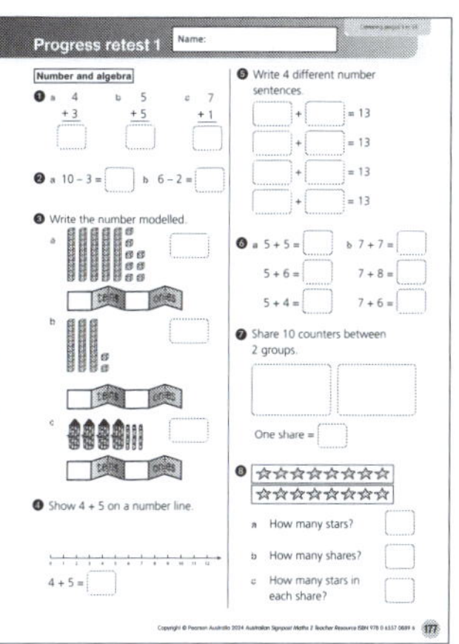

Progress retest 1 Name:

Number and algebra

1 a 4 + 3 = ☐ b 5 + 5 = ☐ c 7 + 1 = ☐

2 a 10 − 3 = ☐ b 6 − 2 = ☐

3 Write the number modelled.
a ☐ tens ☐ ones
b ☐ tens ☐ ones
c ☐ tens ☐ ones

4 Show 4 + 5 on a number line.
4 + 5 = ☐

5 Write 4 different number sentences.
☐ + ☐ = 13
☐ + ☐ = 13
☐ + ☐ = 13
☐ + ☐ = 13

6 a 5 + 5 = ☐ 5 + 6 = ☐ 5 + 4 = ☐
b 7 + 7 = ☐ 7 + 8 = ☐ 7 + 6 = ☐

7 Share 10 counters between 2 groups.
One share = ☐

8
a How many stars? ☐
b How many shares? ☐
c How many stars in each share? ☐

177

Special features of Australian Signpost Maths

- **The traffic light icons**

  These are found on the top right of each worksheet page in the Student Books. They allow students to assess their own progress and give feedback to the teacher.

  - **Green:** I found this work easy.
  - **Orange:** I found some work on the page difficult.
  - **Red:** I don't understand the work on this page.

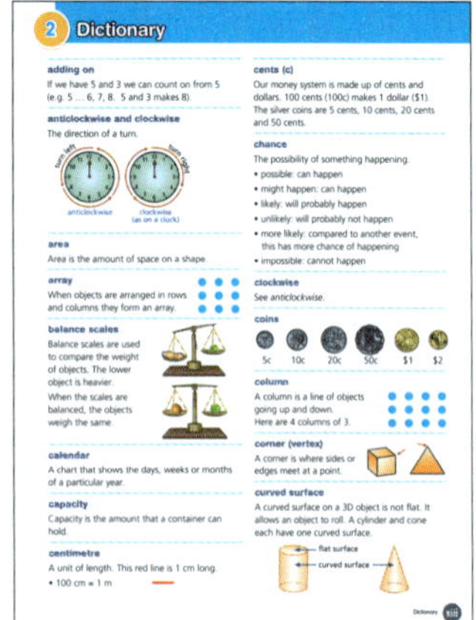

2 Dictionary

- **Dictionary**

  Terms used in the Student Book and terms that should be understood at this level are recorded here to provide a reference for students and teachers. This is found on pages xiii–xviii of this book.

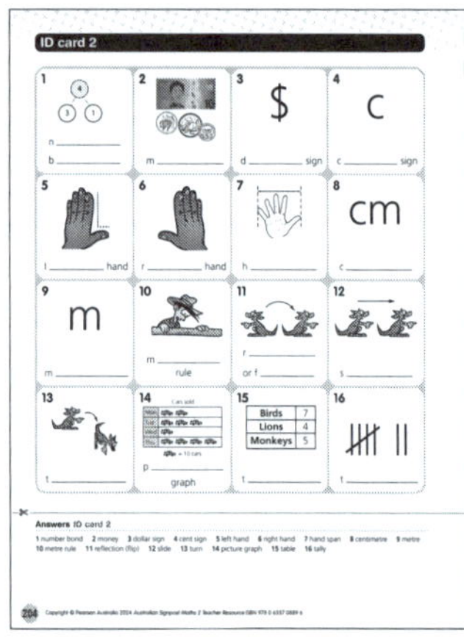

ID card 2

- **ID cards (Years 1 to 6)**

  These cards review the language of Mathematics by asking students to identify common terms, shapes and symbols. They are designed to be reused and are found in the online Teacher Resource and in the front of the Mentals Books.

- **Progress tests**

  These allow the teacher to identify each student's strengths and needs. Cross-references for each question direct teachers and students to the pages where that work is introduced. Tables are provided to record the follow-up that takes place and parallel tests are provided for retesting. These tests can be found in the online Teacher Resource.

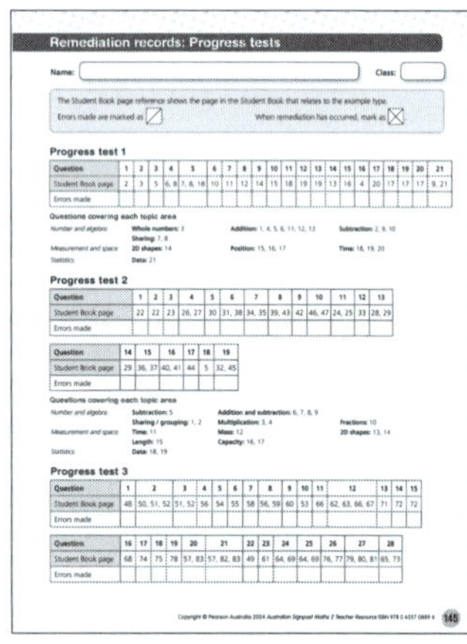

Remediation records: Progress tests

- **Year 2 Consolidation booklet**

  This 32 page booklet is found in the online Teacher Resource. It is designed to reinforce work completed in class and provides practice of important skills and addition and subtraction facts. The booklet can be used when there is limited supervision or when a student finishes classwork early.

- **Answers**

  These are supplied in the online Teacher Resource.

- **Blackline masters (BLM)**

  References are made to the blackline masters in the teaching suggestions provided for each student work page.

- **Differentiation**

  Each student work page has a Teacher Resource page to support it. Cross-references direct the teacher to pages where the concept is introduced and developed. These references may be from the Student Book for the previous year, the current year or the next year.

  The Teacher Resource support pages provide additional learning activities for students who need remediation or extension activities. The blackline masters provide activities to support students of various learning abilities.

- **Cartoons**

  Cartoons are used to motivate and instruct.

Australian Signpost Maths icons

Signpost icons are used throughout the book as cues to the essential nature of exercises and activities, and as a guide to ways of engaging with them. These icons often indicate alternative or more concrete approaches to dealing with concepts.

This icon highlights **important rules and concepts** occurring throughout the book. It often appears with worked examples.

Investigations allow students to **explore and discover** maths concepts.

Activities provide **applications and enrichment**. These activities usually involve the use of concrete materials and partner or group work.

These enjoyable activities are used to **motivate and involve** students in mathematical pursuits. They usually involve games and puzzles.

Structure of the Australian Curriculum, F–6 (v9)

Numeracy elements

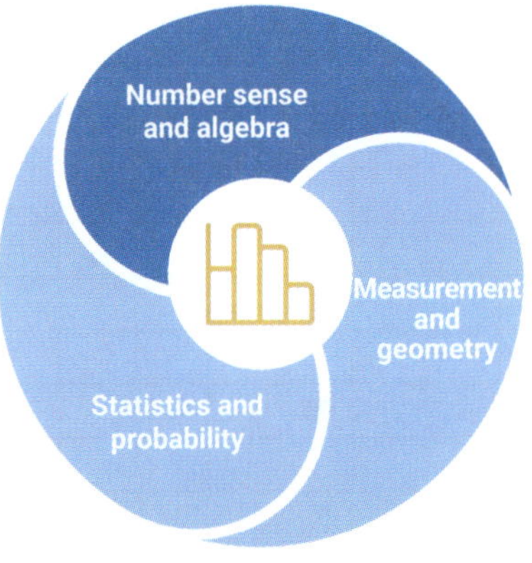

Curriculum content is organised under 6 interrelated strands: Number, Algebra, Measurement, Space, Statistics and Probability.

Sub-elements for Number sense and algebra

- Number and place value
- Counting processes
- Additive strategies
- Multiplicative strategies
- Interpreting fractions
- Number patterns and algebraic thinking
- Understanding money

Sub-elements for Measurement and geometry

- Understanding units of measurement
- Understanding geometric properties
- Positioning and locating
- Measuring time

Sub-elements for Statistics and probability

- Understanding chance
- Interpreting and representing data

The Curriculum strives to develop in students proficiency in Mathematics, highlighting Understanding, Fluency, Reasoning and Problem solving.

Mathematics content of the Australian Curriculum

- It is important that you download the GENERAL CAPABILITIES document from 'Downloads' in the top navigation bar of the website homepage. It contains the tables that list the progression level expectations for each year, F to 10. It also provides the content of all progression levels.
- The LEARNING AREAS download gives a summary of Content descriptions and Elaborations. CROSS-CURRICULUM PRIORITIES can also be found there.

Contents and curriculum overview

KEY

■ (blue)	Number / algebra
■ (green)	Measurement / space
■ (red)	Statistics / probability

Page	Unit	Title	Strand	Number / algebra	Measurement / space	Statistics / probability	Content area	Numbers to 1000 / money	Addition / subtraction	Multiplication / division / fractions	Patterns / tables facts	2D shapes / 3D objects	Position / directions / turns	Length / area / mass	Capacity / volume	Time	Data displays
1	Thinking skills		Critical and creative thinking is covered throughout.														
2	1A	Combinations to 10		■					●								
3	1B	Subtraction to 10		■					●								
4	1C	Position words			■								●				
5	1D	Modelling numbers		■				●									
6	2A	Addition		■					●								
7	2B	Addition to 20		■					●								
8	2C	Addition to 20		■					●								
9	2D	Thinking about graphs				■											●
10	3A	Doubling and near doubling		■						●							
11	3B	Sharing		■						●							
12	3C	Sharing		■						●							
13	3D	2D shapes			■							●					
14	4A	Subtraction		■					●								
15	4B	Subtraction to 20		■					●								
16	4C	Ordinal numbers and calendars			■											●	
17	4D	The calendar			■											●	
18	5A	Addition to 20		■					●								
19	5B	Addition by looking for tens		■					●								
20	5C	Directions			■								●				
21	5D	Using graphs				■											●
Progress test 1: Administer test (see Teacher Resource) then address weaknesses.																	
22	6A	Sharing and grouping		■						●							
23	6B	Groups and rows		■						●							
24	6C	Clocks			■											●	
25	6D	Analog time			■											●	
26	7A	Groups and rows		■						●							
27	7B	Multiplication		■						●							
28	7C	Features of 2D shapes			■							●					
29	7D	Drawing 2D shapes			■							●					

KEY

Key	Strand
■ (blue)	Number / algebra
■ (green)	Measurement / space
■ (orange)	Statistics / probability

Page	Unit	Title	Strand			Content area									
			Number / algebra	Measurement / space	Statistics / probability	Numbers to 1000 / money	Addition / subtraction	Multiplication / division / fractions	Patterns / tables facts	2D shapes / 3D objects	Position / directions / turns	Length / area / mass	Capacity / volume	Time	Data displays
30	8A	Subtraction to 20	■				●								
31	8B	Differences	■				●								
32	8C	Lists, graphs and tables			■										●
33	8D	Comparing masses		■								●			
34	9A	Linking addition and subtraction	■				●								
35	9B	Linking addition and subtraction	■				●								
36	9C	Informal units of length		■								●			
37	9D	Informal units of length		■								●			
38	10A	Addition and subtraction facts	■				●		●						
39	10B	Adding 10s	■				●								
40	10C	Capacity		■									●		
41	10D	Ordering capacities		■									●		
42	11A	How many more?	■				●								
43	11B	Adding and subtracting 10s	■				●								
44	11C	Capacity		■									●		
45	11D	Using tally marks			■										●
46	12A	Half of a group	■					●							
47	12B	Halves	■					●							

Progress test 2: Administer test (see Teacher Resource) then address weaknesses.

Page	Unit	Title	Number / algebra	Measurement / space	Statistics / probability	Numbers to 1000 / money	Addition / subtraction	Multiplication / division / fractions	Patterns / tables facts	2D shapes / 3D objects	Position / directions / turns	Length / area / mass	Capacity / volume	Time	Data displays
48	12C	Problem solving	■					●							
49	12D	Estimating time passed		■										●	
50	13A	Multiplication sign	■					●							
51	13B	Equal groups	■					●							
52	13C	Multiplication	■					●							
53	13D	Patterns	■						●						
54	14A	Using arrays	■					●							
55	14B	Using rows	■					●							
56	14C	Arrays	■					●							
57	14D	Money	■			●									
58	15A	Using skip counting	■					●							
59	15B	Using columns to multiply	■					●							
60	15C	x 2, x 10	■					●	●						
61	15D	Balance scales		■								●			
62	16A	Numbers to 150	■			●									
63	16B	Numbers to 1000	■			●									
64	16C	Informal units of length		■								●			
65	16D	Telling the story from data			■										●

KEY

Colour	Strand
■ (blue)	Number / algebra
■ (green)	Measurement / space
■ (orange)	Statistics / probability

Page	Unit	Title	Strand: Number / algebra	Strand: Measurement / space	Strand: Statistics / probability	Content area: Numbers to 1000 / money	Content area: Addition / subtraction	Content area: Multiplication / division / fractions	Content area: Patterns / tables facts	Content area: 2D shapes / 3D objects	Content area: Position / directions / turns	Content area: Length / area / mass	Content area: Capacity / volume	Content area: Time	Content area: Data displays
66	17A	Numbers to 1000	■			●									
67	17B	Numbers to 1000	■			●									
68	17C	Inverse operations	■				●								
69	17D	Informal units of length		■								●			
70	18A	Numbers to 1000	■			●									
71	18B	Numbers to 1000	■			●									
72	18C	Number patterns	■						●						
73	18D	Gathering data			■										●
74	19A	Number lines	■				●	●							
75	19B	Related problems	■				●								
76	19C	Comparing areas		■								●			
77	19D	Area		■								●			
78	20A	Australian money	■			●									
79	20B	Symmetry		■						●					
80	20C	Symmetry		■						●					
81	20D	Symmetry in our world		■						●					
82	21A	Value of coins	■			●	●								
83	21B	Value of coins	■			●	●								

Progress test 3: Administer test (see Teacher Resource) then address weaknesses.

Page	Unit	Title	Strand: Number / algebra	Strand: Measurement / space	Strand: Statistics / probability	Content area: Numbers to 1000 / money	Content area: Addition / subtraction	Content area: Multiplication / division / fractions	Content area: Patterns / tables facts	Content area: 2D shapes / 3D objects	Content area: Position / directions / turns	Content area: Length / area / mass	Content area: Capacity / volume	Content area: Time	Content area: Data displays
84	21C	Numbers	■			●									
85	21D	Area using informal units		■								●			
86	22A	Amounts to $2	■			●	●								
87	22B	Using groups	■					●							
88	22C	Prisms and cylinders		■						●					
89	22D	3D objects		■						●					
90	23A	Building to the next 10	■				●								
91	23B	Building to the next 10	■				●								
92	23C	Angles		■						●					
93	23D	Using column graphs			■										●
94	24A	Split strategy (addition)	■				●								
95	24B	Split strategy (addition)	■				●								
96	24C	Ordering masses		■								●			
97	24D	Balance scales		■								●			
98	25A	Building to the next 10	■				●								
99	25B	Repeated subtraction	■					●							
100	25C	Turning a shape		■							●				
101	25D	Turning shapes		■							●				

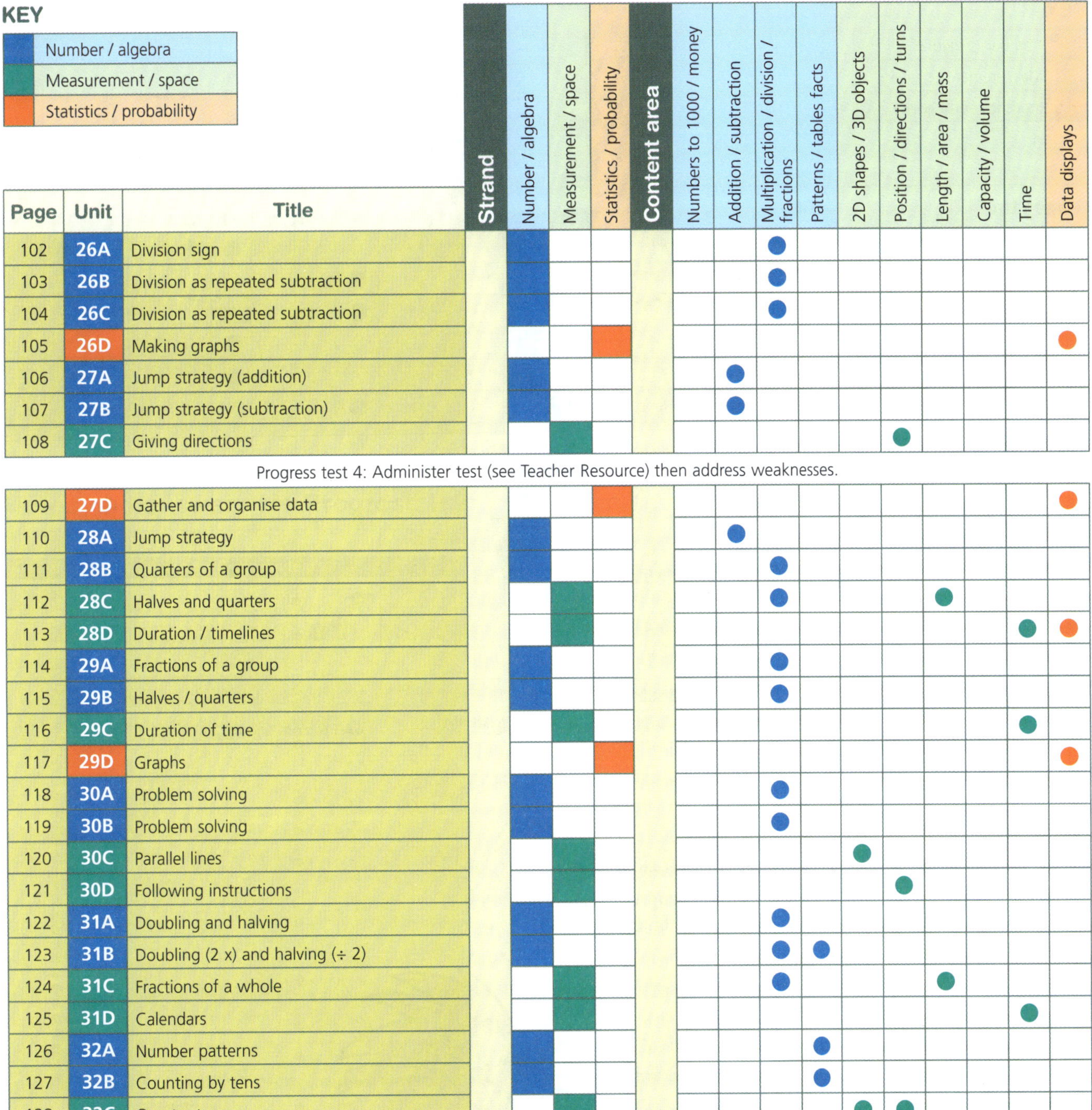

KEY

- Number / algebra
- Measurement / space
- Statistics / probability

Page	Unit	Title	Strand: Number / algebra	Strand: Measurement / space	Strand: Statistics / probability	Numbers to 1000 / money	Addition / subtraction	Multiplication / division / fractions	Patterns / tables facts	2D shapes / 3D objects	Position / directions / turns	Length / area / mass	Capacity / volume	Time	Data displays
102	26A	Division sign	■					●							
103	26B	Division as repeated subtraction	■					●							
104	26C	Division as repeated subtraction	■					●							
105	26D	Making graphs			■										●
106	27A	Jump strategy (addition)	■				●								
107	27B	Jump strategy (subtraction)	■				●								
108	27C	Giving directions		■							●				

Progress test 4: Administer test (see Teacher Resource) then address weaknesses.

Page	Unit	Title	Strand: Number / algebra	Strand: Measurement / space	Strand: Statistics / probability	Numbers to 1000 / money	Addition / subtraction	Multiplication / division / fractions	Patterns / tables facts	2D shapes / 3D objects	Position / directions / turns	Length / area / mass	Capacity / volume	Time	Data displays
109	27D	Gather and organise data			■										●
110	28A	Jump strategy	■				●								
111	28B	Quarters of a group	■					●							
112	28C	Halves and quarters		■				●				●			
113	28D	Duration / timelines		■										●	●
114	29A	Fractions of a group	■					●							
115	29B	Halves / quarters	■					●							
116	29C	Duration of time		■										●	
117	29D	Graphs			■										●
118	30A	Problem solving	■					●							
119	30B	Problem solving	■					●							
120	30C	Parallel lines		■						●					
121	30D	Following instructions		■							●				
122	31A	Doubling and halving	■					●							
123	31B	Doubling (2 x) and halving (÷ 2)	■					●	●						
124	31C	Fractions of a whole		■				●				●			
125	31D	Calendars		■										●	
126	32A	Number patterns	■						●						
127	32B	Counting by tens	■						●						
128	32C	Quarter turns		■						●	●				

Progress test 5: Administer test (see Teacher Resource) then address weaknesses.

KEY

Colour	Strand
■ (blue)	Number / algebra
■ (green)	Measurement / space
■ (orange)	Statistics / probability

Page	Unit	Title	Strand: Number / algebra	Strand: Measurement / space	Strand: Statistics / probability	Content area: Numbers to 1000 / money	Content area: Addition / subtraction	Content area: Multiplication / division / fractions	Content area: Patterns / tables facts	Content area: 2D shapes / 3D objects	Content area: Position / directions / turns	Content area: Length / area / mass	Content area: Capacity / volume	Content area: Time	Content area: Data displays
129	32D	Half and quarter turns		■						●	●			●	
130	33A	Using a strategy	■				●								
131	33B	Choosing a strategy	■				●								
132	33C	Combine and separate shapes		■						●					
133	33D	3D objects		■						●					
134	34A	How many more?	■				●								
135	34B	Inverse strategy, subtraction	■				●								
136	34C	Money	■			●									
137	34D	Comparing objects		■								●	●		
138	35A	Giving directions		■							●				
139	35B	More shapes (extension)		■						●					
140	35C	Problem solving with addition	■				●								
141	35D	Problem solving with groups	■					●							
142		Identifying and addressing areas of need													
144		**1** Addition facts to 20	**2** Subtraction facts to 10					**3** Subtraction facts to 20							
147		**4** Skip counting / number chart	**5** Know your addition facts					**6A** Problem solving							
150		**6B** Problem solving													

Contents cross-reference

Number and algebra

Measurement and space

Statistics and probability

adding on

If we have 5 and 3 we can count on from 5 (e.g. 5 … 6, 7, 8). 5 and 3 makes 8.

angle

The turn between two lines that meet at a corner.

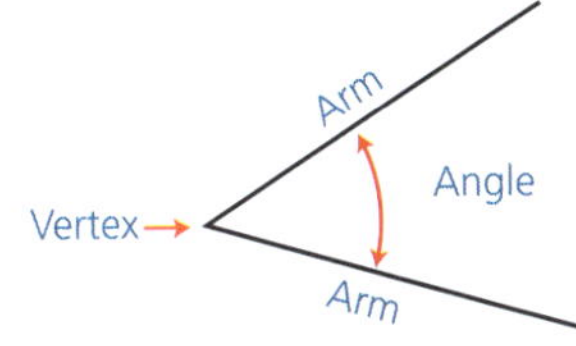

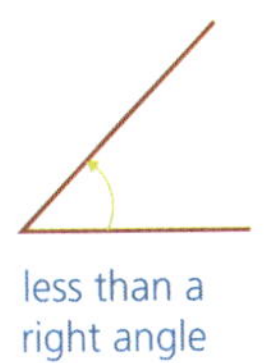
less than a right angle

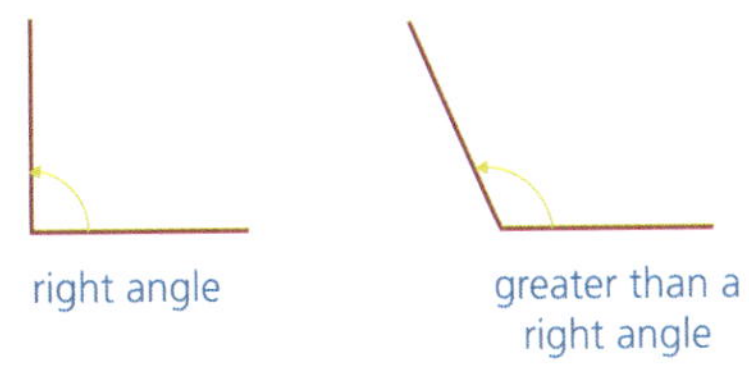
right angle

greater than a right angle

anticlockwise and clockwise

The direction of a turn.

anticlockwise

clockwise (as on a clock)

area

Area is the amount of space on a shape.

array

When objects are arranged in rows and columns they form an array.

balance scales

Balance scales are used to compare the weight of objects. The lower object is heavier.

When the scales are balanced, the objects weigh the same.

calendar

A chart that shows the days, weeks and months of a particular year.

capacity

Capacity is the amount that a container can hold.

cents (c)

Our money system is made up of cents and dollars. 100 cents (100c) makes 1 dollar ($1).

clockwise

See *anticlockwise*.

coins

5c

10c

20c

50c

$1

$2

column

A column is a line of objects going up and down.
Here are 4 columns of 3.

column graph

Groups are compared using the lengths of columns or bars. The graph can be vertical or horizontal.

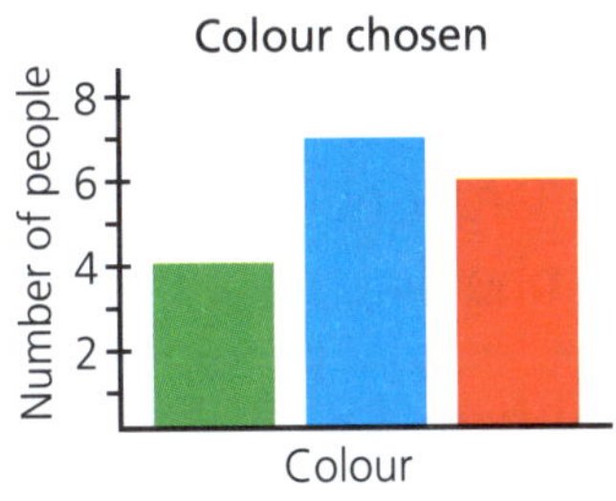

corner (vertex)

A corner is where sides or edges meet at a point.

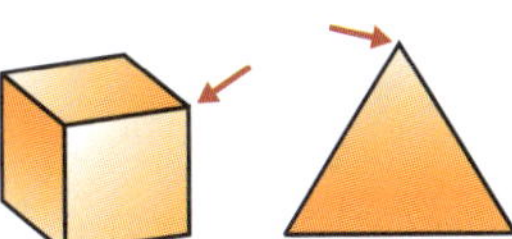

curved surface

A curved surface on a 3D object is not flat. It allows an object to roll. A cylinder and cone each have one curved surface.

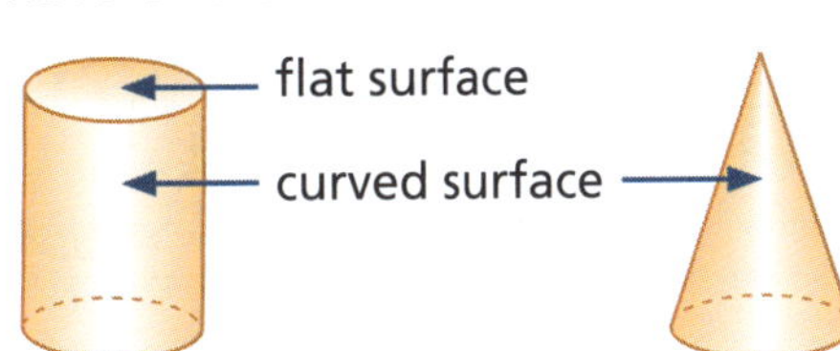

data display

A data display shows categories of objects and allows us to compare them.

Picture graph:

Table:

Dogs	Cats
4	2

date

The date shows the day, the month and the year. For example, 30.5.23 means the 30th day on the 5th month (May) in the year 2023.

difference

How many more?

The difference between 16 and 13 is 3.

For smaller numbers, line up each group in a row to find the difference.

For larger numbers, place the numbers on a number line to find the difference.

dollars ($)

Our money system is made up of cents and dollars.

100 cents (100c) makes 1 dollar ($1).

The gold coins are $1 (1 dollar) and $2 (2 dollars).

double

Double means the same thing twice.
Double 4 means 4 + 4 = 8. That is 2 × 4 = 8.

edge

Two faces of a 3D object meet at an edge.

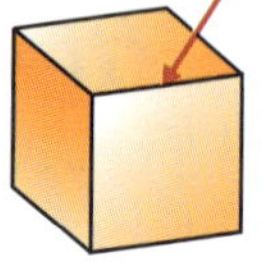

eighth of a whole or collection

One of eight equal parts.

One-eighth of the rectangle is coloured.

One-eighth of this collection is coloured.

equal groups

Groups that have the same number of members.

equals sign (=)

The equals sign means "makes", "is equal to" or "is the same as".

For example, 2 + 3 = 4 + 1.

estimate

A good guess.

face

A flat surface that has straight sides (e.g. the side of a box).

flat surface

A cylinder has 2 flat surfaces, one on both ends, and one curved surface.

A cube has 6 flat surfaces.

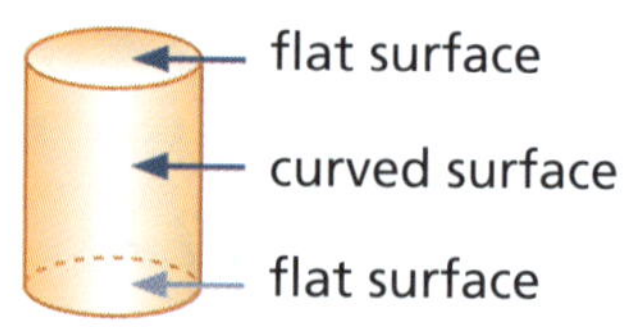

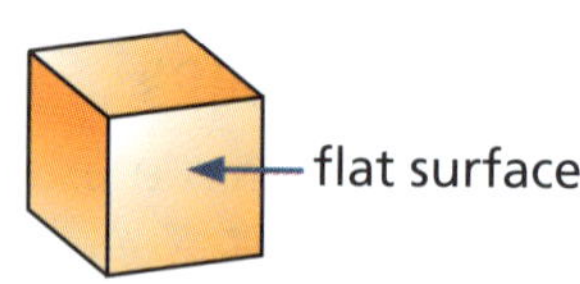

friends of ten

Numbers that add together to make 10.
The friends of 10 are 1 and 9, 2 and 8, 3 and 7, 4 and 6, 5 and 5, 6 and 4, 7 and 3, 8 and 2, 9 and 1.

graph

See *data display*.

half of a whole or collection

One of two equal parts.

One-half of the rectangle is coloured.

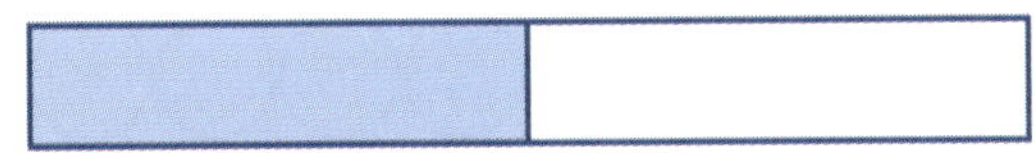

One-half of the collection is coloured.

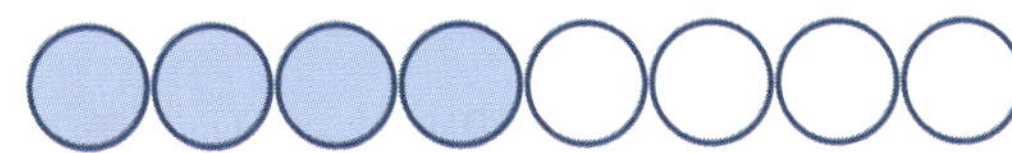

Half of 8 is 4. Another way to say this is 8 divided by 2 is 4. That is 8 ÷ 2 = 4.

halfway point

The halfway point is the middle position.

hefting

To compare masses by lifting them with your hands.

hour

Hours are used to measure the length of time. 60 minutes is the same as one hour.

There are 24 hours in one day.

left and right

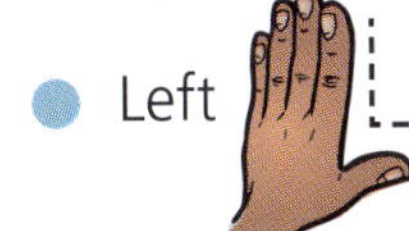

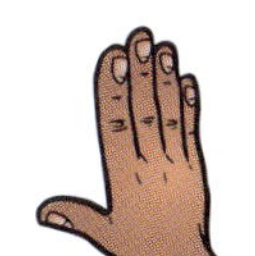

multiplication sign (×)

The multiplication sign is used to combine equal groups. × means "groups of".

3 groups of 5, or 3 × 5, or 3 fives.

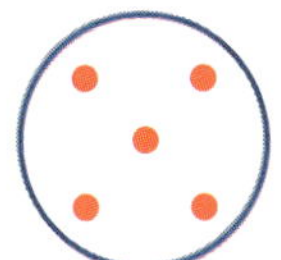

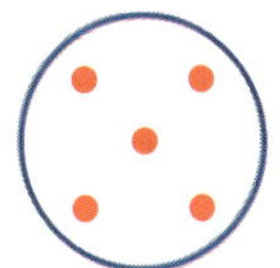

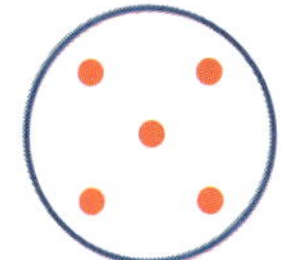

notes

$5

$10

$20

$50

$100

number bonds

These show how a number can be broken up into parts (e.g. the top number, 4, can be broken up into 3 and 1).

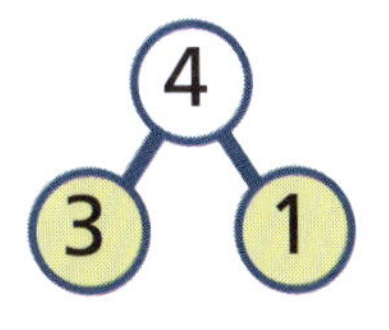

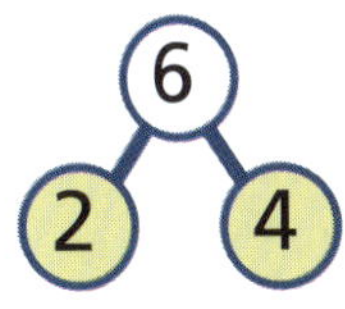

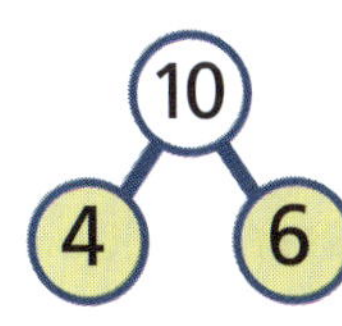

number line

A line that shows numbers in order. Number lines can be used for many things (e.g. counting, adding, subtracting and multiplying).

number sentence

A number sentence can use words, numerals and symbols (e.g. 4 and 6 makes 10. This can be written as 4 + 6 = 10).

numeral

A numeral is a symbol that stands for a number such as 7, 18, 92, 120 or vii.

odd and even numbers

Odd numbers end in 1, 3, 5, 7 or 9 (e.g. 49).

Even numbers end in 2, 4, 6, 8 or 0 (e.g. 32).

ordinal numbers

Ordinal numbers describe the order or position of something.

1st, 2nd, 3rd, 4th, 5th …

parallel lines

Straight lines that do not meet. A parallelogram has opposite sides parallel.

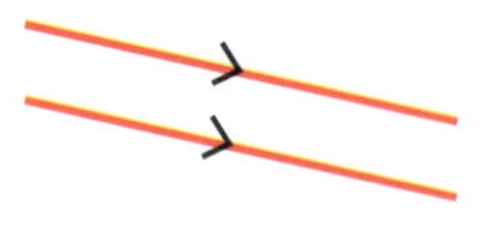

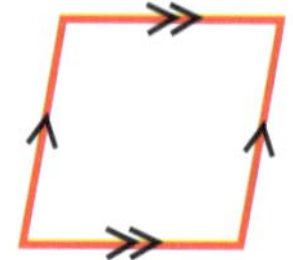

pattern

A pattern is a group of numbers, objects, shapes, colours, sounds or actions that are repeated over and over again.

place value

The position of each digit of a numeral holds a different value.

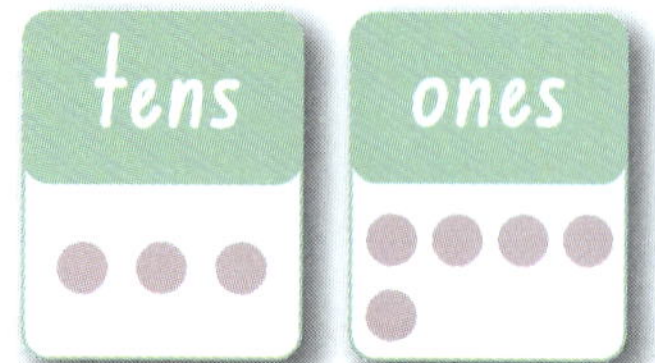

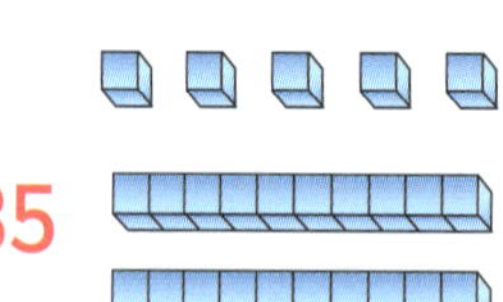

place-value blocks

These are used to represent numbers.

ones block 

tens block 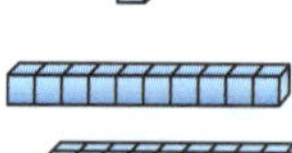

hundreds block 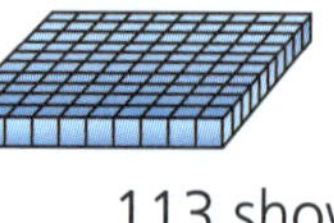

42 shown as

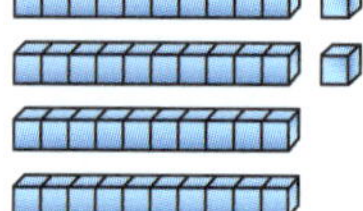

113 shown as

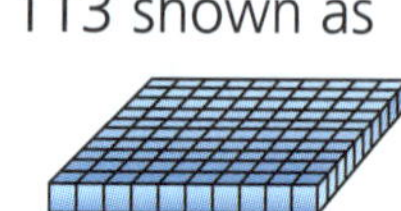

quarter of a whole or collection

One of four equal parts.

One-quarter of the rectangle is coloured.

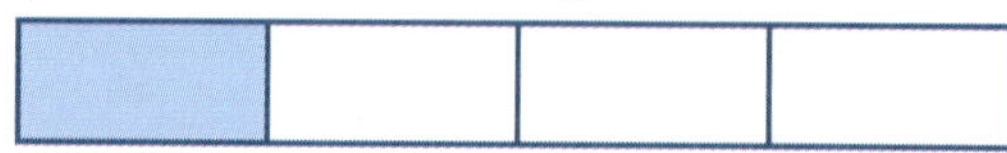

One-quarter of the collection is coloured.

A quarter of 8 is 2. Another way to say this is 8 divided by 4 is 2. That is $8 \div 4 = 2$.

Three-quarters of the rectangle is coloured.

Three-quarters of the collection is coloured.

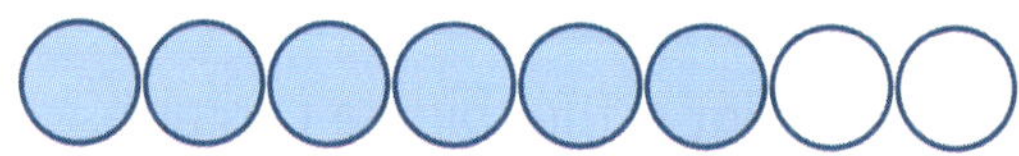

right and left

Left

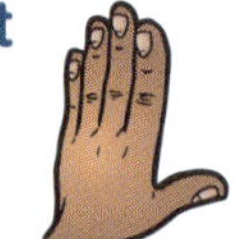

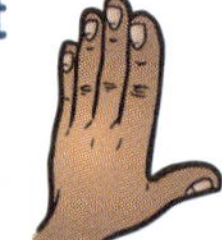

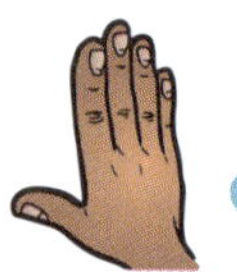

row

A row is a line of objects going across.
Here are 2 rows of 5.

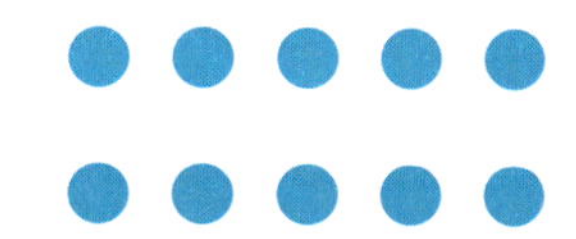

seconds

Seconds are used to measure time passed.
60 seconds is the same as 1 minute.

sharing

When sharing, we make sure that each share is the same size.

2 people could share these 6 balls. Each person would get 3 balls.

If two groups are not the same, we can make fair shares by moving items from the larger group to the smaller group.

straight line

A straight line has no bends or curves.

symmetry

A shape has symmetry when one side is the mirror-image of the other. It can be folded so that the two halves match, exactly.

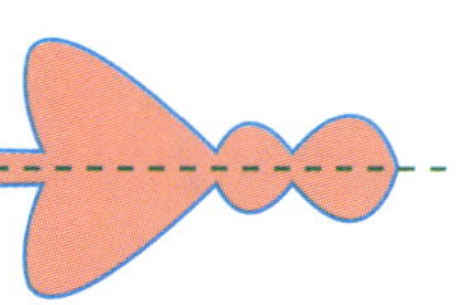

take away (subtract or minus)

When we remove objects from a group we call this "take away".

tally marks

Tally marks are used to keep count. Groups of 5 are used.

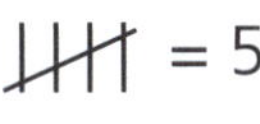

three-dimensional (3D) objects

3D objects are three-dimensional. They have length, width and height.

spheres (ball-shaped objects) are curved and round. They can roll.

cubes (box-shaped objects) have 6 square faces. They can slide and stack.

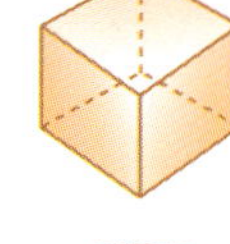

cylinders (can-shaped objects) have 2 flat surfaces and 1 curved surface. They can roll, slide and stack.

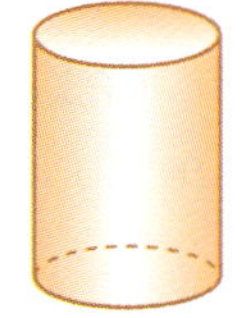

cones (cone-shaped objects) have 1 flat surface and 1 curved surface. They can roll and slide.

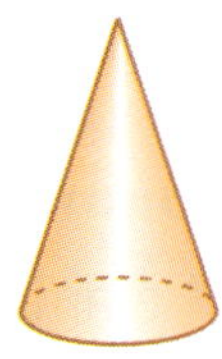

prisms

A prism has rectangular faces joining two identical bases at the two ends.

hexagonal prism

triangular prism

time words

morning	day
afternoon	night

Days			
Sunday	Monday	Tuesday	Wednesday
Thursday	Friday	Saturday	

Months			
January	February	March	April
May	June	July	August
September	October	November	December

Seasons			
Summer	Autumn	Winter	Spring

- clocks

analog clock / digital clock

3 o'clock

- o'clock

When the long hand (minute hand) is pointing to 12, the time is an "o'clock" time. The short hand (hour hand) points to the hour (e.g. the hour hand above is pointing to the 3 so it is 3 o'clock).

half past 3

- half past

When the long hand is pointing to the 6, the time is a "half past" time. The short hand on this clock points halfway between the 3 and the 4 so it is half past 3.

quarter past 6

- quarter past

When the long hand is pointing to the 3, then the time is "quarter past" the hour. The short hand on this clock is a quarter of the way from 6 to 7, so it is a quarter past 6.

quarter to 7

- quarter to

When the long hand is pointing to the 9, then the time is "quarter to" the next hour. The short hand on this clock is a quarter of the way from the next number 7, so it is a quarter to 7.

total

The number of items altogether. The result once everything has been added.

turn

Moving a shape in a clockwise or anticlockwise direction.

- quarter turn

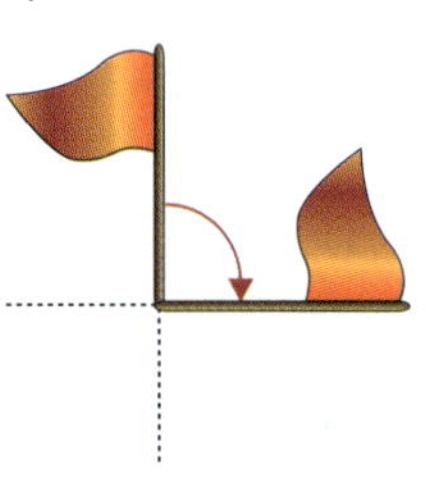

- half turn

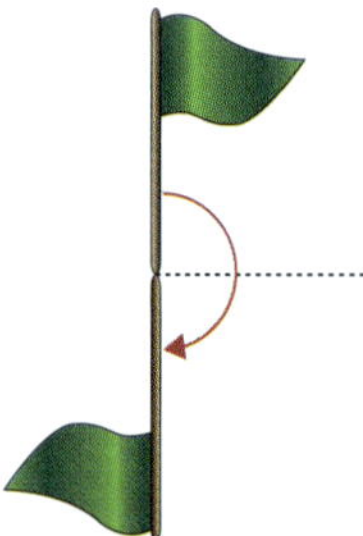

- three-quarter turn

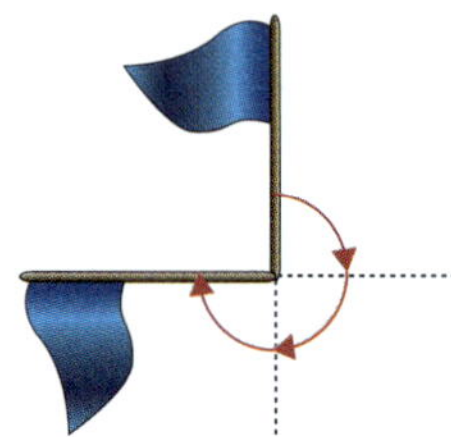

- full turn

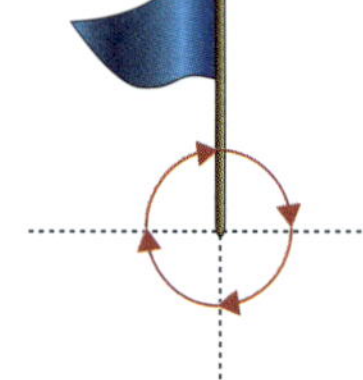

two-dimensional (2D) shapes

Flat shapes are two-dimensional. They have length and width.

circle
1 curved side

triangle
3 sides
3 corners

square
4 equal sides
4 corners

rectangle
2 equal long sides and 2 equal short sides, like a stretched square

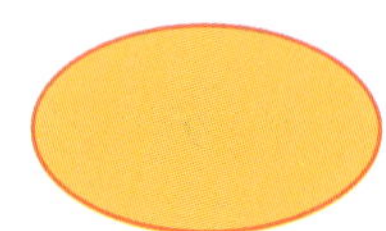

oval
1 curved side, like a squashed circle

pentagon
5 sides
5 corners

hexagon
6 sides
6 corners

octagon
8 sides
8 corners

quadrilaterals
4 sides and 4 corners. Squares and rectangles are quadrilaterals.

vertex

A corner. The plural of vertex is vertices.

volume

The amount of space an object takes up.

year

There are 365 days in a year and 366 days in a leap year (which is every 4th year). There are 12 months in a year.

Little robbers

1. What were the mice planning to do?
2. Do you think the mouse on stilts could reach the pie?
3. Explain how the mice carried out their plan.
4. Do you think the mice would take only a part of the pie? Why?
5. Does the police officer think the mice took the missing pie? Why or why not?
6. How do you think the stilts could be made?
7. Which of these questions do you like the best? Why do you like it?

 • *AUSTRALIAN SIGNPOST MATHS 2* • ISBN 9780655708766

1A Combinations to 10

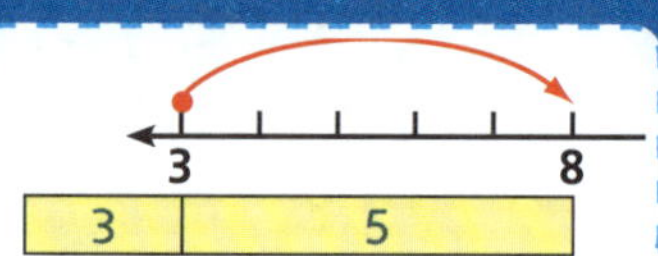

1 Count on from the largest number to complete these.

a $1 + 6 = \square$ b $2 + 2 = \square$ c $3 + 4 = \square$ d $1 + 3 = \square$ e $4 + 5 = \square$

f $4 + 4 = \square$ g $6 + 3 = \square$ h $5 + 4 = \square$ i $6 + 1 = \square$ j $0 + 5 = \square$

k $2 + 7 = \square$ l $5 + 1 = \square$ m $2 + 5 = \square$ n $3 + 6 = \square$ o $7 + 0 = \square$

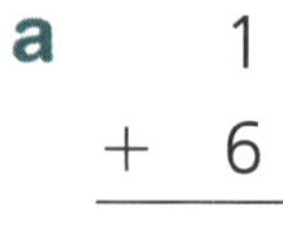

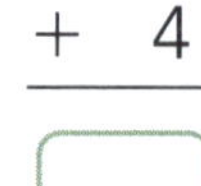
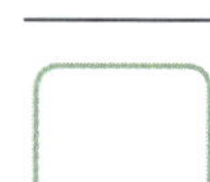
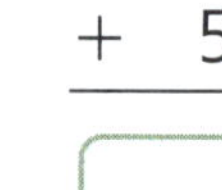
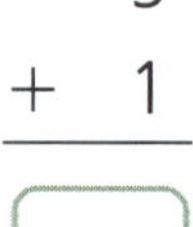
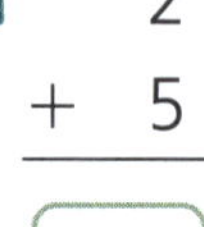
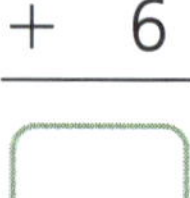
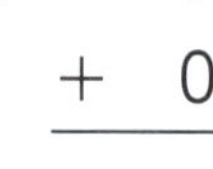
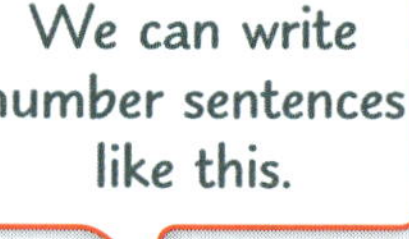

Discuss word problems for these number sentences.

2 Finish the **number story** for each question below.

a  +    ☐ lollies + ☐ lollies equals ☐ lollies.

b 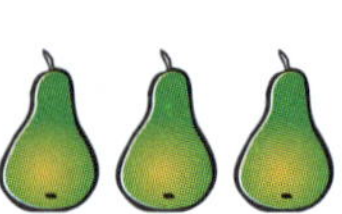 + 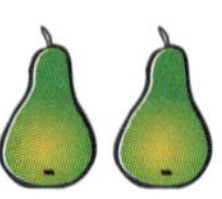  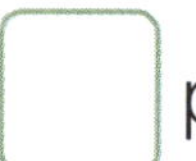 ☐ pears + ☐ pears equals ☐ pears.

Use objects to model your own addition stories.

 • *AUSTRALIAN SIGNPOST MATHS 2* • ISBN 9780655708766

1B Subtraction to 10

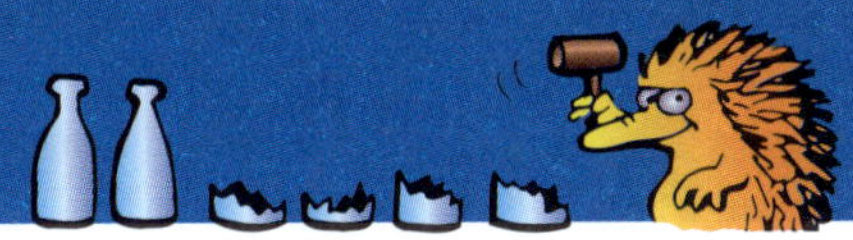
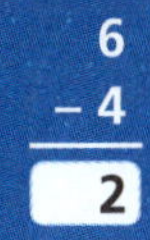

1 You could use counting on or counting back to complete these.

a 6 – 4 = ☐ **b** 8 – 3 = ☐ **c** 9 – 6 = ☐

d 10 – 7 = ☐ **e** 9 – 5 = ☐ **f** 10 – 8 = ☐

g 7 – 4 = ☐ **h** 10 – 4 = ☐ **i** 9 – 3 = ☐

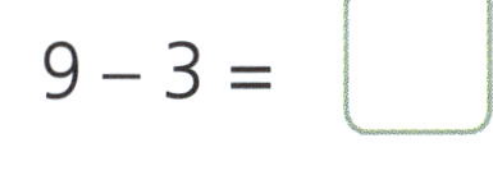

2

a	**b**	**c**	**d**	**e**	**f**
5 − 3 = ☐	7 − 1 = ☐	10 − 3 = ☐	5 − 4 = ☐	6 − 3 = ☐	9 − 8 = ☐

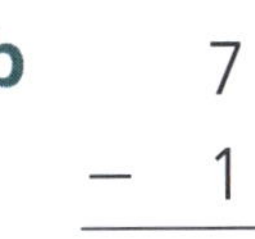
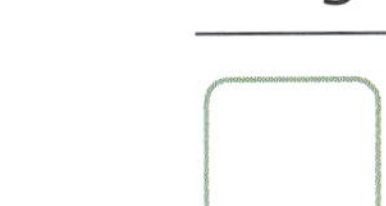
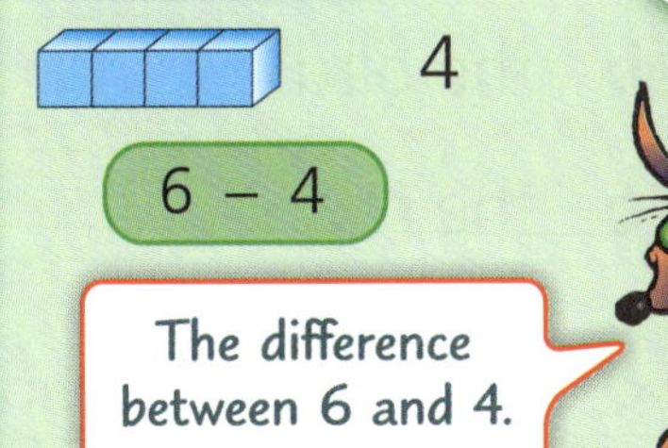

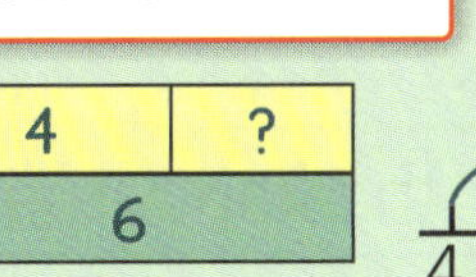

g	**h**	**i**	**j**	**k**
9 − 4 = ☐	9 − 7 = ☐	10 − 6 = ☐	7 − 3 = ☐	8 − 5 = ☐

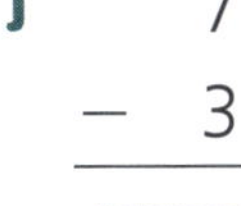

3

a	**b**	**c**	**d**
8 pegs − 4 pegs = ☐	8 bugs − 2 bugs = ☐	9 cats − 2 cats = ☐	10 bears − 5 bears = ☐

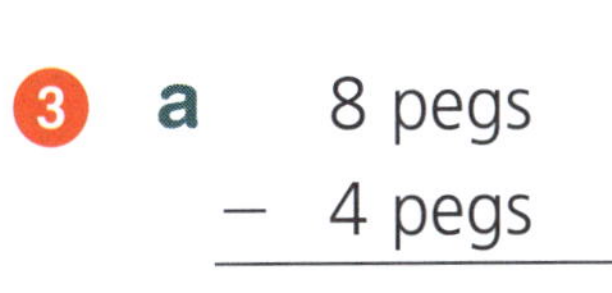
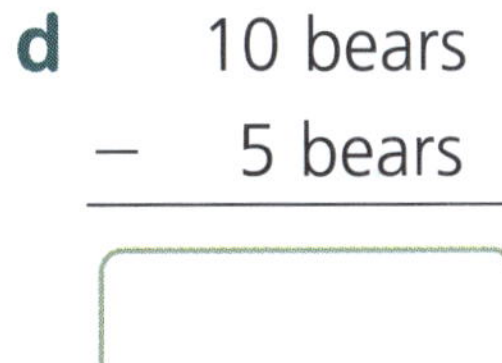

4

a

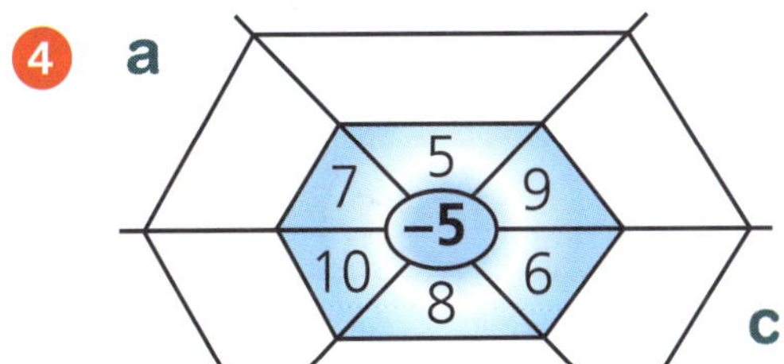

b

c

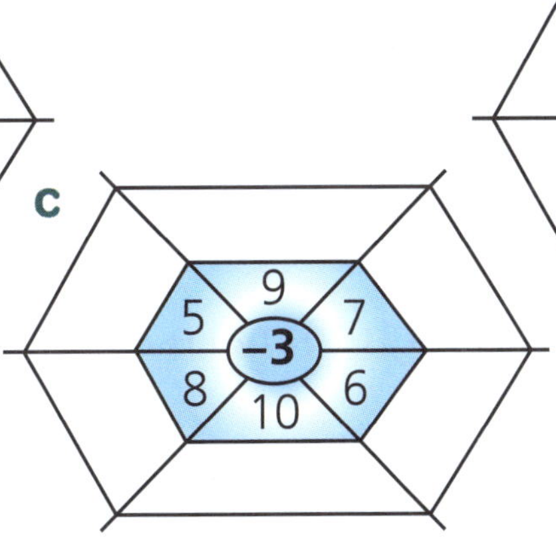

Discuss word problems for the number sentences on this page.

1C Position words

beside	next to	left	right	centre	middle
above	on	onto	on top of	below	beneath
under	underneath	bottom	back to back	in front of	upside down
behind	between	close to	forward	near	far
further away	up	high	low	in	inside

1 Use some of these words to give the position of:

a the emu

b the bird

c the rocks

d the kangaroo lying down

e the kangaroo standing up

f the long grass plant

2 Describe the position of the animals in this picture.

For example, the kangaroo (13) is in front of the tree.

3 a Use plasticine or playdough to make a simple model of the picture in Question 1.

b Make a model of your bedroom or another room at home.

 • *AUSTRALIAN SIGNPOST MATHS 2* • ISBN 9780655708766

1D Modelling numbers

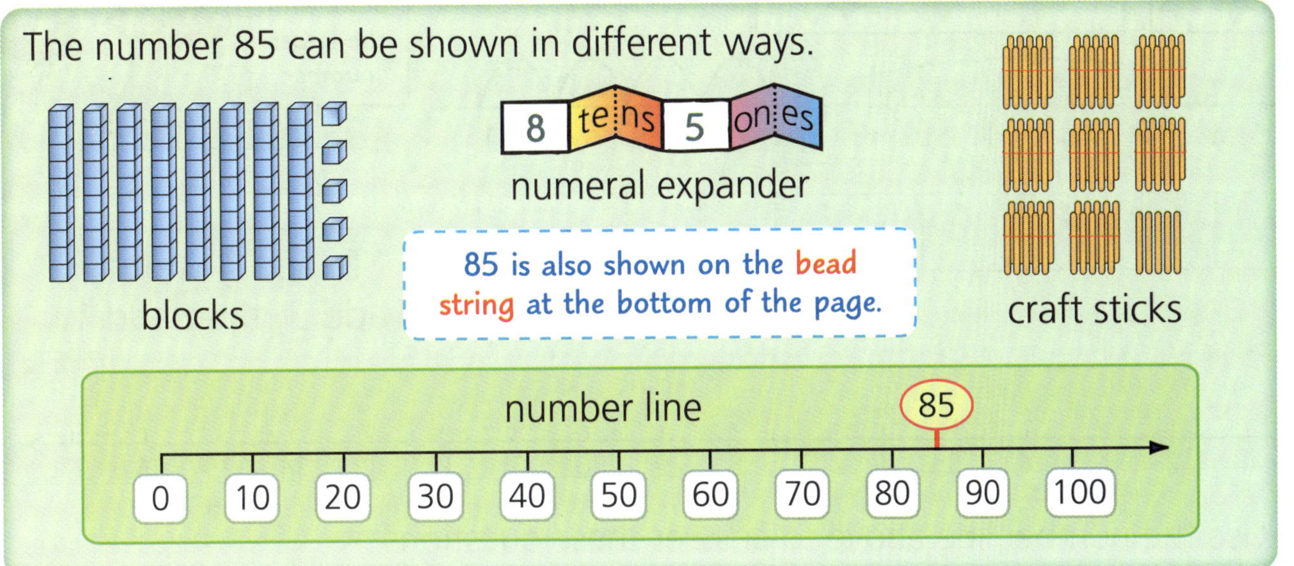

1 Write the number modelled and fill in the numeral expander.

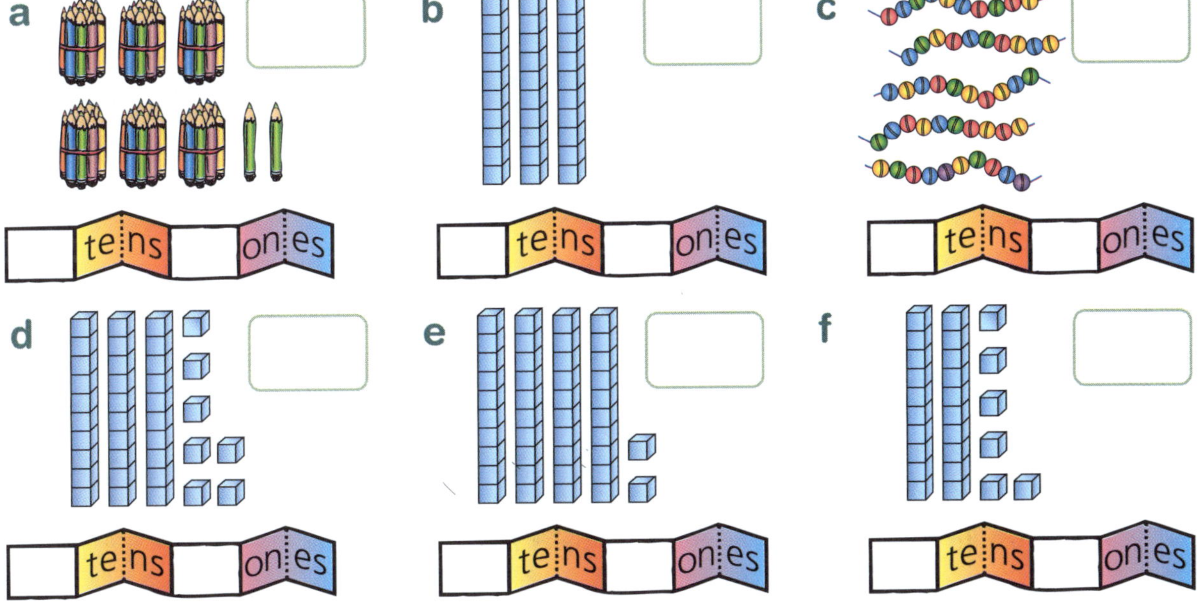

2 Every 10th bead around this page is coloured red. Colour bead number:

a 16 b 35 c 49 d 62 e 74 f 92

3 Tick the bead that comes before:

a 10 b 30 c 65 d 78 e 95 f 108

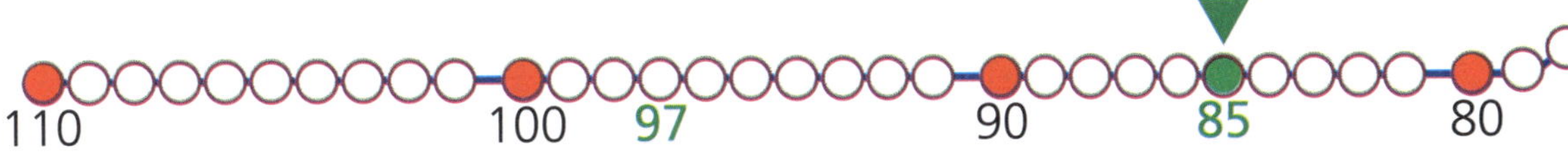

40 50 58 60 70

and = and
2 + 4 is the same as 4 + 2

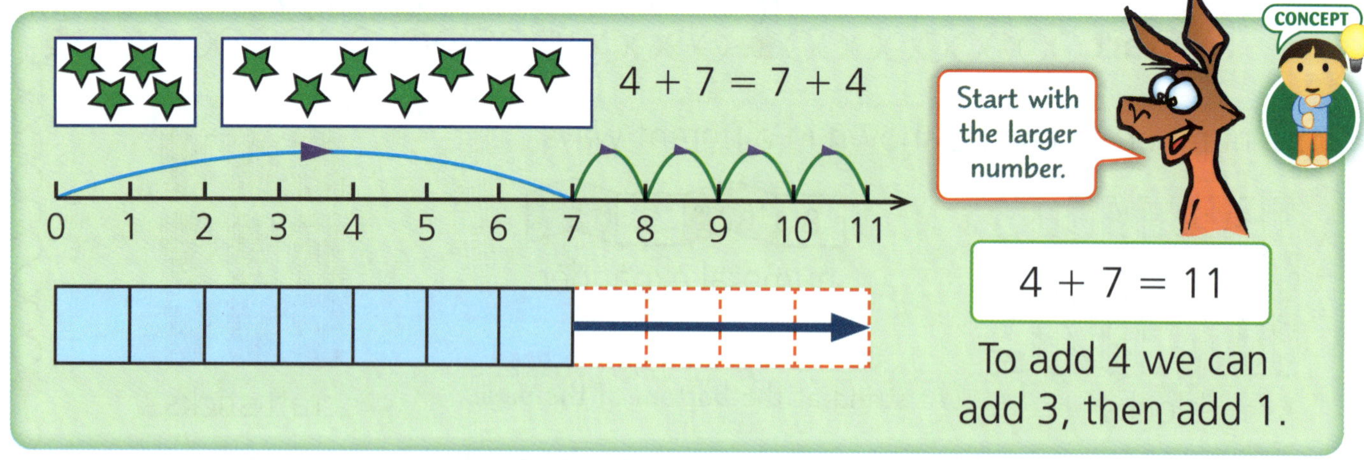

0 1 2 3 4 5 6 7 8 9 10 11 12 13 14 15 16 17

1 Use the number line above to answer these questions.

a 3 and 6 makes ☐. **b** 5 and 5 makes ☐.

c 9 + 2 = ☐ **d** 7 + 4 = ☐ **e** 8 + 5 = ☐

f 8 + 3 = ☐ **g** 7 + 7 = ☐ **h** 9 + 4 = ☐

i 8 + 7 = ☐ **j** 7 + 8 = ☐ **k** 9 + 8 = ☐

l 8 + 6 = ☐ **m** 4 + 7 = ☐ **n** 2 + 9 = ☐

Use the number line to add to ten then add on the rest.

Example:
7 + **5** = (7 + **3**) + **2**
= 12

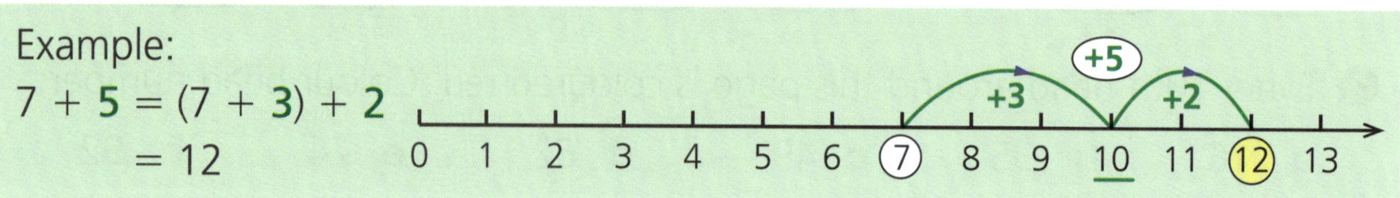

o 6 + 7 = ☐ **p** 9 + 5 = ☐ **q** 5 + 7 = ☐

r 6 + 5 = ☐ **s** 4 + 8 = ☐ **t** 3 + 9 = ☐

Addition to 20

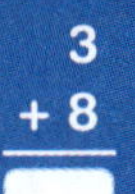

$\begin{array}{r} 3 \\ +\ 8 \\ \hline \square \end{array}$ 3 + 8 = ☐

1 Use counters or counting on to complete each number sentence.

a 4 + 9 = ☐ **b** 6 + 8 = ☐ **c** 7 + 9 = ☐

d 7 + ☐ = 14 **e** 9 + ☐ = 15 **f** 8 + ☐ = 12

g 5 + ☐ = 13 **h** 9 + ☐ = 18 **i** 10 + ☐ = 18

2

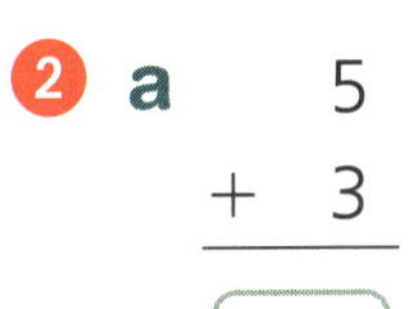

a $\begin{array}{r} 5 \\ +\ 3 \\ \hline \square \end{array}$ **b** $\begin{array}{r} 8 \\ +\ 4 \\ \hline \square \end{array}$ **c** $\begin{array}{r} 7 \\ +\ 8 \\ \hline \square \end{array}$

d $\begin{array}{r} 5 \\ +\ 9 \\ \hline \square \end{array}$ **e** $\begin{array}{r} 9 \\ +\ 9 \\ \hline \square \end{array}$ **f** $\begin{array}{r} 7 \\ +\ 6 \\ \hline \square \end{array}$

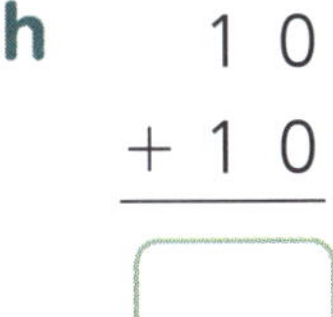

g $\begin{array}{r} 6 \\ +\ 7 \\ \hline \square \end{array}$ **h** $\begin{array}{r} 10 \\ +\ 10 \\ \hline \square \end{array}$ **i** $\begin{array}{r} 12 \\ +\ 3 \\ \hline \square \end{array}$

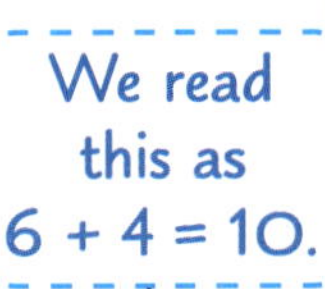

$\begin{array}{r} 6 \\ +\ 4 \\ \hline 10 \end{array}$

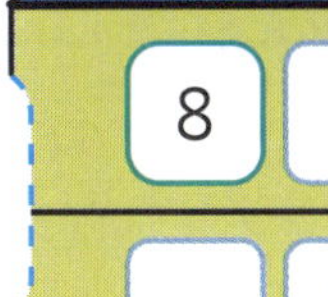

11	
8	☐
☐	7
6	☐
3	☐
2	☐
5	☐
☐	4

3 Write a different true number sentence each time.

a 12 = ☐ + ☐ **b** 15 = ☐ + ☐

12 = ☐ + ☐ 15 = ☐ + ☐

12 = ☐ + ☐ 15 = ☐ + ☐

12 = ☐ + ☐ 15 = ☐ + ☐

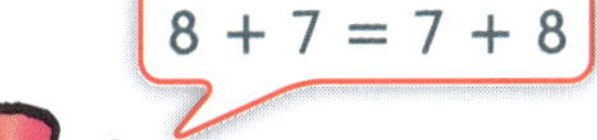

4 Complete these number bond houses.

13				
	8	☐	6	☐
	7	☐	9	☐

14				
	8	☐	6	☐
	7	☐	9	☐

16				
	8	☐	6	☐
	7	☐	9	☐

2C Addition to 20

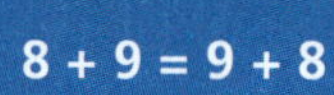

CONCEPT

8 + 5 Start at 8 and count on.

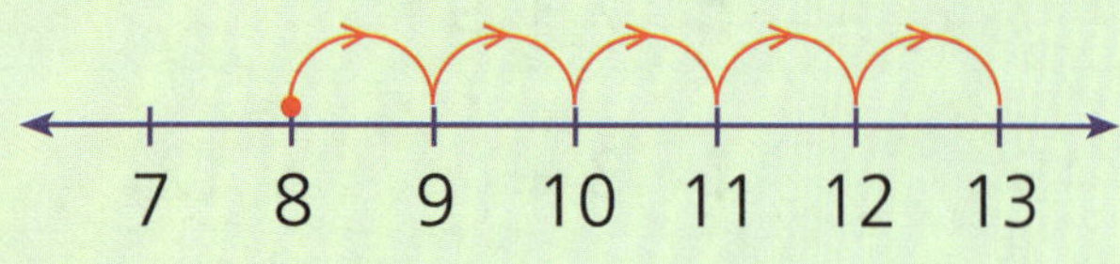

$$\begin{array}{r} 8 \\ +\ 5 \\ \hline 13 \end{array}$$

We read this as 8 + 5 = 13.

1 Use the number line to count on from the larger number.

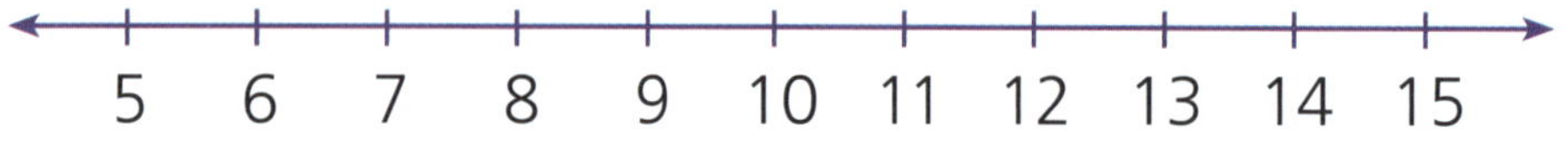

Learn your addition tables.

a 7 + 6 = ☐

b 4 + 7 = ☐

c 3 + 9 = ☐

d 8 + 4 = ☐

e 5 + 6 = ☐

f 4 + 8 = ☐

g 9 + 2 = ☐

h 6 + 8 = ☐

i 2 + 9 = ☐

j 7 + 8 = ☐

2 Use counters to find numbers for the windows.

3 a An ant has 6 legs.
Find different ways its legs can be grouped.

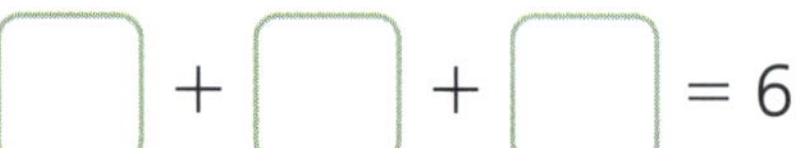

☐ + ☐ + ☐ = 6

☐ + ☐ + ☐ = 6

b An octopus has 8 legs.
Find different ways its legs can be grouped.

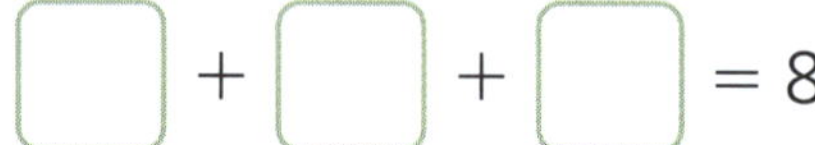

2D Thinking about graphs

Words: baseline
equal spacing
same-sized symbols

1

B

In the pond

Tadpoles

Frogs

Fish

Which of these do you think is the better picture graph?

Why do you think so?

2 **a** Each smiley face stands for a sticker.
What is wrong with this graph?

Number of stickers given

Alana Deepak Brand

b Complete this table.

Name	Number
Alana	
Deepak	
Brand	

c Draw a better graph.
Colour one face for each sticker.

3A Doubling and near doubling

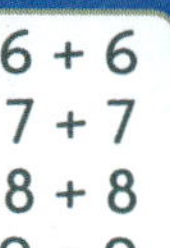

Learn your doubles.

6 + 7 = 6 + 6 + 1
7 + 8 = 7 + 7 + 1
8 + 9 = 8 + 8 + 1

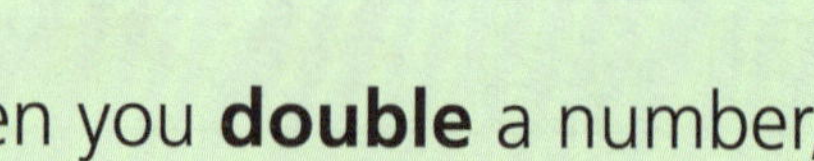
When you **double** a number, the answer will be **even**.

1 Complete each number sentence.

a double 3

☐ + ☐ = ☐

b double 6

☐ + ☐ = ☐

c double 1

☐ + ☐ = ☐

d double 7

☐ + ☐ = ☐

e double 9

☐ + ☐ = ☐

f double 8

☐ + ☐ = ☐

2

a $\begin{array}{r} 2 \\ +\ 2 \\ \hline \end{array}$ ☐

b $\begin{array}{r} 4 \\ +\ 4 \\ \hline \end{array}$ ☐

c $\begin{array}{r} 0 \\ +\ 0 \\ \hline \end{array}$ ☐

d $\begin{array}{r} 5 \\ +\ 5 \\ \hline \end{array}$ ☐

e $\begin{array}{r} 10 \\ +\ 10 \\ \hline \end{array}$ ☐

3

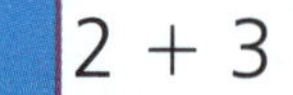

 • *AUSTRALIAN SIGNPOST MATHS 2* • ISBN 9780655708766

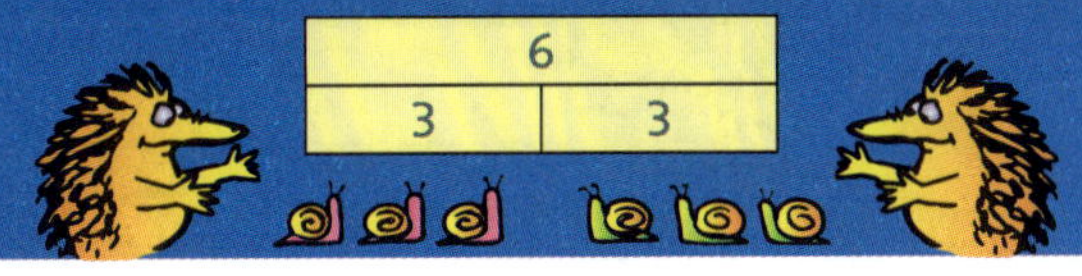

CONCEPT

When sharing fairly, each person is given the same amount.
Some counters could be left over.

?	?	?
9		

1 Share 6 counters among 3 boxes. One share = ☐

☐ ☐ ☐

If we combine the shares again, how many counters would we have? ☐

2 Share 20 counters between 2 groups.

☐ ☐ One share = ☐

If we combine the shares again, how many counters would we have? ☐

3 Share 25 counters between 2 groups.

☐ ☐ One share = ☐
and ☐ left over

INVESTIGATION

Share 12 counters:

12

a between 2 people One share = ☐

b among 3 people One share = ☐

c among 5 people One share = ☐ and ☐ left over

 • *AUSTRALIAN SIGNPOST MATHS 2* • ISBN 9780655708766

3C Sharing

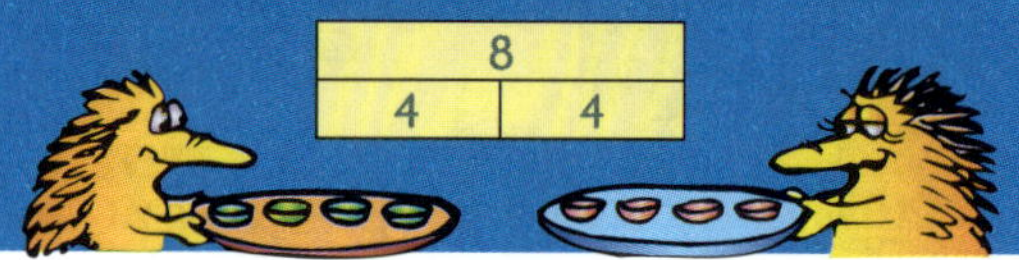

When we share, each person is given the same number of items.

1 Circle each share, then answer the questions.

a Shared among 4

How many stars? ☐

How many shares? ☐

How many stars in each share? ☐

b Shared among 4

How many caps? ☐

How many shares? ☐

How many caps in each share? ☐

c Shared between 2

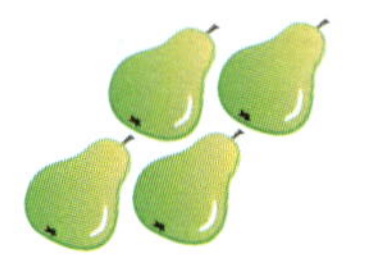

How many pears? ☐

How many shares? ☐

How many pears in each share? ☐

d Shared among 4

How many fish? ☐

How many shares? ☐

How many fish in each share? ☐

e Shared between 2

How many stars? ☐

How many shares? ☐

How many stars in each share? ☐

f Shared among 4

How many cups? ☐

How many shares? ☐

How many cups in each share? ☐

INVESTIGATION

Use 18 counters. What is one share if they are shared:

a among 3? ☐ counters **b** among 6? ☐ counters

Use 20 counters. What is one share if they are shared:

c among 5? ☐ counters **d** among 4? ☐ counters

 • *AUSTRALIAN SIGNPOST MATHS 2* • ISBN 9780655708766

3D 2D shapes

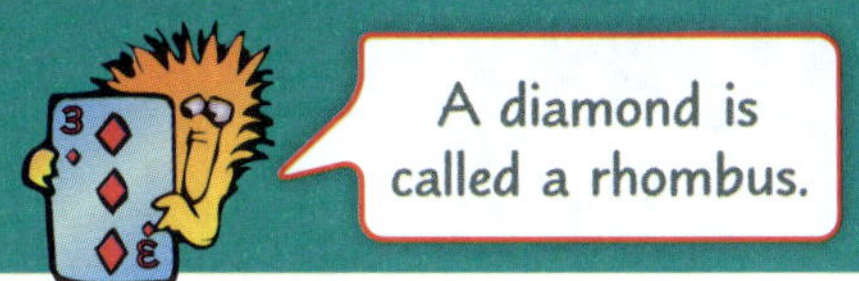

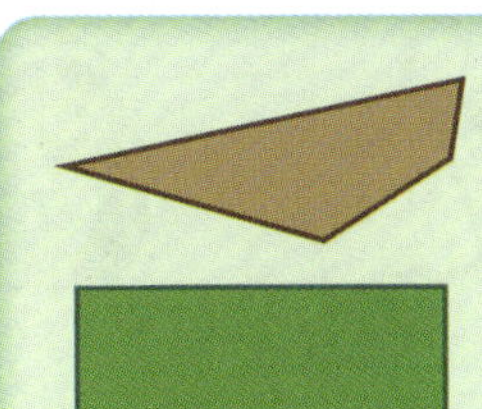

Quadrilateral: 4 straight sides
4 vertices (corners)

Rectangle: opposite sides equal
4 vertices (corners)

Hexagon: 6 straight sides
6 vertices (corners)

1. In this picture, find how many:

   a circles
   b triangles
   c squares
   d hexagons
   e pentagons
   f octagons

   Discuss their features.

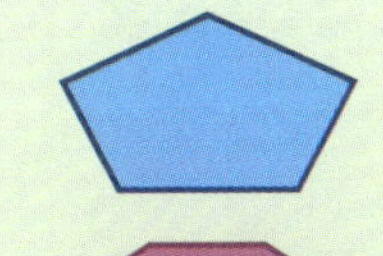

Pentagon: 5 straight sides, 5 vertices

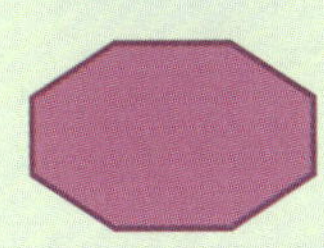

Octagon: 8 straight sides, 8 vertices

Are the number of sides and vertices always the same?

2. Write the name of each shape.

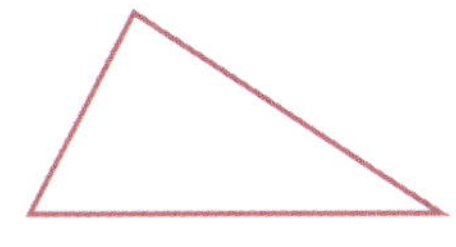

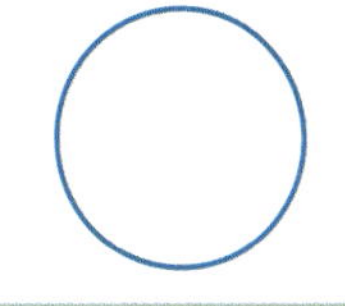

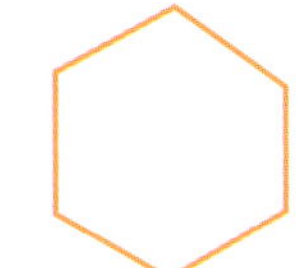

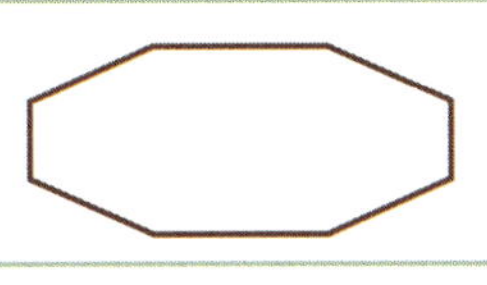

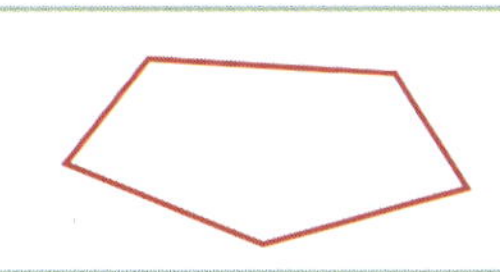

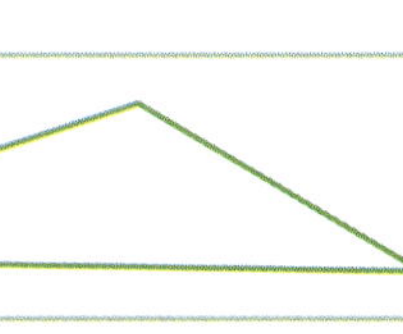

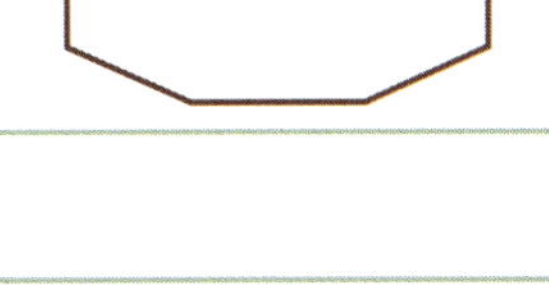

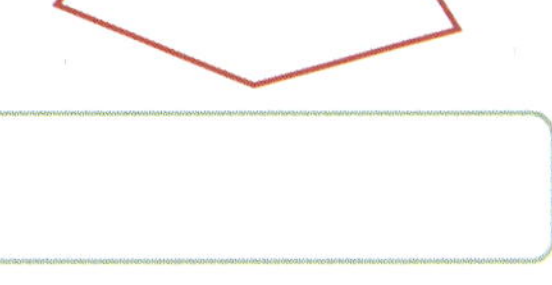

4A Subtraction

If 6 + 8 = 14 then 14 – 8 = 6.

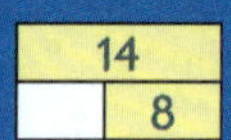

CONCEPT

11 take away 4 leaves 7.

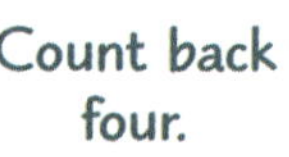

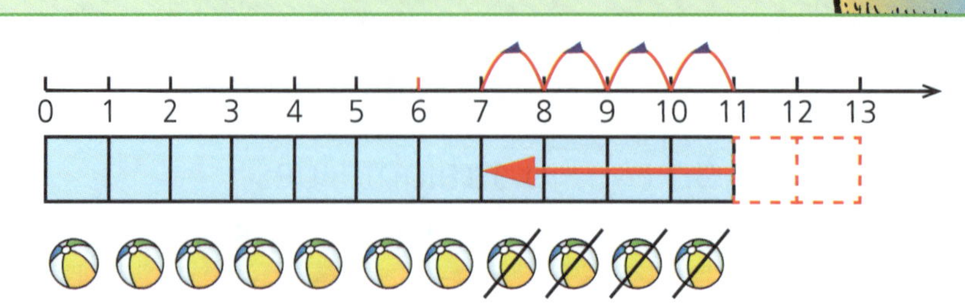

0 1 2 3 4 5 6 7 8 9 10 11 12 13 14 15 16 17

1 Use the number line above to answer these questions.

a 13 minus 4 equals ☐.   **b** 12 minus 3 equals ☐.

c 11 – 6 = ☐   **d** 15 – 8 = ☐   **e** 12 – 4 = ☐

f 10 – 7 = ☐   **g** 14 – 7 = ☐   **h** 16 – 9 = ☐

i 11 – 3 = ☐   **j** 13 – 6 = ☐   **k** 13 – 5 = ☐

l 17 – 9 = ☐   **m** 16 – 8 = ☐   **n** 14 – 6 = ☐

You can subtract to the 10, then take away the rest.

13 – **7** = (13 – **3**) – **4**
  = 6

–7 –4 –3
0 1 2 3 4 5 6 7 8 9 10 11 12 13

o 12 – 7 = ☐   **p** 13 – 8 = ☐   **q** 17 – 8 = ☐

r 14 – 8 = ☐   **s** 16 – 7 = ☐   **t** 15 – 6 = ☐

 • *AUSTRALIAN SIGNPOST MATHS 2* • ISBN 9780655708766

Subtraction to 20

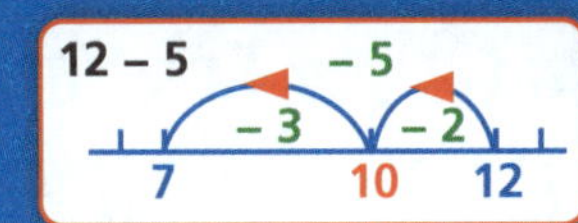

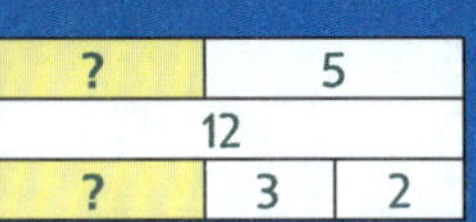

Billy had 12 apples.

He ate 5.

How many did he have left?

12 – 5 = 7

$$\begin{array}{r} 12 \\ -\ 5 \\ \hline 7 \end{array}$$

1 **a** 10 bottles
8 broken
How many left?
☐ – ☐ = ☐

b 12 flowers
7 picked
How many left?
☐ – ☐ = ☐

c 9 cakes
6 eaten
How many left?
☐ – ☐ = ☐

d 15 balls
6 lost
How many left?

e 13 pencils
8 broken
How many left?
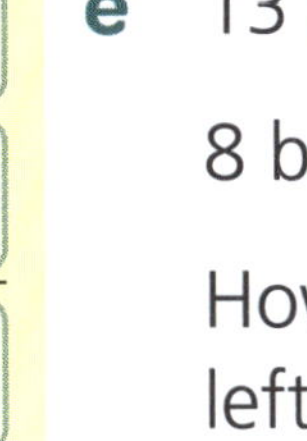

f 14 mice
7 caught
How many left?
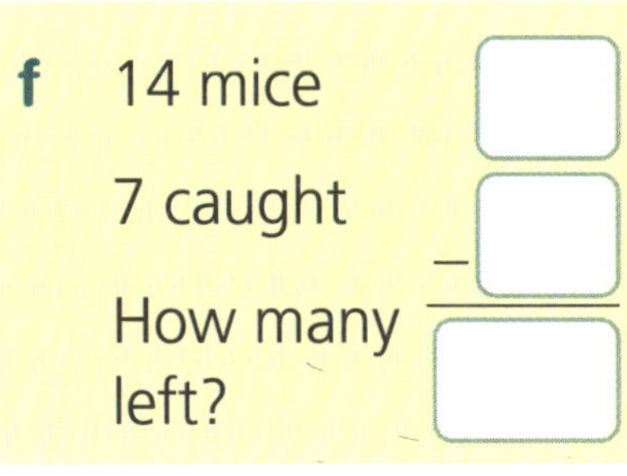

g 16 nuts
9 eaten
How many left?

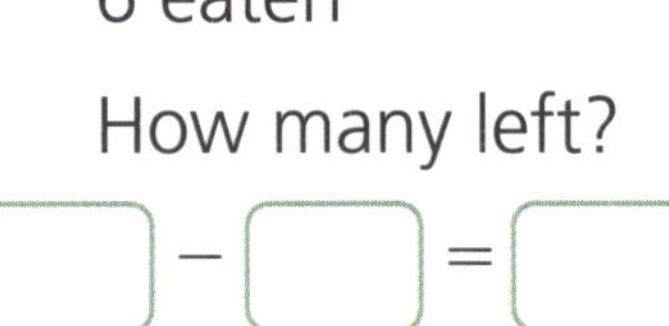

Challenge a friend to answer these questions quickly.

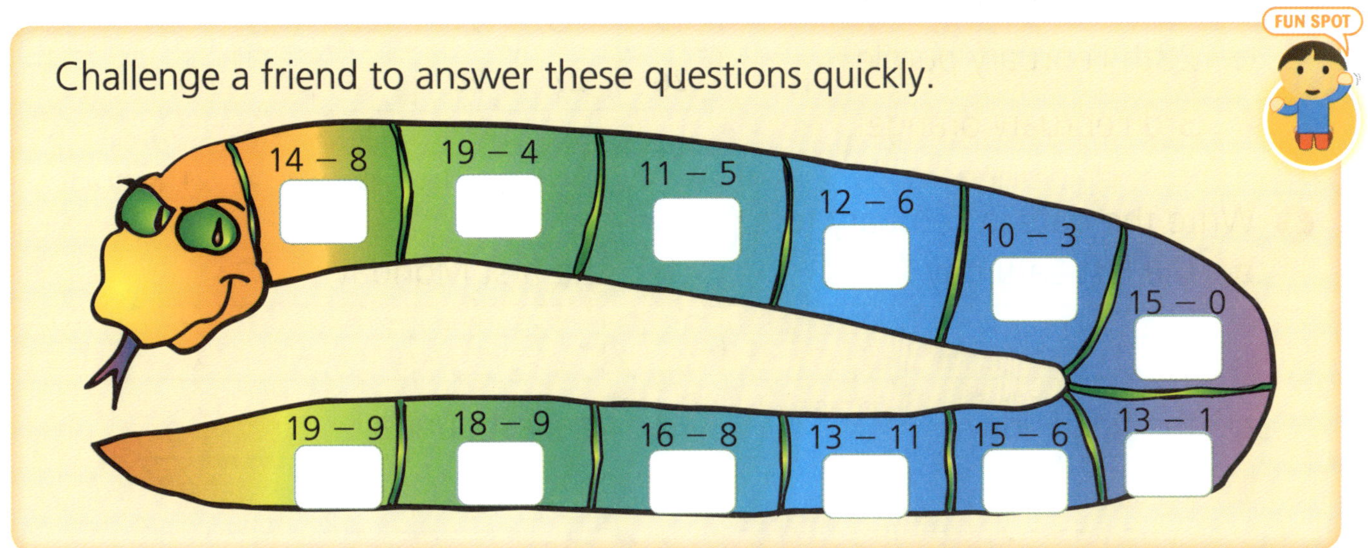

4C Ordinal numbers and calendars

1 **a** Write the ordinal number for each dinosaur.

1st

Colour:

b the 3rd dinosaur green

c the 6th dinosaur red

d the 2nd dinosaur blue

e the 10th dinosaur purple

f the 4th dinosaur orange

g the 1st dinosaur pink

2 Write the ordinal number for:

a  **b** 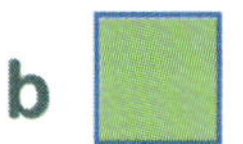  **c** 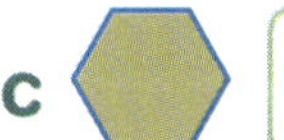  **d** 

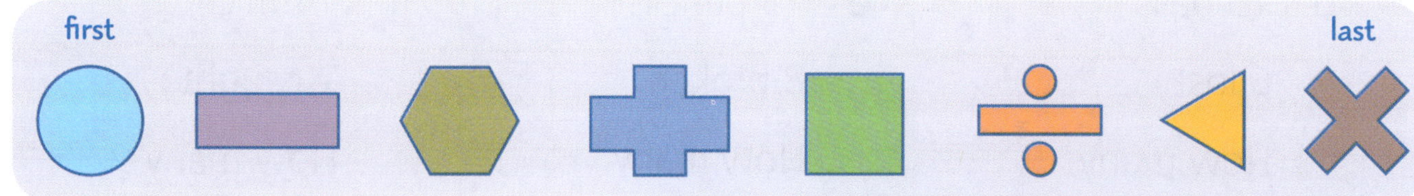

3 Colour:

a 21st February red

b 2nd February green

c 19th February blue

d 26th February yellow

e 28th February purple

f 3rd February orange

February						
Sun	Mon	Tues	Wed	Thurs	Fri	Sat
			1	2	3	4
5	6	7	8	9	10	11
12	13	14	15	16	17	18
19	20	21	22	23	24	25
26	27	28				

21st February = 21 February

4 Write the date in February for:

a the last Saturday

b the first Monday

c the first Friday

d the last Sunday

4D The calendar

Learn this poem about the days in each month.

Here is a calendar for November. Fill in the missing numbers.

November						
Sun	Mon	Tues	Wed	Thurs	Fri	Sat
1	2		4	5	6	7
15	16	17	18		20	21
22	23		25	26	27	28
29	30					

Next year, November starts on a different day.

30 days has
September,
April, June and
November.
All the rest
have 31
Except February alone,
Which has 28
days clear,
And 29 days each
leap year.

1. **a** How many days are in November? ☐

   b How many Sundays are there in this month? ☐

   How many weeks is it from 2nd of November until:

   c 23rd November? ☐ **d** 16th November? ☐ **e** 30th November? ☐

   How many days is it from 4th of November until:

   f 28th November? ☐ **g** 17th November? ☐ **h** 22nd November? ☐

   On what day is:

   i 4th November? ☐ **j** 21st November? ☐ **k** 29th November? ☐

2. Would you use minutes, hours, days or months to measure:

   a the time it takes for a trip to the zoo? ☐

   b the time it takes for eggs to hatch? ☐

   c the time it takes to build a house? ☐

   d the time it takes to cook a sausage? ☐

3. How many days from 23rd November until the end of the year? ☐

 • *AUSTRALIAN SIGNPOST MATHS 2* • ISBN 9780655708766

	+4	+5	+6	+7	+8	+9
8	12	13	14	15	16	17
9	13	14	15	16	17	18

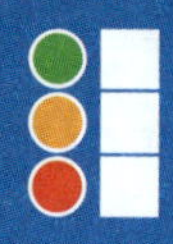

1. Draw a picture and complete the number sentences.

   a Milly got 8 pencils from Dad, 6 from Mum and 5 from Bess.
   How many did Milly get altogether?

   ☐ + ☐ + ☐ = ☐

   Working

   b Ben had 6 DVDs. Dom gave him 4 DVDs and Ravi gave him 8.
   How many DVDs does Ben have altogether?

   ☐ + ☐ + ☐ = ☐

   Working

2. Count on or use doubles to complete.

   a 3 + 4 + 3 = ☐ **b** 10 + 2 + 2 = ☐ **c** 6 + 1 + 6 = ☐

   d 4 + 3 + 5 = ☐ **e** 8 + 4 + 2 = ☐ **f** 6 + 4 + 4 = ☐

   g 4 + 3 + 4 = ☐ **h** 1 + 6 + 4 = ☐ **i** 3 + 6 + 2 = ☐

3. Write three number sentences for each total.

   a
   ☐ + ☐ = 15
   ☐ + ☐ = 15
   ☐ + ☐ = 15

   b
   ☐ + ☐ = 17
   ☐ + ☐ = 17
   ☐ + ☐ = 17

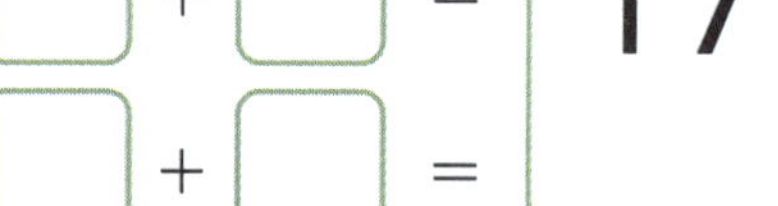

   c
   ☐ + ☐ = 16
   ☐ + ☐ = 16
   ☐ + ☐ = 16

   d
   ☐ + ☐ = 18
   ☐ + ☐ = 18
   ☐ + ☐ = 18

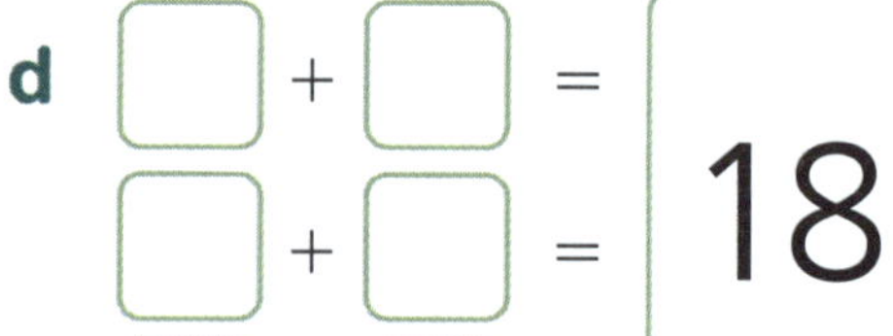

4. Complete these addition facts.

	+4	+5	+6	+7	+8	+9
6						
7						

	+8	+9
8		
9		

5B Addition by looking for tens

Do you know the friends of ten?

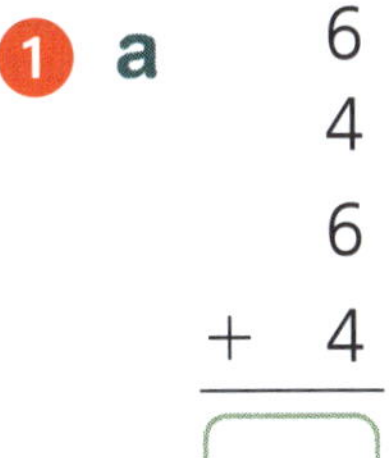

1

	a	b	c	d	e	f
	6	3	5	7	4	9
	4	3	9	3	8	7
	6	2	3	4	2	1
+	4	7	1	5	2	2
	☐	☐	☐	☐	☐	☐

	g	h	i	j	k
	4	3	5	3	6
	5	9	7	6	6
	6	8	8	9	5
+	7	1	5	4	4
	☐	☐	☐	☐	☐

2

	a	b	c	d	e
	$5	$9	$2	$8	$7
	$7	$3	$6	$4	$6
	$5	$1	$7	$2	$4
+	$3	$2	$3	$7	$5
	☐	☐	☐	☐	☐

3 **a** 8 cows, 3 sheep, 2 goats, 7 pigs. How many animals? ☐

b 2 fish, 9 mice, 7 birds, 1 emu. What is the total number? ☐

4 True (T) or false (F)?

a 6 + 7 + 3 + 4 + 5 = 5 + 4 + 7 + 6 + 3 ☐

b 2 + 5 + 8 + 5 + 3 = 3 + 8 + 2 + 3 + 7 ☐

c 3 + 9 + 1 + 9 + 7 = 9 + 5 + 2 + 8 + 5 ☐

We can add them in any order.

 • *AUSTRALIAN SIGNPOST MATHS 2* • ISBN 9780655708766

5C Directions

Left

Right

Finish

40
7
2
1

Start

1 Move the shortest way from *Start* to *Finish*, not crossing any walls. In the column on the left, write the numbers you pass through.

Finish

40	39	38	37
33	34	35	36
32	31	30	29
25	26	27	28
24	23	22	21
17	18	19	20
16	15	14	13
9	10	11	12
8	7	6	5
1	2	3	4

Start

Start writing the answers from the bottom.

2 3U means 3 up.
3D means 3 down.
2R means 2 right.
4L means 4 left.
Draw the path below on the grid.
3R, 2U, 2L, 1U, 3R

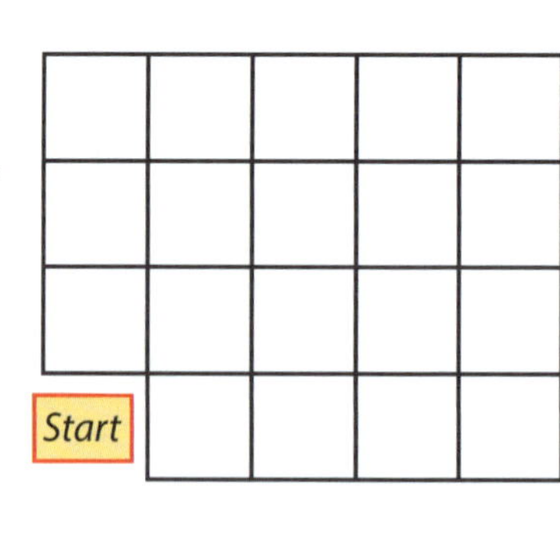

3 On this grid, follow the path and write the letters you pass through.
1R, 1U, 1L, 2U, 2R

i	n	g	a	g
k	p	s	i	n
l	a	s	t	i
Start	t	e	a	r

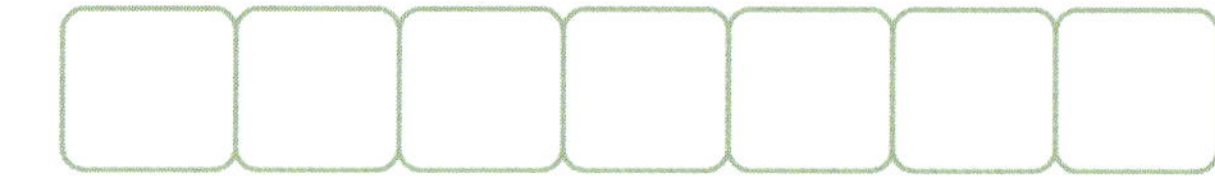

4 On this grid, follow the path and write the letters you pass through.
2R, 1U, 1R, 2U, 1L.

s	f	t	i	s
p	l	l	p	d
e	e	n	d	e
Start	s	a	y	s

5 Write paths that make words in Question 3.

Write paths that make words in Question 4.

5D Using graphs

1 How many:

a sandwiches?

b pies?

c apples?

d altogether?

e more pies than apples?

Food in the classroom

f Complete the table below to show the food in the classroom.

Food in the classroom	
Sandwiches	
Pies	
Apples	

g What other foods could be in a classroom?

2 Each student put a candle above their month of birth to make this graph.

Jan	Feb	Mar	Apr	May	Jun	Jul	Aug	Sep	Oct	Nov	Dec
🕯🕯🕯		🕯	🕯🕯	🕯🕯	🕯	🕯🕯	🕯🕯	🕯	🕯🕯	🕯	🕯🕯

How many students were born in:

a January?

b November?

c February?

d How many students are there altogether?

Discuss how your class could find out:

- the most popular colours of the cars passing the school.
- the number of each colour in a box of Smarties (or M&Ms).

6A Sharing and grouping

For grouping, we ask how many groups can be made?

Sharing

8 stickers were shared between Zoe and Lakshmi.

They got **4** each.

Grouping

I had 8 stickers. How many people could take 2 stickers?

4 groups of 2 makes 8.

4 people could take stickers.

1. Draw lines to show how you would share these collections equally.

a 6 apples
2 children

☐ each

b 10 stickers
2 children

☐ each

c 12 balls
3 children

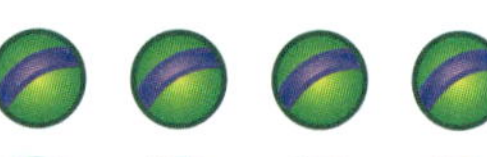
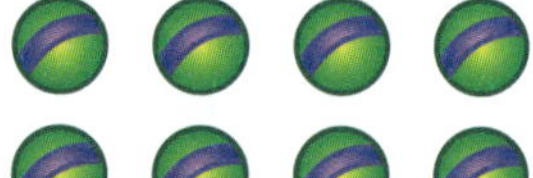

☐ each

2. Circle groups that have been made.

a

6 apples.
How many children could take 2 apples? ☐

b

10 stickers.
How many children could take 2 stickers? ☐

c

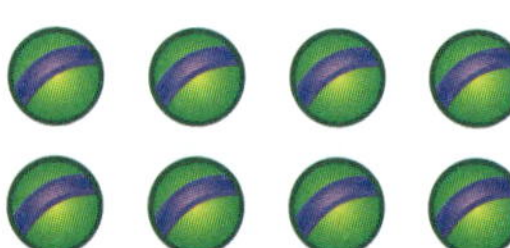
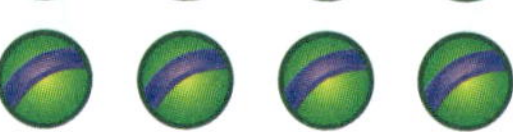

12 balls.
How many children could take 3 balls? ☐

3. Show how you could divide this array into two equal groups.
Write what you did.

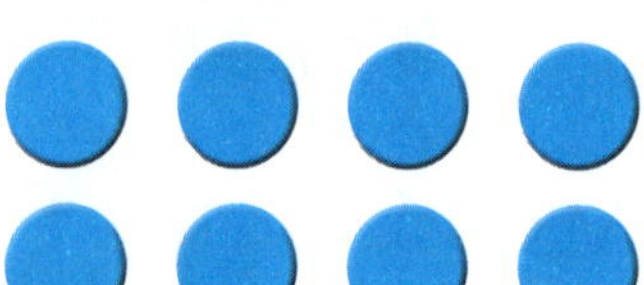

 • *AUSTRALIAN SIGNPOST MATHS 2* • ISBN 9780655708766

6B Groups and rows

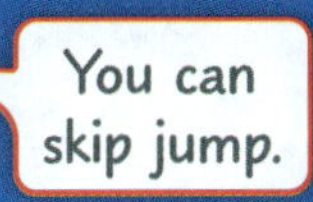

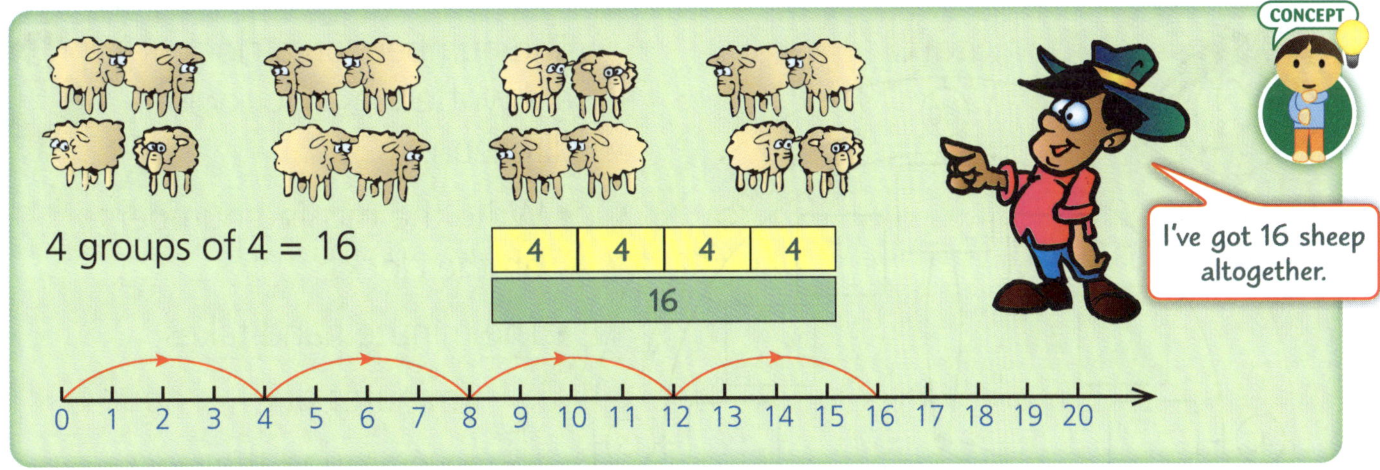

1. Use a number line or number chart to complete these.

a

☐ + ☐ + ☐

3 groups of 3 = ☐

b

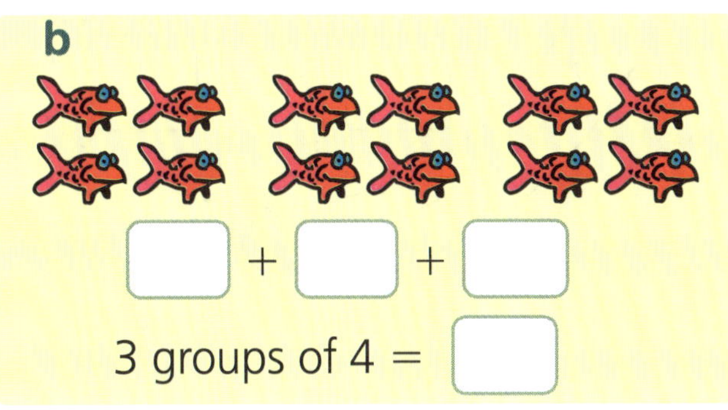

☐ + ☐ + ☐

3 groups of 4 = ☐

c

6 groups of 3 = ☐

d

4 rows of 5 = ☐ or

5 columns of 4 = ☐

e

☐ rows of ☐ = ☐

☐ columns of ☐ = ☐

2. Use counters to solve these problems.

a 3 groups of 5 balls = ☐ balls

b 2 rows of 7 trees = ☐ trees

c 3 groups of 8 ants = ☐ ants

d 4 rows of 6 people = ☐ people

 • *AUSTRALIAN SIGNPOST MATHS 2* • ISBN 9780655708766

Clocks

9 o'clock

9 fifteen

9 thirty

9 forty-five

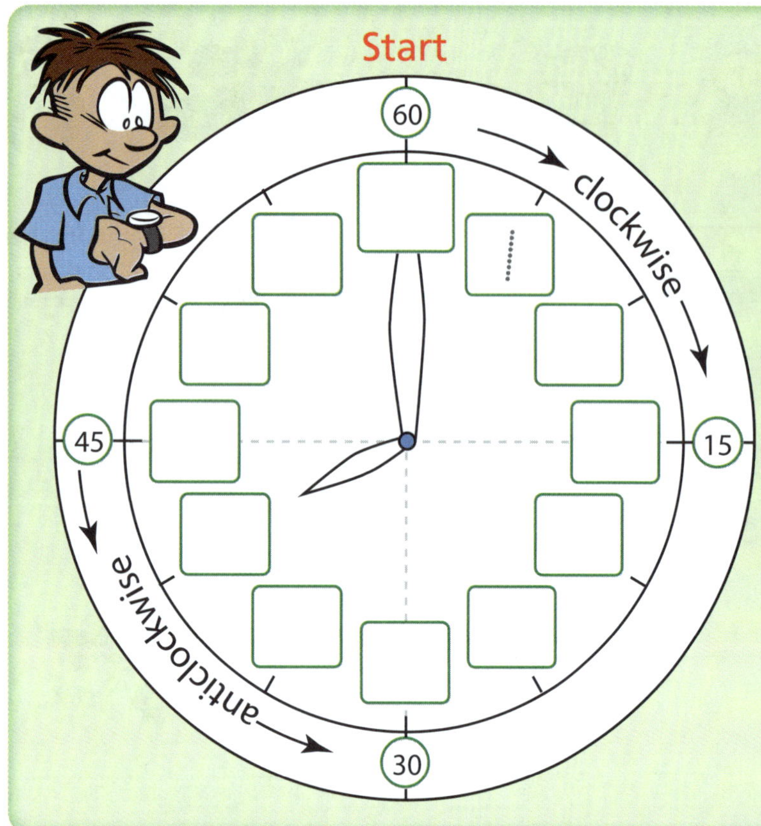

The numbers on a clock are written in a clockwise direction.

- Write the missing numbers on the clock.
- The minute hand takes ☐ minutes or ☐ hour to move around the clock.
- The hour hand takes ☐ hours to move around the clock.

Colour the minute hand blue.

Colour the hour hand red.

1 **a** At a quarter past, the minute hand has moved ☐ minutes around the clock from 12. The minute hand has moved quarter / half of the way around the clock. This is a quarter turn to the right. Colour the first quarter of the clock green.

b At half past, the minute hand has moved ☐ minutes around the clock from 12. The minute hand has moved quarter / half of the way around the clock. Colour the border on the clock yellow to show a half turn to the right from 12.

2 Write the time shown. **Word list:** • quarter past • half past • quarter to

a

b

c

d

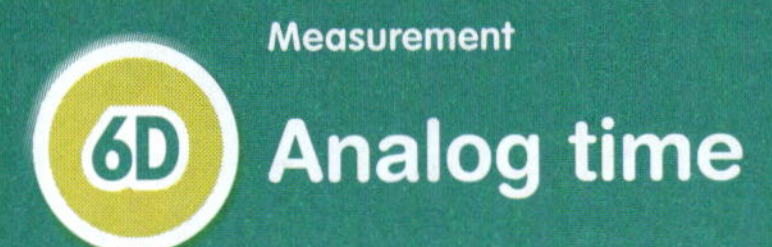

Analog time

quarter past 8

half past 8

quarter to 9

1 Write the time shown.

a 

b 

c 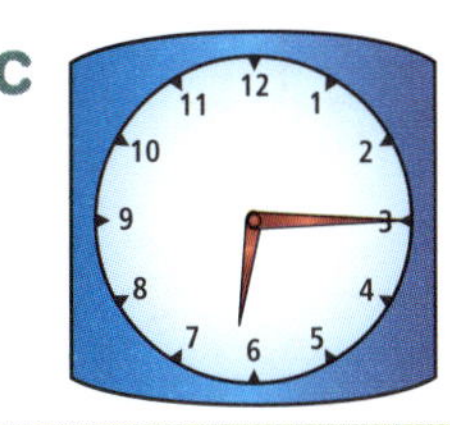

d 

e 

f 

g 

h 

2 Draw the time shown.

a 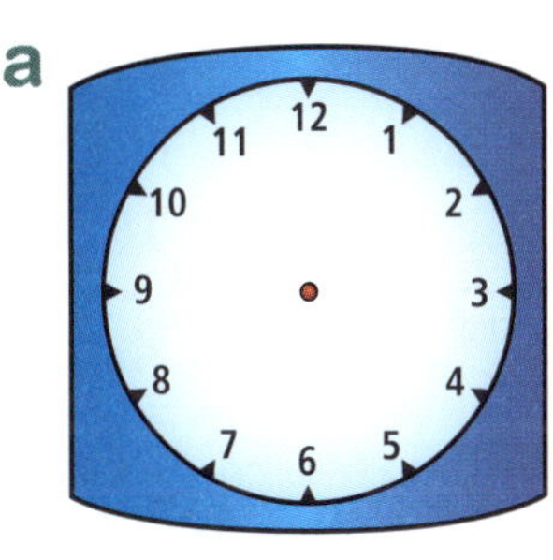

quarter to 5

b 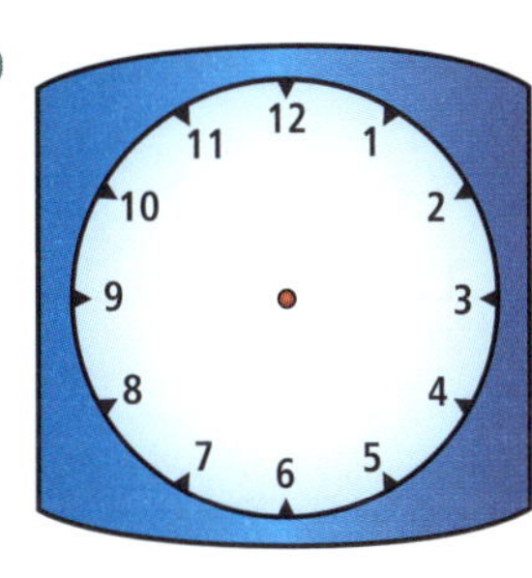

half past 1

c 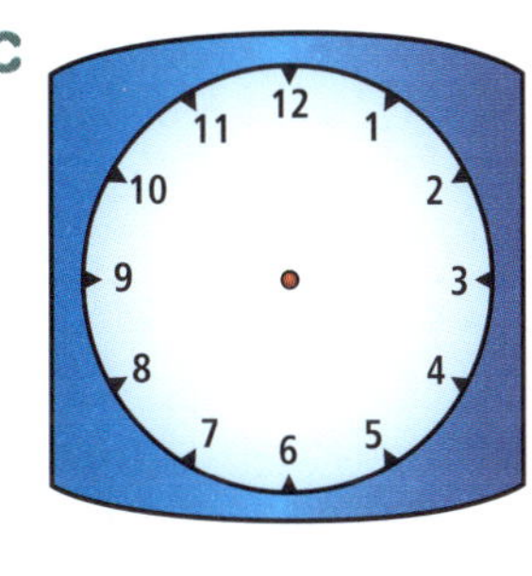

quarter past 4

3 Complete. The smaller hand shows hours. The larger hand shows minutes.

Time	Hour hand points to:	Minute hand points to:
quarter past 2	just past ☐	☐
quarter to 2	just before ☐	☐
half past 2	halfway between ☐ and ☐	☐

7A Groups and rows

three groups of four
4 + 4 + 4

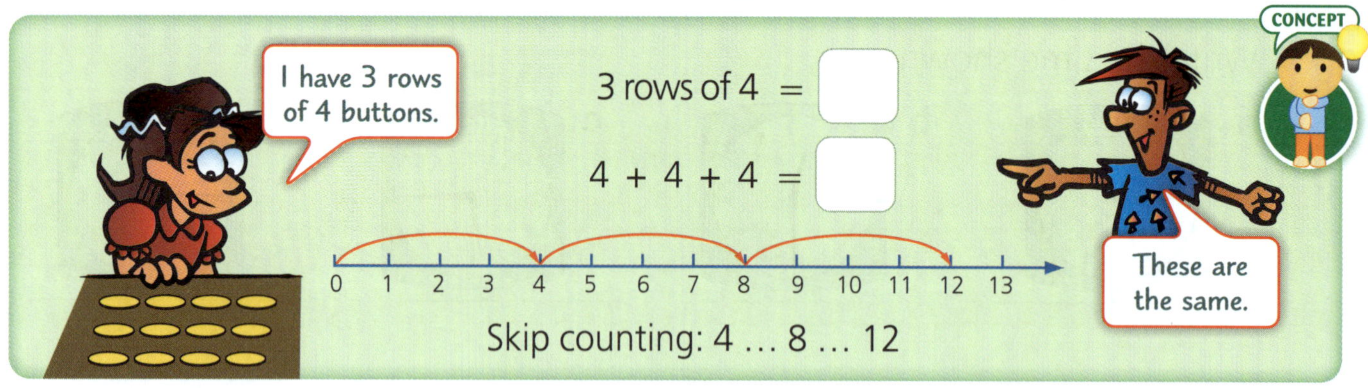

1 Complete:

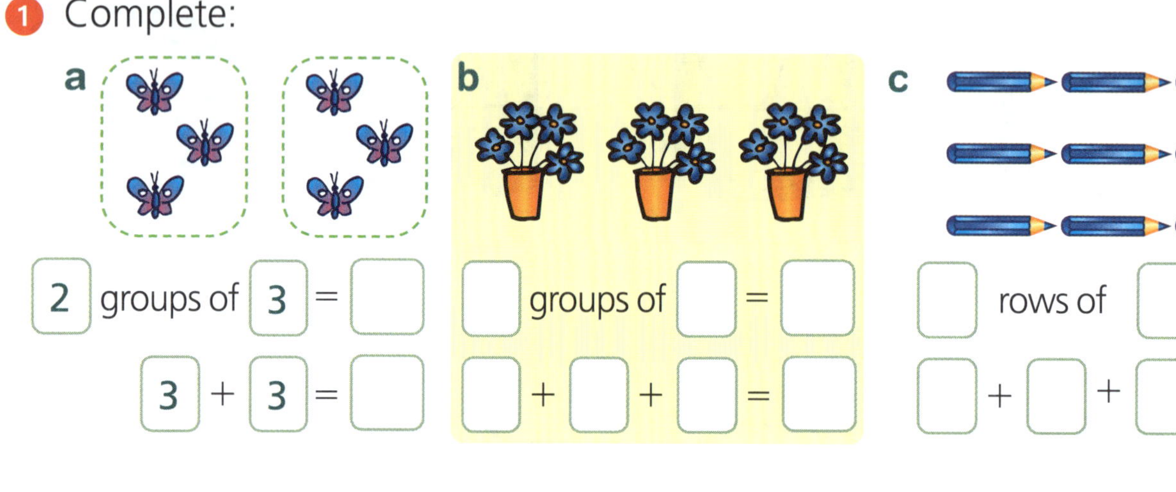

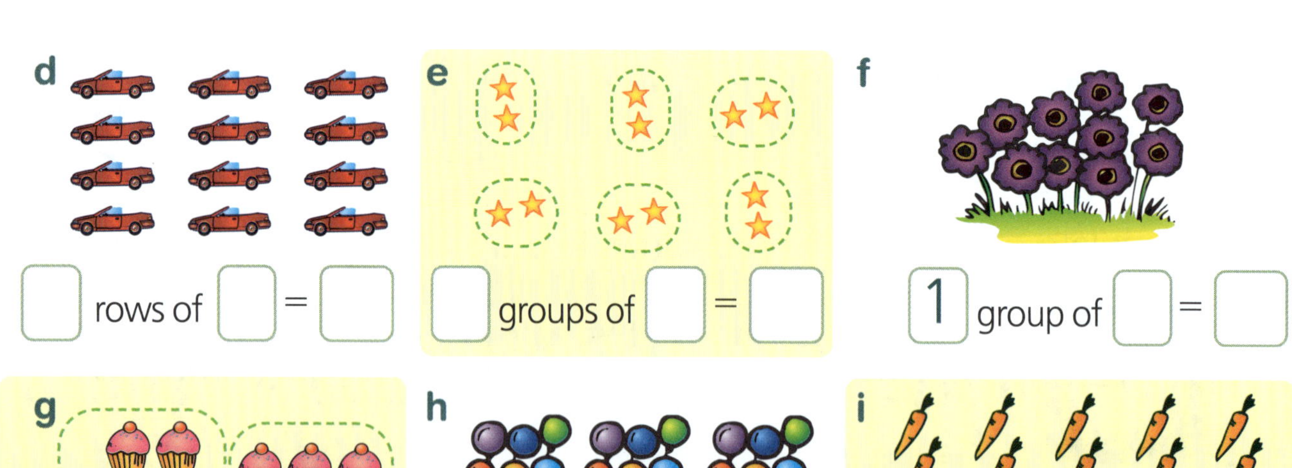

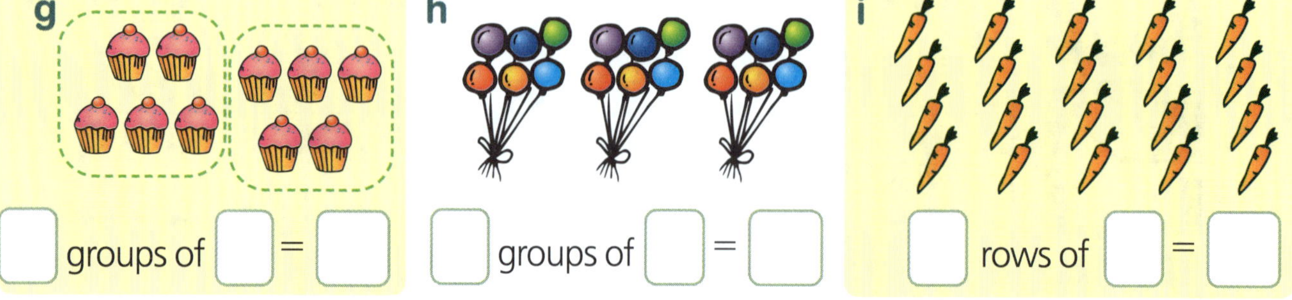

7B Multiplication

1 Use the drawings above to complete these number sentences.

a ☐ groups of ☐ flying birds = ☐ flying birds

b ☐ groups of ☐ cows = ☐ cows

c ☐ rows of ☐ frogs = ☐ frogs

d 1 group of ☐ cockatoos = ☐ cockatoos

e 1 group of ☐ fish = ☐ fish

f ☐ groups of ☐ turtles = ☐ turtles

g ☐ rows of ☐ trees = ☐ trees

2 groups of 4
= double 4
= 4 + 4

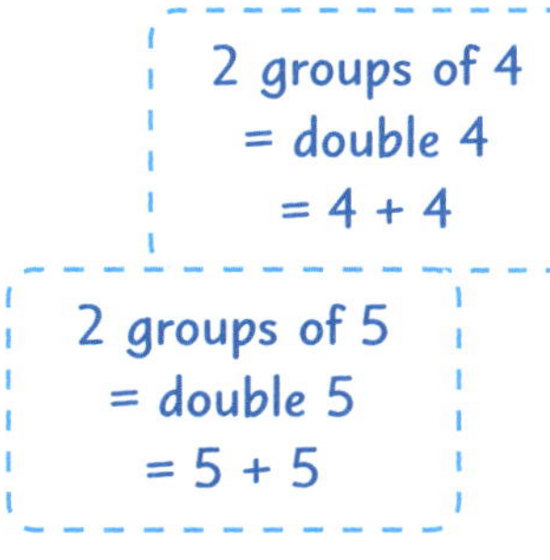

2 groups of 5
= double 5
= 5 + 5

INVESTIGATION

Use the groups above to make up other problems.

a 2 groups of 4 cockatoos = ☐ cockatoos

b ☐ groups of ☐ ☐ = ☐ ☐

c ☐ groups of ☐ ☐ = ☐ ☐

7C Features of 2D shapes

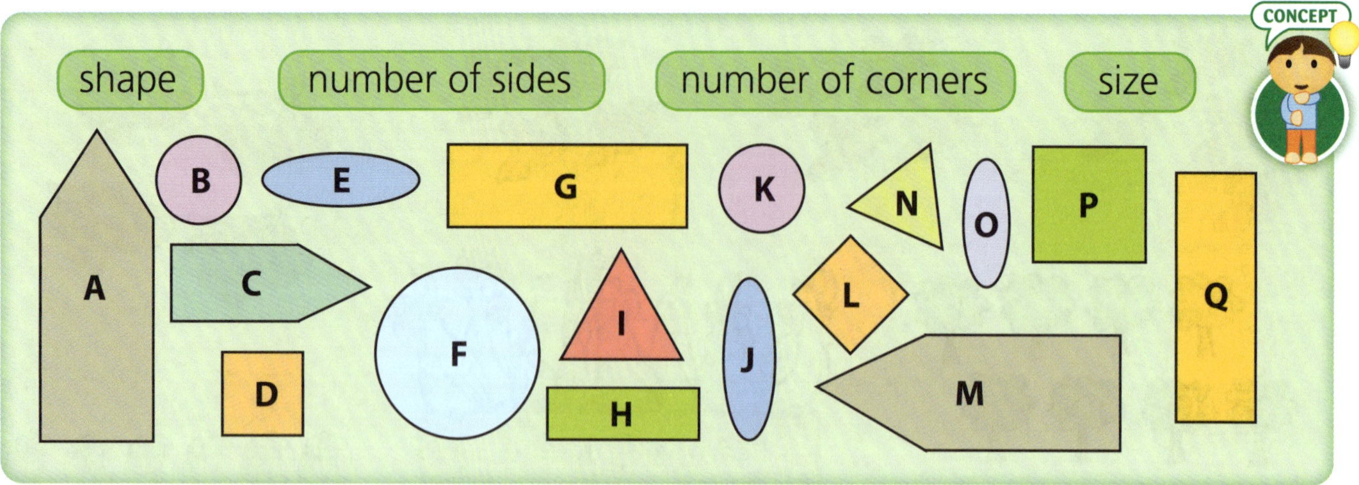

1. Look at these blocks.
   - **a** Which have the same shape as E?
   - **b** Which have the same shape as K?
   - **c** Which has the same shape as I?
   - **d** Which have the same shape as G?
   - **e** Which has the same shape and size as B?
   - **f** Which has the same shape and size as A?
   - **g** Which has the same shape and size as G?
   - **h** Which have the same shape as P?
   - **i** Which have the same shape as M?
   - **j** Which have four corners (vertices)?

2. What is the name of:
   - **a** shape A?
   - **b** shape B?
   - **c** shape Q?
   - **d** shape N?
   - **e** shape D?
   - **f** shape J?

7D Drawing 2D shapes

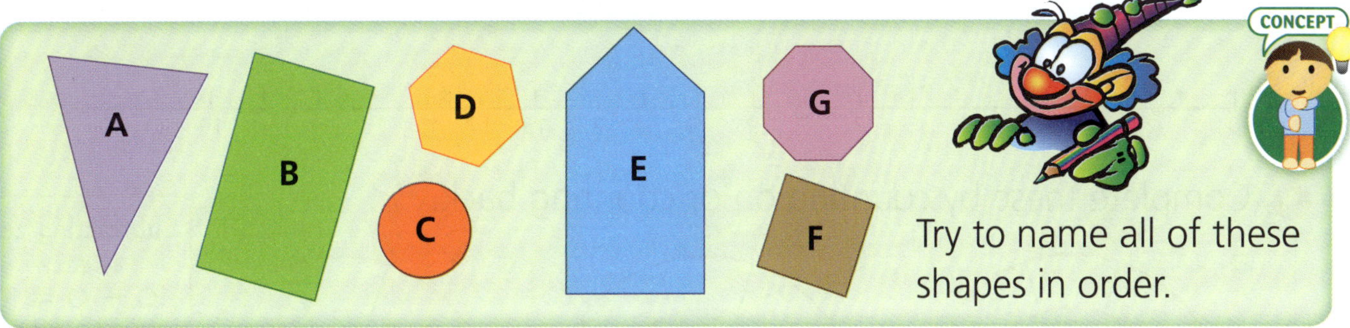

1. Use a ruler to draw these shapes. Use the dots to help.

   a triangle

   b rectangle

   c hexagon

   d pentagon

   e octagon

   f quadrilateral

ACTIVITY

Use the shapes to add to this design. Try to name shapes A to F.

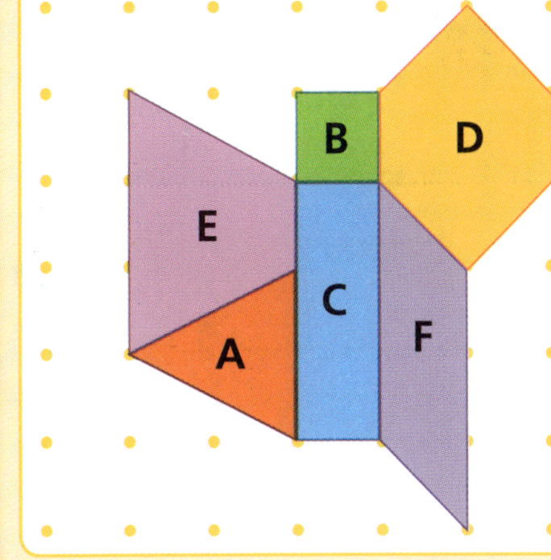

 • *AUSTRALIAN SIGNPOST MATHS 2* • ISBN 9780655708766

Subtraction to 20

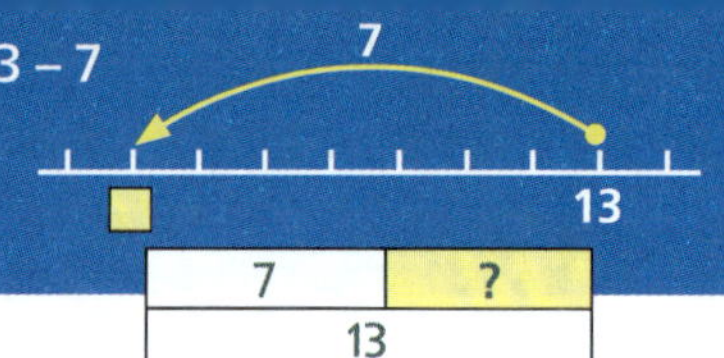

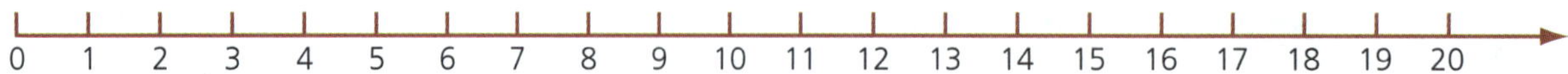

1 Complete these by counting on or counting back.

a

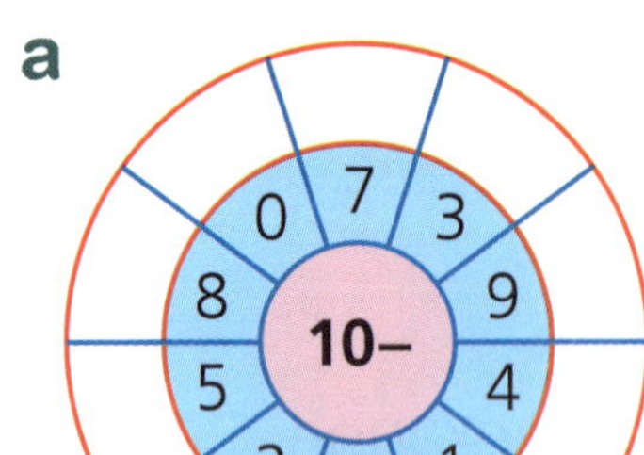

b

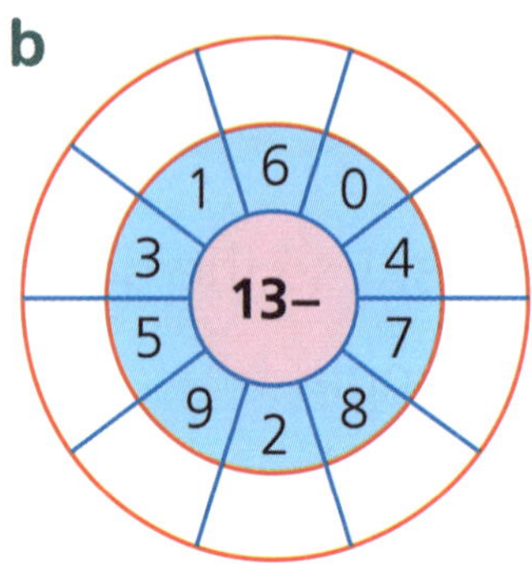

c

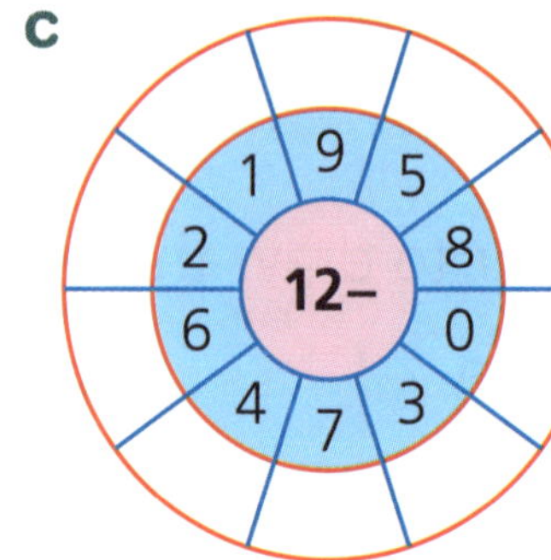

Subtracting zero is easy.
10 – 0 = 10

2 Colour the boxes. 10 = red, 9 = blue, 8 = green, 7 = yellow

14 – 4	13 – 4	9 – 2	13 – 6	11 – 4	16 – 7	20 – 10
12 – 3	15 – 5	14 – 5	12 – 5	15 – 6	19 – 9	17 – 8
11 – 3	12 – 4	16 – 6	19 – 10	18 – 8	14 – 6	16 – 8
8 – 1	15 – 7	18 – 9	17 – 7	11 – 2	10 – 3	13 – 5

3 Use this code to find the message.

A	E	H	I	K	L	M	S	T
8	6	2	3	9	4	5	7	10

10 – 7 = ☐

Ask:
7 plus what makes 10?

7 + ☐ = 10

Message:

10–7		12–8	9–6	11–2	10–4		8–3	9–1	10–0	7–5	9–2

FUN SPOT

Make a message of your own using the code.

 • *AUSTRALIAN SIGNPOST MATHS 2* • ISBN 9780655708766

8B Differences

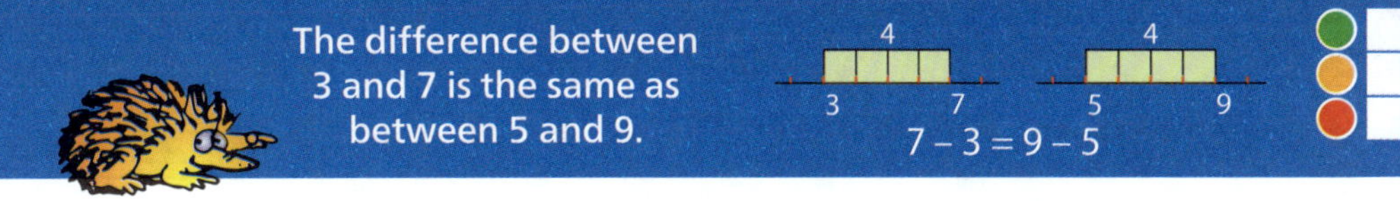

CONCEPT

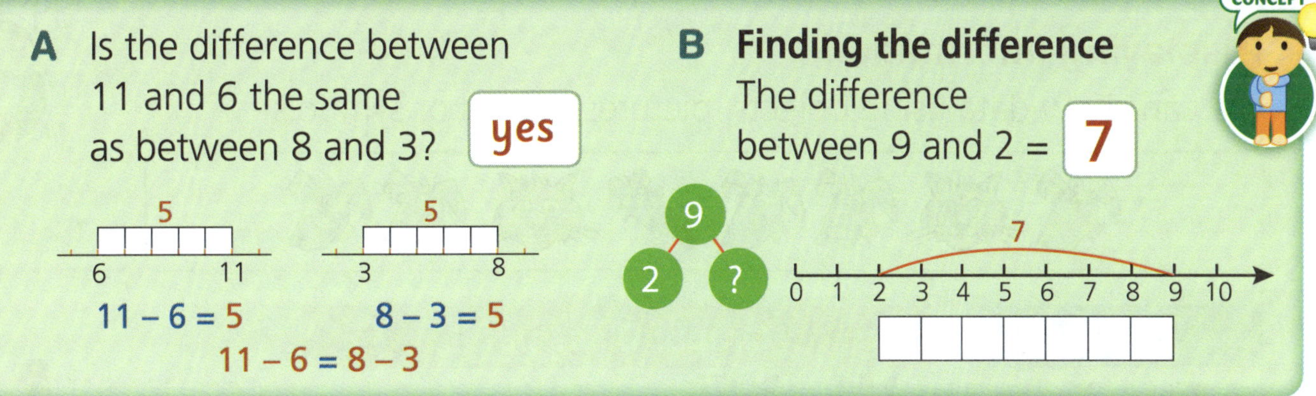

1

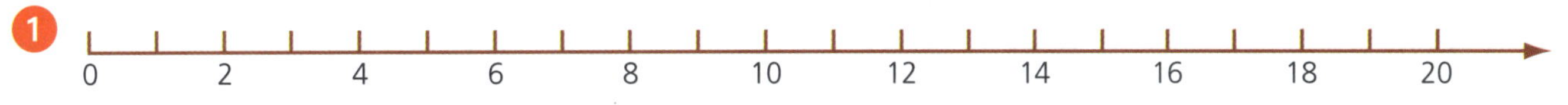

a The difference between 10 and 6 = ☐.

b The difference between 15 and 8 = ☐.

c The difference between 12 and 6 = ☐.

2

14 – 8 is the difference between 8 and 14.

2, 5

7 8 9 10 11 12 13 14 15

2 + 5 = 7 so
14 – 8 = 7

a Is the difference between 7 and 4 the same as between 17 and 14? ☐

b Is the difference between 8 and 5 the same as between 16 and 13? ☐

c Is the difference between 12 and 8 the same as between 11 and 5? ☐

3 Fill in the diagram using addition facts.

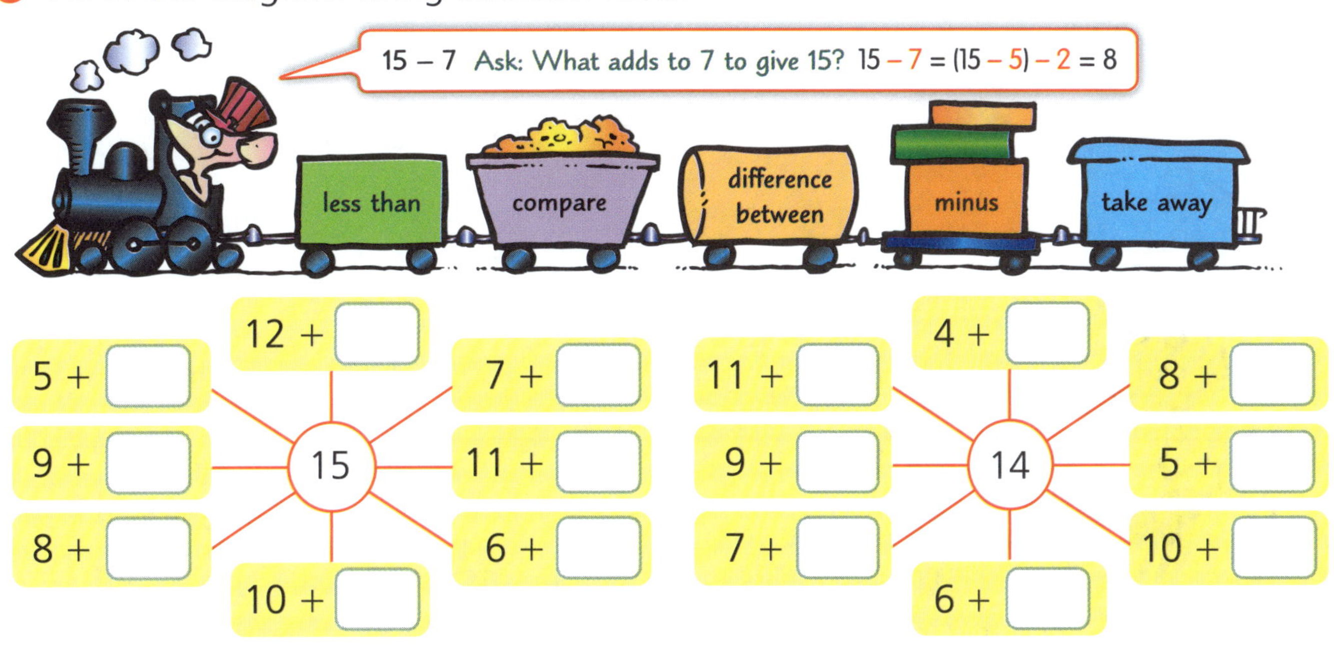

 • *AUSTRALIAN SIGNPOST MATHS 2* • ISBN 9780655708766

Lists, graphs and tables

CONCEPT

Displaying information

We can show data using objects, pictures, words or symbols.

Table

Pet	Number
Cat	2
Dog	5
Rat	1

Graph: Class pets

List

Dog, Cat, Dog, Dog, Rat, Cat, Dog, Dog

We might ask why there were only 8 pets.

Use the data above to answer these questions.

a How many cats? ☐

b How many more dogs than cats? ☐

1. Students were asked which animal they liked best out of **elephant**, **lion** and **monkey**. Use the list to finish the graph and table.

List

Monkey, Lion, Lion, Monkey, Elephant, Lion, Monkey, Elephant, Elephant, Elephant, Lion, Elephant, Monkey, Elephant, Monkey

Animal	Number
Elephant	
Lion	
Monkey	

Discuss the results. Could some students have a different favourite?

8D Comparing masses

Why would I need more ones blocks than marbles?

ACTIVITY

1 a Handle two objects like these and **estimate** which one is heavier.

I estimate the ______ to be heavier than the ______.

pencil case   lunch box

b Use marbles and a balance scale to find the mass of each object.

The ______ has a mass equal to ______ marbles.

The ______ has a mass equal to ______ marbles.

2 Choose three pairs of objects in the classroom.

- Estimate which object is heavier in each pair by hefting.
- Check by using a balance scale and marbles.
- Complete this chart.

Estimate by hefting	Number of units	Was your estimate correct?
______ is heavier than ______	______ ______	☐ Yes ☐ No
______ is heavier than ______	______ ______	☐ Yes ☐ No
______ is heavier than ______	______ ______	☐ Yes ☐ No

INVESTIGATION

Estimating mass

Choose two objects. Estimate what their mass would be using marbles. Use a balance scale to measure. How close were your estimates?

Object	Estimate	Real mass	Difference
	marbles	marbles	marbles
	marbles	marbles	marbles

9A Linking addition and subtraction

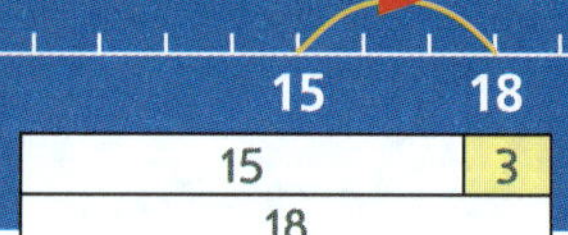

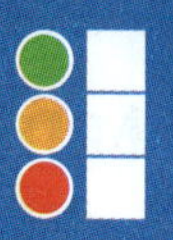

CONCEPT

If 8 + 12 = 20 then 12 + 8 = 20

20 − 8 = 12

20 − 12 = 8

8	12
20	

13 + 6 = 19

6 + 13 = 19

19 − 6 = 13

19 − 13 = 6

These are linked.

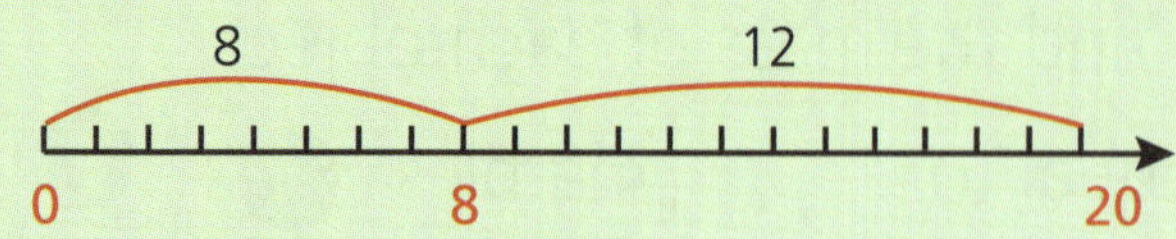

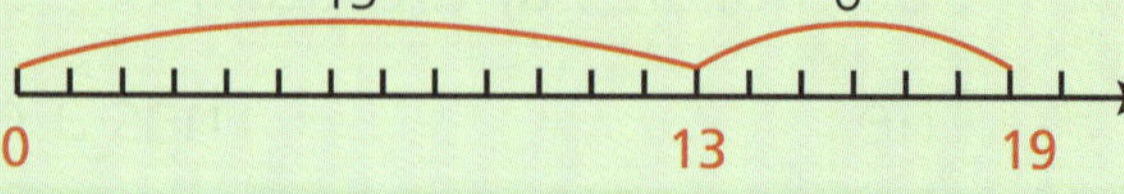

1 **a** If 7 + 15 = 22 then 15 + 7 = ☐

7	15
22	

22 − 7 = ☐

22 − 15 = ☐

7 + 15 = ☐

b 9 + 8 = ☐

8 + 9 = ☐

17 − 9 = ☐

17 − 8 = ☐

2 Use the pictures to help fill in the missing numerals.

a

☐ + ☐ = ☐

☐ + ☐ = ☐

☐ − ☐ = ☐

☐ − ☐ = ☐

b

☐ + ☐ = ☐

☐ + ☐ = ☐

☐ − ☐ = ☐

☐ − ☐ = ☐

3 Write two addition and two subtraction facts for this picture.

☐ + ☐ = ☐   ☐ − ☐ = ☐

☐ + ☐ = ☐   ☐ − ☐ = ☐

4 Write two addition and two subtraction facts for this picture.

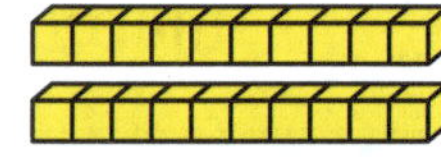

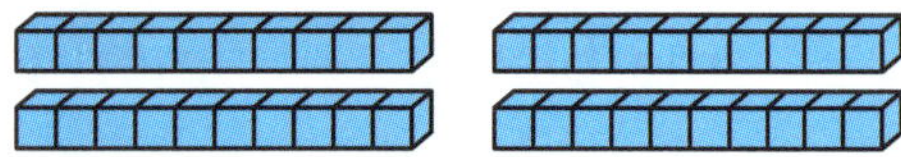

☐ + ☐ = ☐   ☐ − ☐ = ☐

☐ + ☐ = ☐   ☐ − ☐ = ☐

9B Linking addition and subtraction

1 Write two linking subtraction number sentences for each addition.

a 8 + 7 = 15
- ___ – ___ = ___
- ___ – ___ = ___

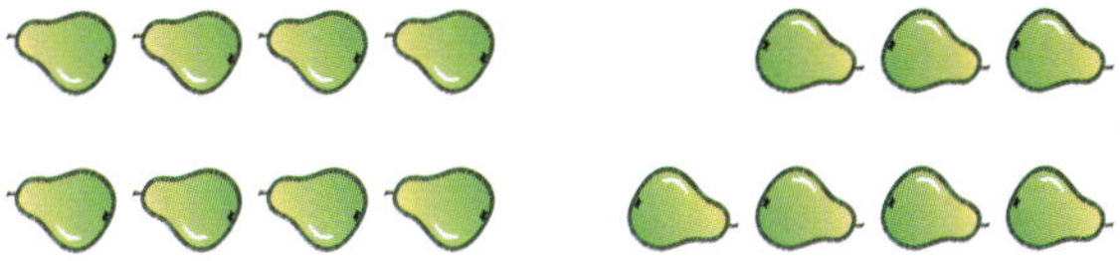

b 6 + 8 = 14
- ___ – ___ = ___
- ___ – ___ = ___

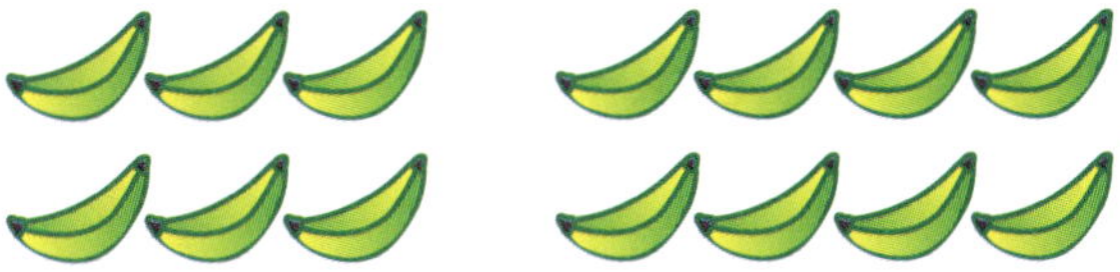

c 7 + 5 = 12
- ___ – ___ = ___
- ___ – ___ = ___

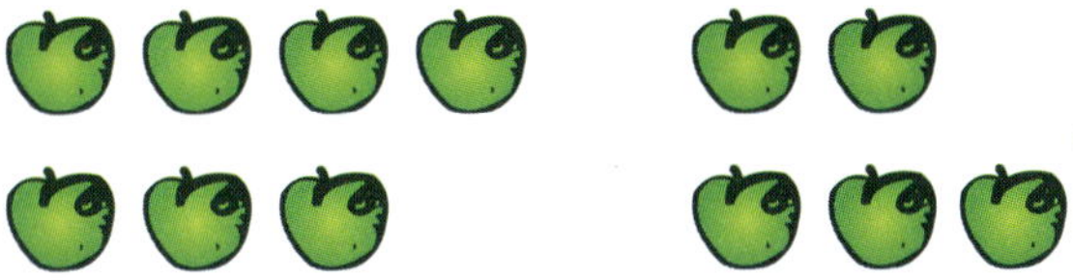

d 14 + 6 = 20
- ___ – ___ = ___
- ___ – ___ = ___

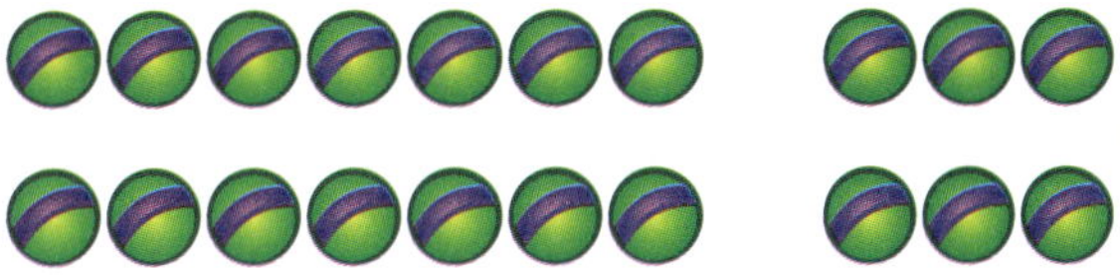

e 22 + 9 = 31
- ___ – ___ = ___
- ___ – ___ = ___

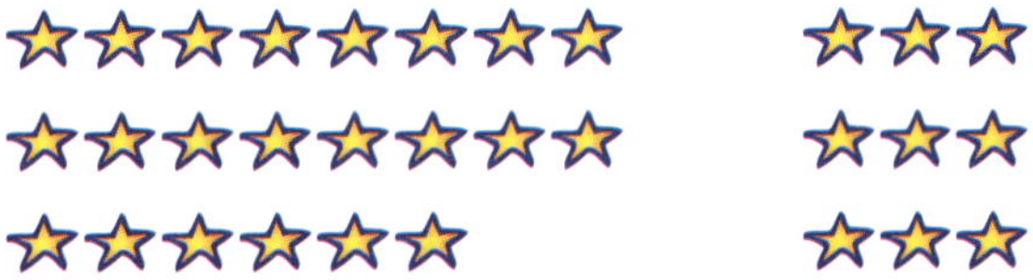

f 17 + 9 = 26
- ___ – ___ = ___
- ___ – ___ = ___

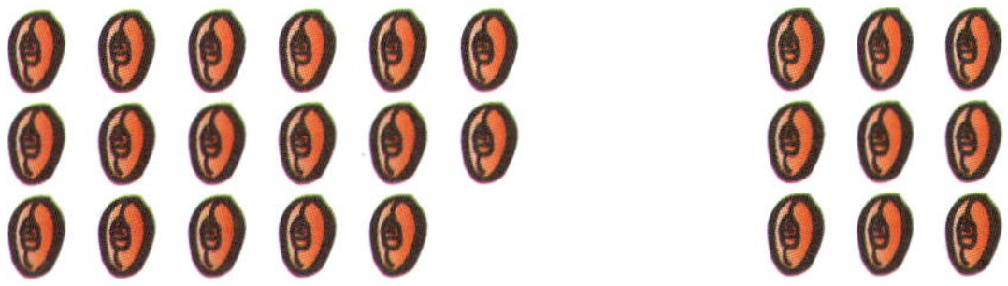

Make linked number sentences of your own.

 • *AUSTRALIAN SIGNPOST MATHS 2* • ISBN 9780655708766

9C Informal units of length

8 squares long

CONCEPT

How many times will the width of my finger fit along my pencil?

[ ] finger widths

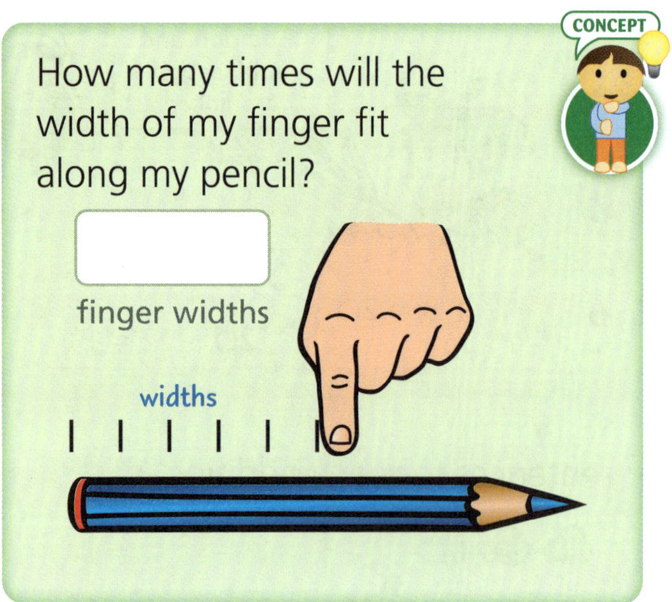

1 Use the different measuring units to find the length of your pencil.

Unit used	Length of your pencil
place-value ones blocks	[ ] blocks
paperclips	[ ] paperclips
finger widths	[ ] finger widths

2 Use hand spans to measure the length of:

	Guess	Check
a this book		
b a bag		
c a window		
d your arm.		

Order these lengths from shortest to longest.

ACTIVITY

Estimate then measure how many steps from where you are to:

	Guess	Check
a the school canteen		
b the lunch seats		
c the library.		

Each step should be the same length.

Order these distances from shortest to longest.

9D Informal units of length

1. Use the different measuring units to find the length of your desk.

Unit used	Length of your desk
this book	☐ books
a pencil	☐ pencils
finger lengths	☐ fingers

CONCEPT

2. Use your hand span to measure the length of each object.

Your desk	☐ hand spans
Teacher's desk	☐ hand spans

Which is longer? ____________

Cupboard	☐ hand spans
Door	☐ hand spans

Which is shorter? ____________

3. Estimate, then use craft sticks to measure these lengths.

a

Estimate: ☐ sticks

Measure: ☐ sticks

b

Estimate: ☐ sticks

Measure: ☐ sticks

c

Estimate: ☐ sticks

Measure: ☐ sticks

ACTIVITY

Use string to compare the length of objects in the room.

____________ is longer than ____________.

____________ is longer than ____________.

 • *AUSTRALIAN SIGNPOST MATHS 2* • ISBN 9780655708766

10A Addition and subtraction facts

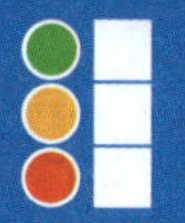

Are you a tables champion?

Memorise your addition facts up to 10 + 10.

Once you learn your addition tables, use them for subtraction.

- If 6 + 7 = 13, then 13 − 6 = 7 and 13 − 7 = 6.
- If 8 + 9 = 17, then 17 − 8 = 9 and 17 − 9 = 8.

1. Use a pencil to join each question to the correct answer. You could practise your tables facts by rubbing out your answers and doing them again.

a +

Question		Answer
2 + 6		1
4 + 6		7
0 + 1		8
5 + 7		9
5 + 6		10
0 + 7		11
4 + 5		12
7 + 10		15
8 + 7		17
10 + 10		18
9 + 9		20
Scores:		

b +

Question		Answer
2 + 3		4
4 + 3		5
2 + 2		7
5 + 4		9
8 + 5		8
8 + 0		10
7 + 5		11
1 + 9		12
10 + 5		13
6 + 5		15
10 + 9		19
Scores:		

c +

Question		Answer
3 + 6		6
2 + 8		7
4 + 2		8
5 + 2		9
4 + 7		10
3 + 5		11
9 + 6		12
6 + 6		13
8 + 8		14
7 + 6		15
10 + 4		16
Scores:		

d +

Question		Answer
3 + 4		5
6 + 2		6
4 + 5		7
3 + 2		8
2 + 4		9
8 + 4		10
4 + 9		11
5 + 5		12
4 + 7		13
7 + 8		14
5 + 9		15
Scores:		

e −

Question		Answer
8 − 6		1
10 − 4		0
1 − 0		2
12 − 5		4
11 − 6		6
7 − 7		5
9 − 5		7
17 − 7		8
15 − 7		10
11 − 8		9
18 − 9		3
Scores:		

f −

Question		Answer
5 − 2		2
7 − 3		3
4 − 2		4
9 − 4		5
13 − 5		0
8 − 8		1
12 − 5		6
10 − 9		7
15 − 5		8
11 − 5		10
19 − 10		9
Scores:		

g −

Question		Answer
6 − 4		0
5 − 2		1
10 − 9		2
7 − 7		3
9 − 3		4
7 − 3		5
10 − 3		6
14 − 5		7
9 − 4		8
18 − 8		9
10 − 2		10
Scores:		

h −

Question		Answer
6 − 5		0
9 − 9		1
6 − 3		2
8 − 6		3
8 − 4		4
16 − 9		5
9 − 4		6
16 − 7		7
17 − 7		8
10 − 4		9
17 − 9		10
Scores:		

10B Adding 10s

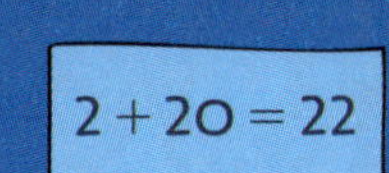

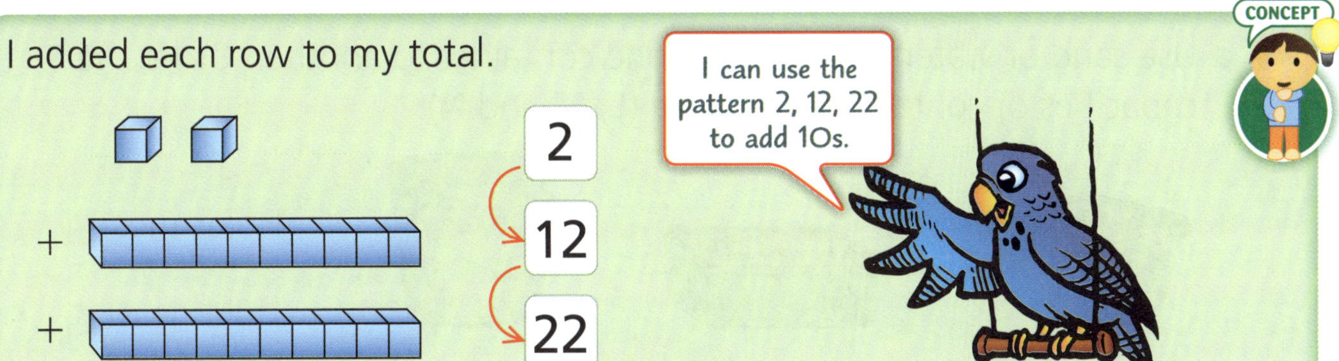

1. Write the totals, adding another 10 for each row.

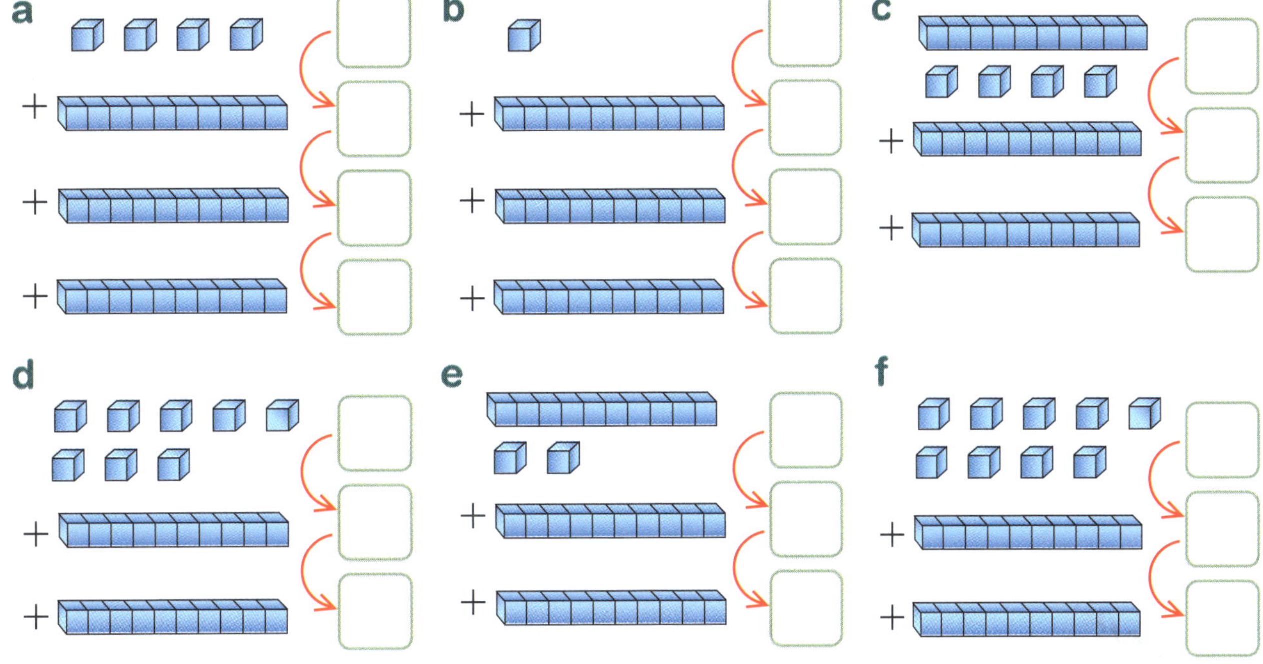

2. Add 20 to each number.

a 3 ☐ **b** 36 ☐ **c** 17 ☐ **d** 52 ☐ **e** 94 ☐

3. Add 30 to each number.

a 1 ☐ **b** 35 ☐ **c** 68 ☐ **d** 19 ☐ **e** 33 ☐

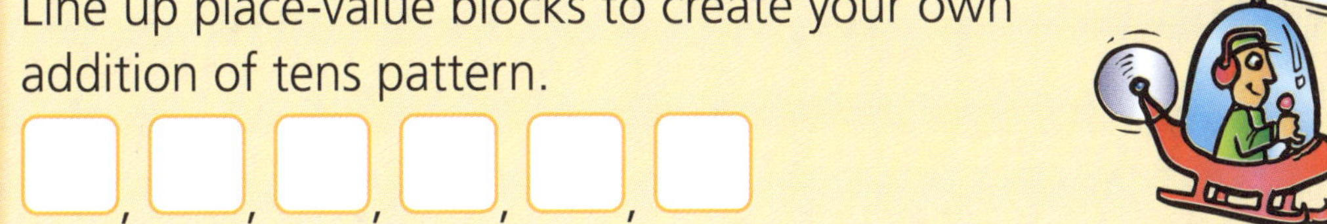

10C Capacity

Capacity is how much a container can hold.

1 a Use sand or water to pour from one container to another. Order the capacities of containers like these (**L**, **M** and **N**).

L container **M** lunch box **N** bucket

Holds most: ☐

Holds least: ☐

b Would you use a spoon, a cup or a milk container as the unit to measure the capacities of the containers? ☐ Discuss.

c Use a cup to estimate and measure each container.

Container		Estimate	Count
L	☐	☐ cups	☐ cups
M	☐	☐ cups	☐ cups
N	☐	☐ cups	☐ cups

Use a full cup each time so that each unit is the same.

d The ☐ holds the least and the ☐ holds the most.

Was the cup a good unit to use to measure these containers?

e The bucket holds ☐ more cups than the lunch box.

f The container holds ☐ more cups than the lunch box.

2 Explain what you did to measure the capacity of the bucket.

 AUSTRALIAN SIGNPOST MATHS 2 • ISBN 9780655708766

10D Ordering capacities

Order the capacities from smallest to largest.

1 Choose sets of three containers and measure the capacity of each. Record your results in the table below.

Use a full cup each time

a

Container	Estimate	Count
	cups	cups
	cups	cups
	cups	cups

b

Container	Estimate	Count
	cups	cups
	cups	cups
	cups	cups

2 Order each set of containers above from "holds least" to "holds most".

a 1 ______ 2 ______ 3 ______

b 1 ______ 2 ______ 3 ______

3 Tina recorded these results. Answer the following questions.

Container	Number	Comment
large pot	15 cups	2nd largest
bucket	11 cups	holds least
box	26 cups	holds most

a Which container held 15 cups? ______

b Which container held 26 cups? ______

c Which container held less than the large pot? ______

d Which container held more than the large pot? ______

e Order the containers from smallest to largest.

1 ______ 2 ______ 3 ______

 • *AUSTRALIAN SIGNPOST MATHS 2* • ISBN 9780655708766

11A How many more?

27 + (3 + 5) = 35
so 27 + 8 = 35

CONCEPT

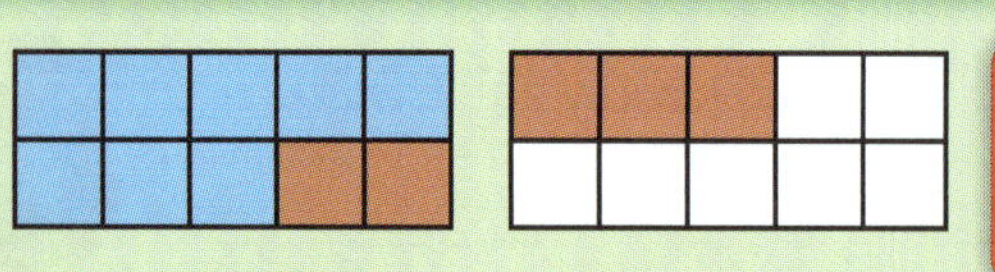

8 + ☐ = 13

I have 8 fish. How many more to make 13?

18 + ☐ = 23

We can say 8 + 2 gives 10, and 3 more makes 13.

so 8 + 5 = 13

18 + 2 gives 20, and 3 makes 23.

so 18 + 5 = 23

1 Find the missing numbers.

a 3 + ☐ = 10 **b** 8 + ☐ = 10 **c** 7 + ☐ = 10

d 16 + ☐ = 20 **e** 14 + ☐ = 20 **f** 19 + ☐ = 20

g 37 + ☐ = 40 **h** 28 + ☐ = 30 **i** 45 + ☐ = 50

2 Find the missing numbers by first counting on to the next ten.

a 3 + ☐ = 12 **b** 8 + ☐ = 14 **c** 7 + ☐ = 15

d 16 + ☐ = 22 **e** 14 + ☐ = 21 **f** 19 + ☐ = 27

g 37 + ☐ = 45 **h** 28 + ☐ = 33 **i** 45 + ☐ = 52

3 Use the method above to find the answers.

a 22 – 16 = ☐ **b** 21 – 14 = ☐

c 45 – 37 = ☐ **d** 33 – 28 = ☐

e 32 – 29 = ☐ **f** 66 – 59 = ☐

g 51 – 49 = ☐ **h** 74 – 66 = ☐

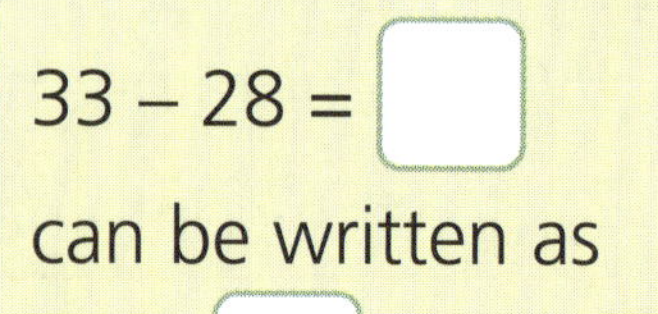

33 – 28 = ☐ can be written as 28 + ☐ = 33.

11B Adding and subtracting 10s

+10 45 + 10 = 55

−10 45 − 10 = 35

We can use the columns to add 10s or take away 10s.

31, 21 — 31 − 10 = 21

9, 19, 29, 39 — 9 + 30 = 39

43, 33, 23, 13 — 43 − 30 = 13

1	2	3	4	5	6	7	8	9	10
11	12	13	14	15	16	17	18	19	20
21	22	23	24	25	26	27	28	29	30
31	32	33	34	35	36	37	38	39	40
41	42	43	44	45	46	47	48	49	50

1 Help Banjo find the answers by adding or subtracting 10.

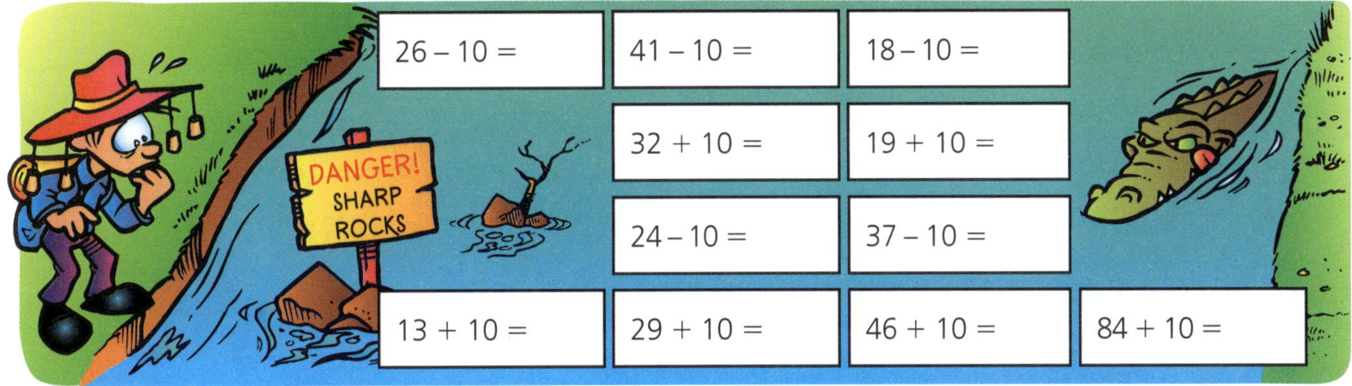

26 − 10 =

41 − 10 =

18 − 10 =

32 + 10 =

19 + 10 =

24 − 10 =

37 − 10 =

13 + 10 =

29 + 10 =

46 + 10 =

84 + 10 =

2 Continue these patterns.

a 15, 25, 35, ☐, ☐, ☐

b 59, 49, 39, ☐, ☐, ☐

c 37, 47, 57, ☐, ☐, ☐

d 81, 71, 61, ☐, ☐, ☐

3 Use 10s patterns to complete these.

a 12 + 20 → 12, 22, 32 so 12 + 20 = ☐

b 27 + 30 → 27, 37, 47, 57 so 27 + 30 = ☐

c 51 − 20 → 51, 41, 31 so 51 − 20 = ☐

d 85 − 30 → 85, 75, 65, 55 so 85 − 30 = ☐

e 43 + 40 = ☐

f 74 − 40 = ☐

g 38 + 40 = ☐

h True or false? 34 + 30 = 94 − 30 ☐

 • *AUSTRALIAN SIGNPOST MATHS 2* • ISBN 9780655708766

11C Capacity

To find which holds more, pour the contents of one into the other.

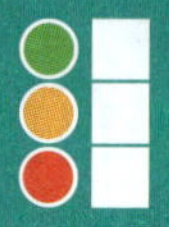

1 Dipping into water:

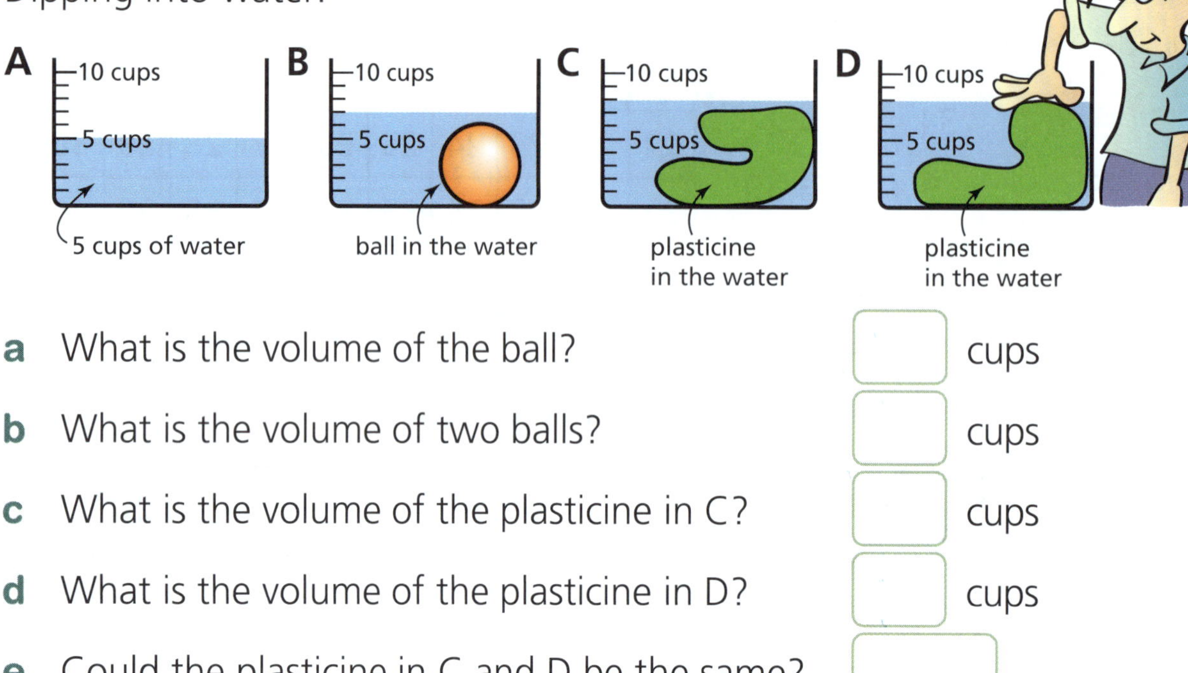

a What is the volume of the ball? ☐ cups

b What is the volume of two balls? ☐ cups

c What is the volume of the plasticine in C? ☐ cups

d What is the volume of the plasticine in D? ☐ cups

e Could the plasticine in C and D be the same? ☐

2 When the water from A is poured into D it reaches Level A.

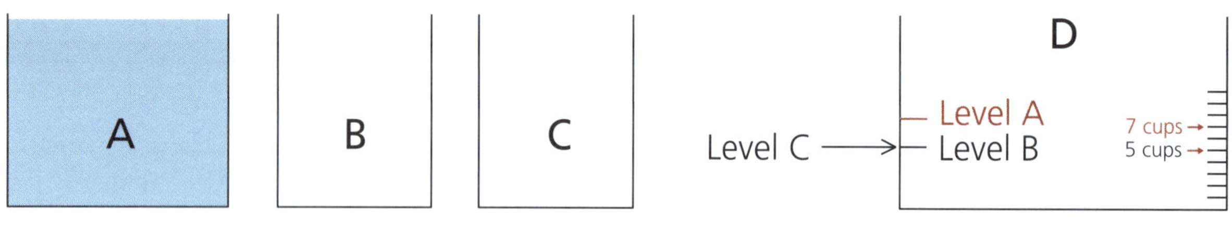

a What is the capacity of:

A ☐ cups? **B** ☐ cups? **C** ☐ cups

b Does container B have the same capacity as container A? ☐

c Which container has the same capacity as container C? ☐

d Which container has the greatest capacity? ☐

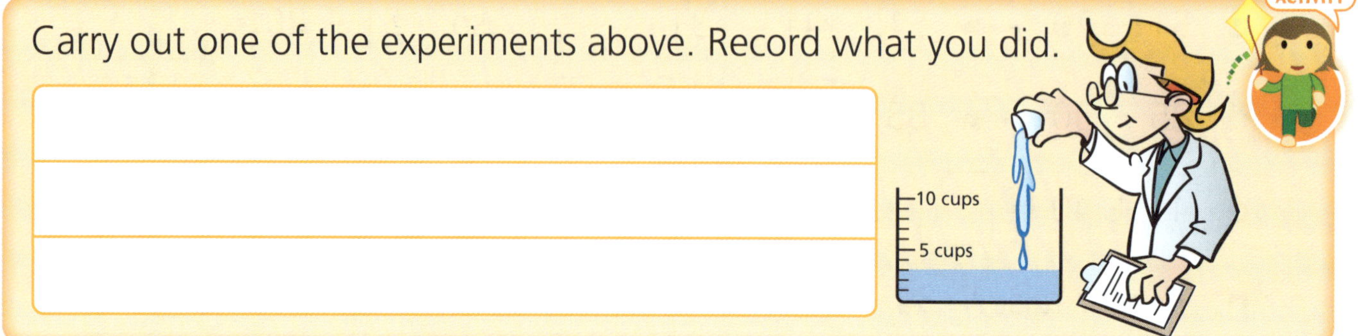

Carry out one of the experiments above. Record what you did.

11D Using tally marks

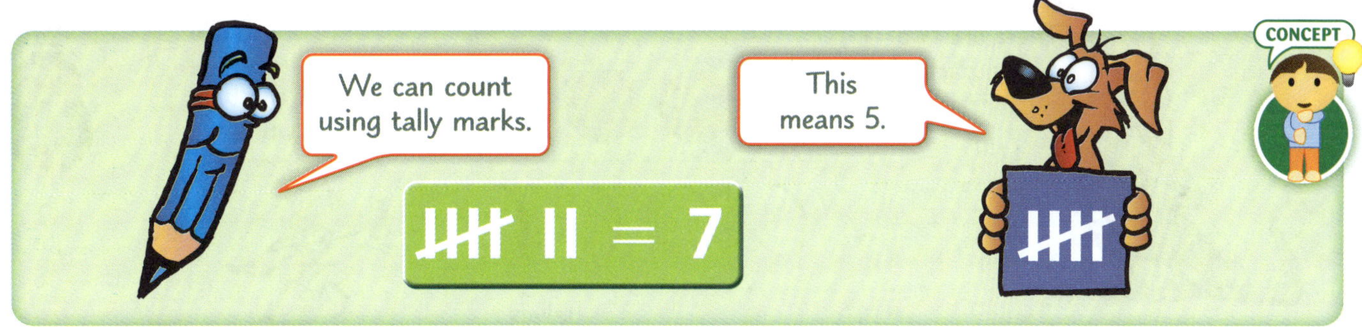

1. Write the number shown by each tally.

a ||| ☐ b 𝍸 |  c 𝍸 𝍸 ☐

d 𝍸 |||| ☐ e 𝍸 𝍸 | ☐ f 𝍸 | ☐

2. Cross off one ball at a time and put a tally mark in the table.

Christmas balls	Number
red	
blue	
green	
orange	

O	G	G	R	G	B	G
G	B	G	G	B	G	R
B	G	R	R	G	G	B
R	G	O	G	B	R	G
G	B	G	R	G	G	R
B	R	R	B	R	O	O

How many of the balls are:

a red? ☐ b blue? ☐ c green? ☐

d orange? ☐ e How many balls altogether? 

Make a tally

Complete this tally for the people in your class. You can decide who has light hair and who has dark hair.

Hair colour	Number
light	
dark	

12A Half of a group

Two halves make the whole collection.

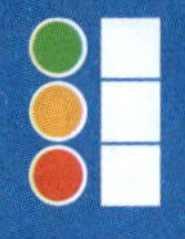

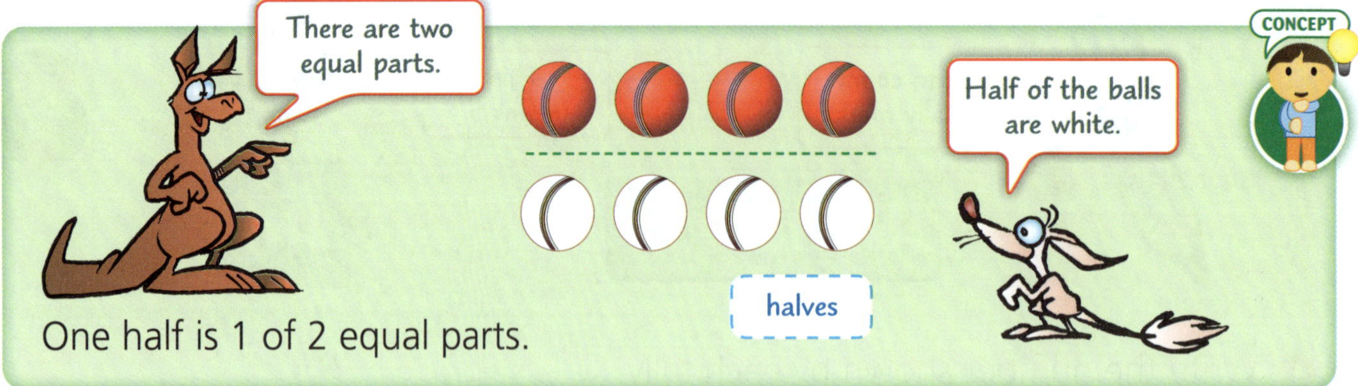

1 Circle the groups that are divided into halves.

Colour one half of each of the circled groups.

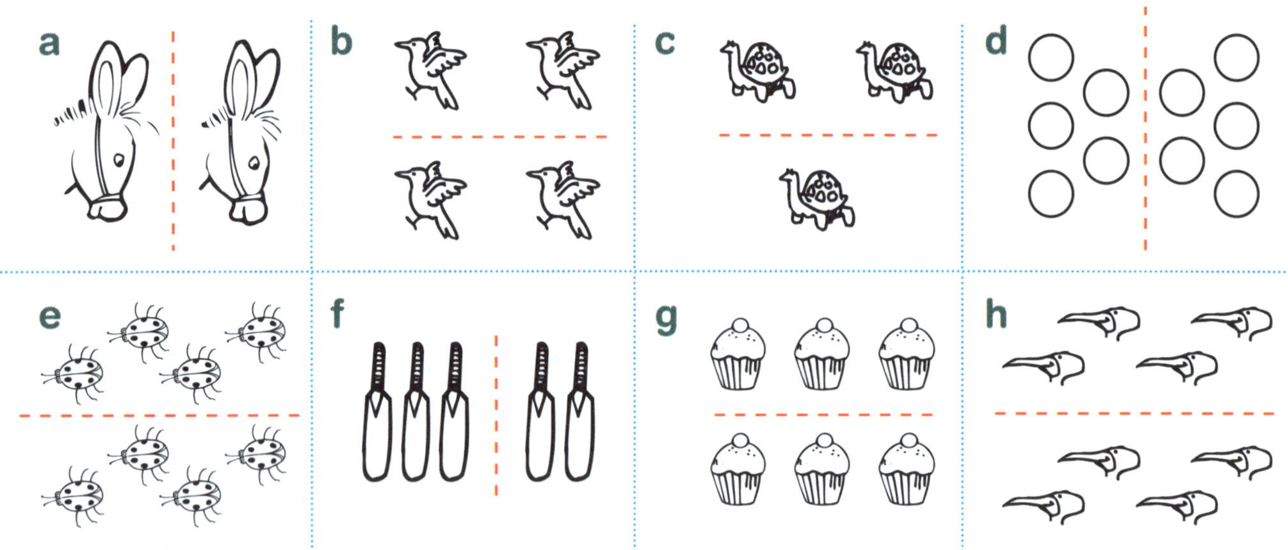

2 Circle half of each group.

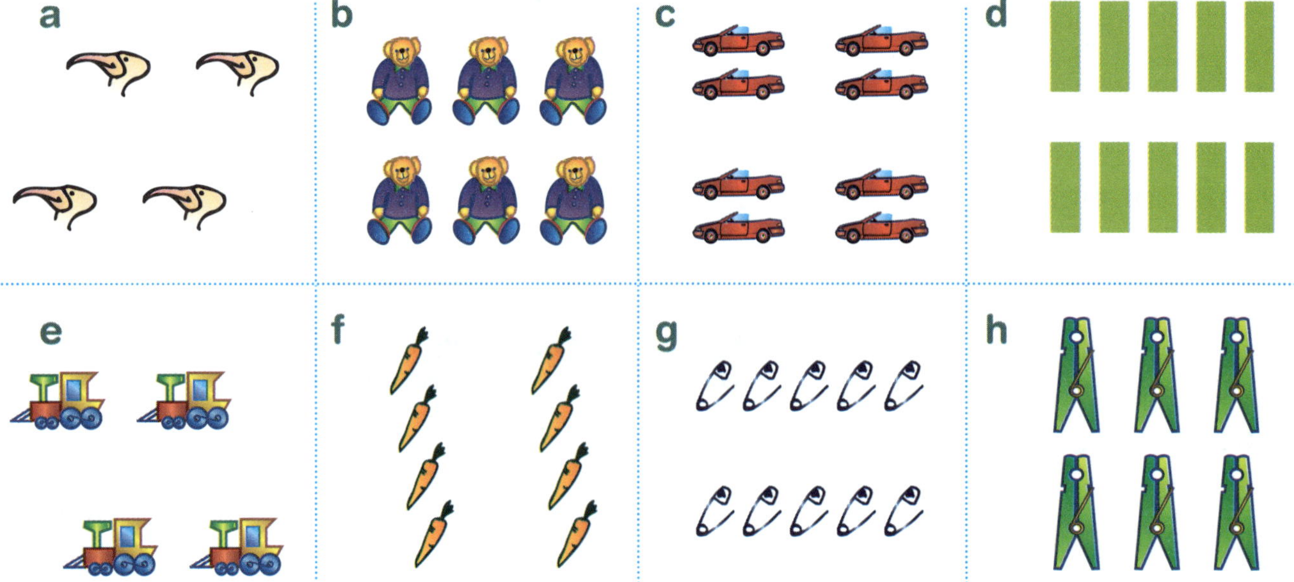

 • *AUSTRALIAN SIGNPOST MATHS 2* • ISBN 9780655708766

Halves

half half

Two halves make one whole.

CONCEPT

One half is one of two equal parts.

1 Draw a line to halve each group.

a b c d e

2 Circle half of each collection.

a b c

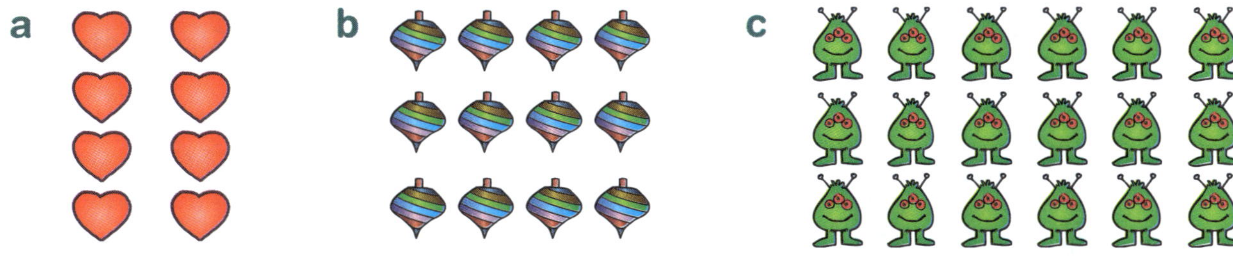

3 True or false?

When two halves of a collection are put together you have the whole collection.

FUN SPOT

Share a collection of 20 counters into two halves.
Count each half.

What is half of 20 counters?

Find half of other collections.

 • AUSTRALIAN SIGNPOST MATHS 2 • ISBN 9780655708766

3 → 6 → 9
holds 3 | holds 3 | holds 3

You can skip count by 3.

CONCEPT

Each bag has 5 apples.

To find how many apples are in 4 bags, we count the 5 apples four times, 5 + 5 + 5 + 5 or skip count by 5s.

1 Use the picture above to find how many apples are in:

a 2 bags ☐ **b** 3 bags ☐ **c** 4 bags ☐

5	5

5	5	5

5	5	5	5

2

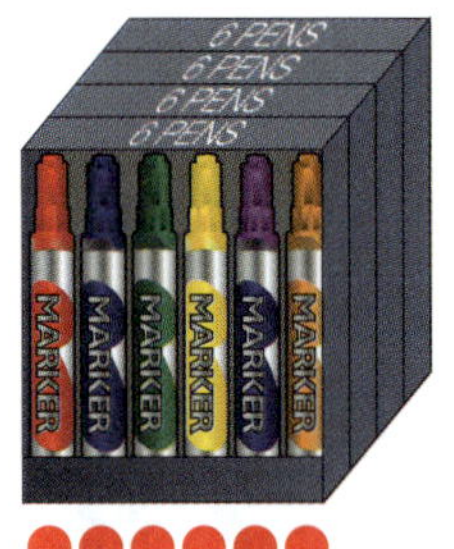

In each packet there are 6 pens.
How many pens are in:

a 2 packets? ☐ **b** 3 packets? ☐

c 4 packets? ☐ **d** 5 packets? ☐

3

In each pod there are 4 peas.
How many peas are in:

a 2 pods? ☐ **b** 3 pods? ☐

c 4 pods? ☐ **d** 5 pods? ☐

e 6 pods? ☐ **f** 10 pods? ☐

4

In each can there are 3 tennis balls.
How many balls are in:

a 2 cans? ☐ **b** 3 cans? ☐

c 4 cans? ☐ **d** 5 cans? ☐

e 6 cans? ☐ **f** 10 cans? ☐

 ISBN 9780655708766

12D Estimating time passed

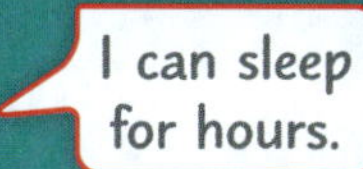

ACTIVITY

1 Work in groups of three. As one person writes their name, the other two clap. Record the number of claps.

Number of claps for friend 1	
Number of claps for friend 2	

Who took the least time to write their name? ______

2 Use clapping to time other events. First estimate the time it will take.

Event	Estimate	Claps

3 Practise saying "1 second, 2 seconds, 3 seconds …" so that each count takes 1 second.

a Count like this for 1 minute (60 seconds). What number did you reach? ______

b Repeat the activity in Question 1 using this form of counting.

Number of seconds for friend 1	
Number of seconds for friend 2	

1 second, 2 seconds, 3 seconds, 4 seconds …

4 Would these events take minutes or hours to complete? Match.

a day at school	minutes	brushing your teeth
recess	hours	painting a house
a party		eating an apple

  ISBN 9780655708766

13A Multiplication sign

X means
- groups of
- rows of or
- columns of

1. Complete these number sentences.

× means "groups of".

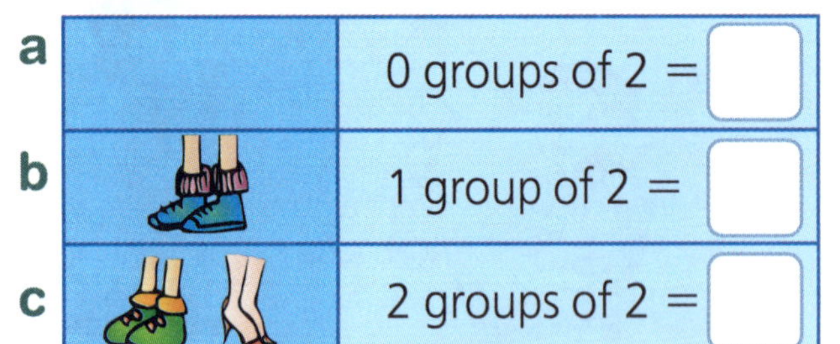

a		0 groups of 2 = ☐
b		1 group of 2 = ☐
c		2 groups of 2 = ☐

d		3 × 2 = ☐
e		4 × ☐ = ☐
f		☐ × ☐ = ☐

2. Draw pictures to show each story. Complete the number sentences.

a 3 vases of 4 flowers each

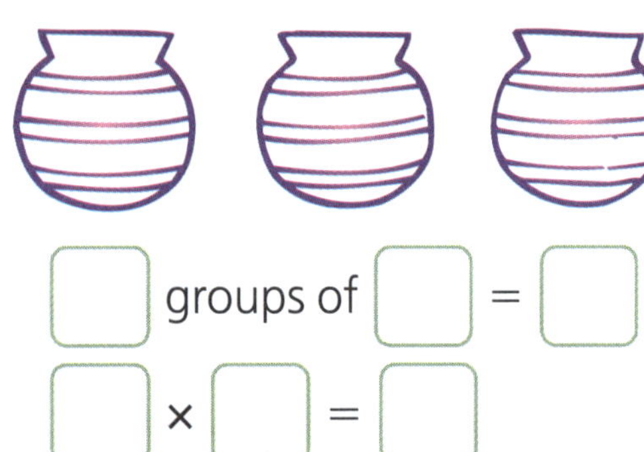

☐ groups of ☐ = ☐

☐ × ☐ = ☐

b 2 boxes with 6 balls in each

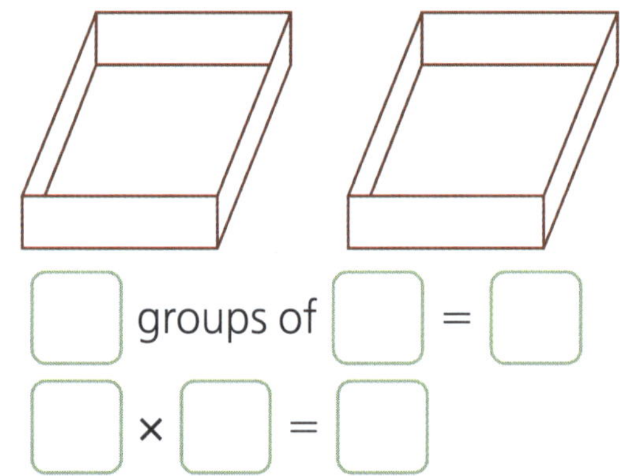

☐ groups of ☐ = ☐

☐ × ☐ = ☐

3. Match each group with the correct number sentence.

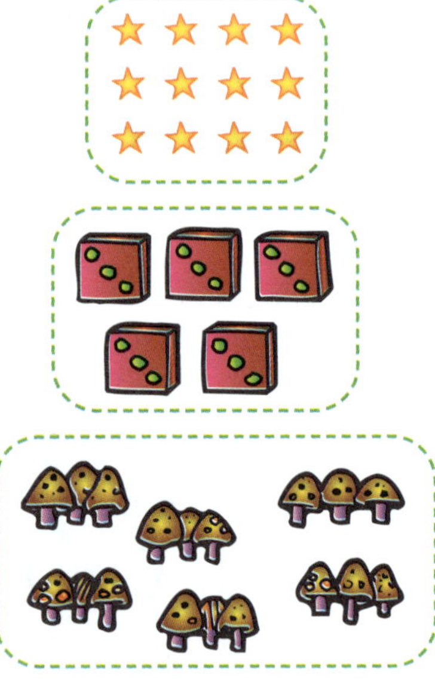

2 × 9 = 18

5 × 2 = 10

6 × 3 = 18

2 × 6 = 12

3 × 4 = 12

5 × 3 = 15

4. Use counters to make arrays to answer these questions.

a 3 × 7 = ☐ b 4 × 6 = ☐ c 5 × 3 = ☐

13B Equal groups

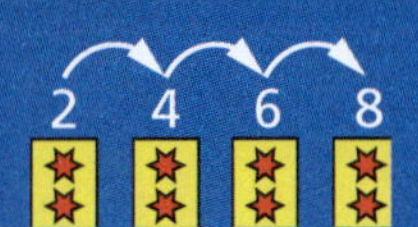

2 groups of 2 = 2 x 2 = 4
3 groups of 2 = 3 x 2 = 6
4 groups of 2 = 4 x 2 = 8

1 Complete the number sentences. **x** means "groups of" or "rows of".

a 

☐ × ☐ = ☐

b 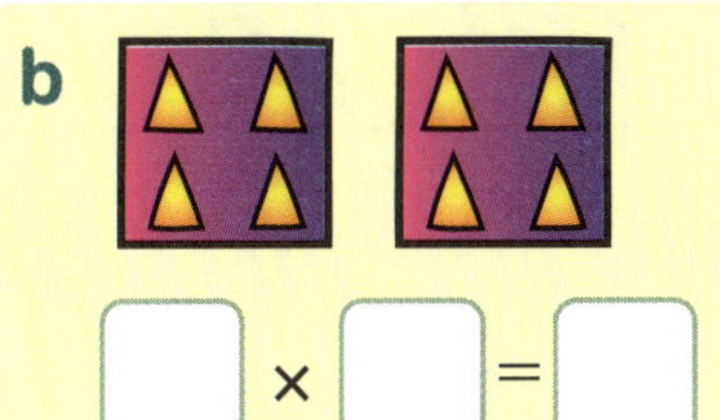

☐ × ☐ = ☐

c 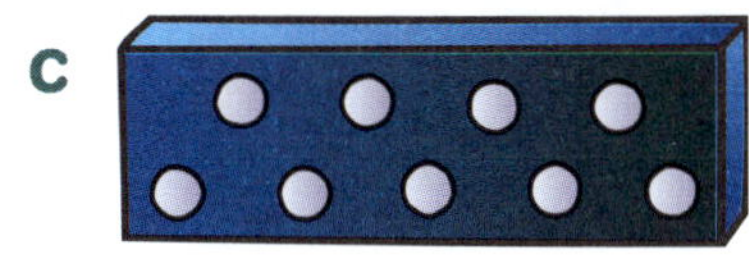

1 × ☐ = ☐

d 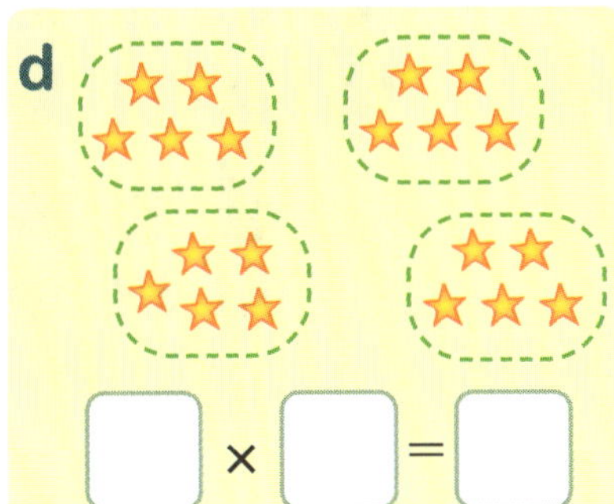

☐ × ☐ = ☐

e 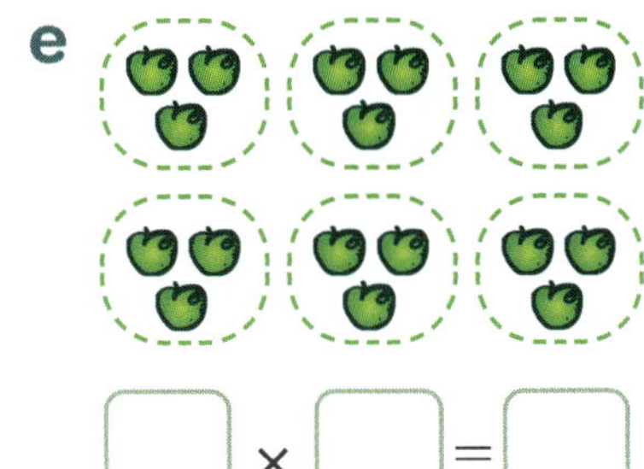

☐ × ☐ = ☐

f 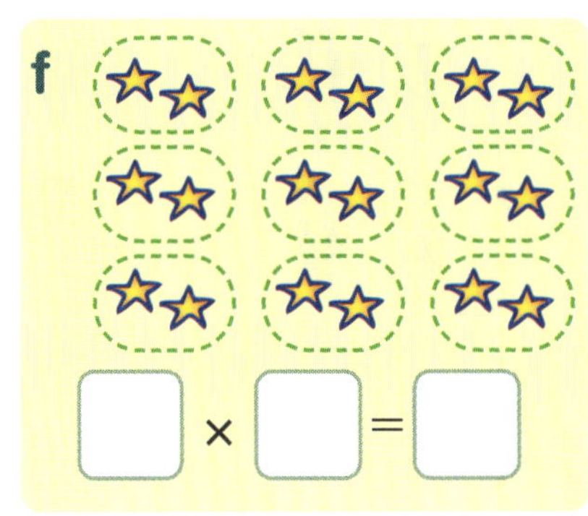

☐ × ☐ = ☐

g 

☐ × ☐ = ☐

h 

☐ × ☐ = ☐

i 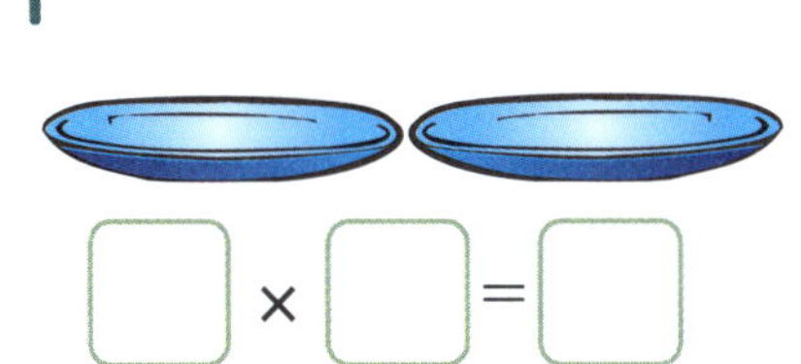

☐ × ☐ = ☐

2 Draw pictures to show these.

a

b

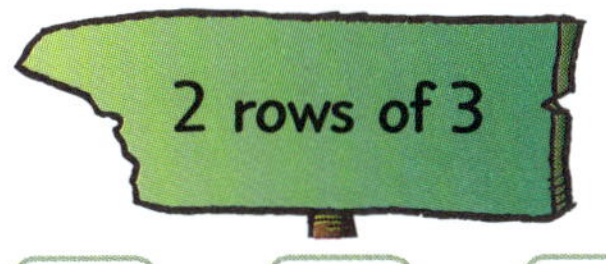

☐ × ☐ = ☐

☐ × ☐ = ☐

INVESTIGATION

Use the dots to help you complete the number sentences.

2 × 6 = ☐

3 × 4 = ☐

4 × 3 = ☐

6 × 2 = ☐

13C Multiplication

This is called a number sentence.

1 Write a number sentence for each part.

a

$\square \times \square = \square$

b

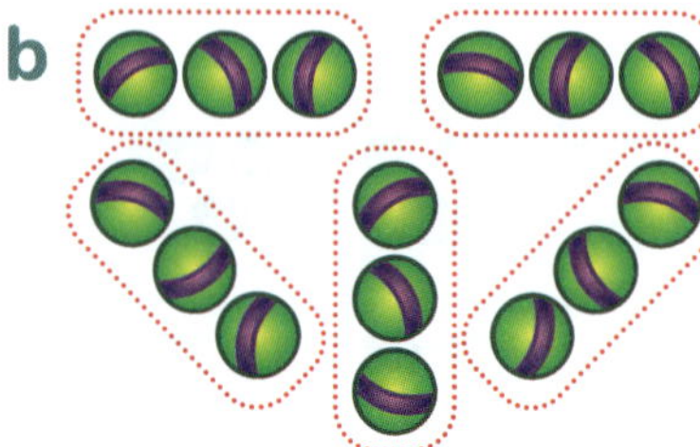

$\square \times \square = \square$

c

$\square \times \square = \square$

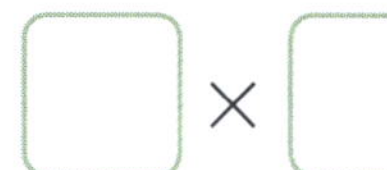

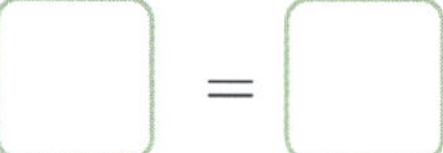

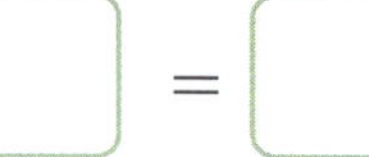

d

$\square \times \square = \square$

2 Write four different number sentences about these dogs.

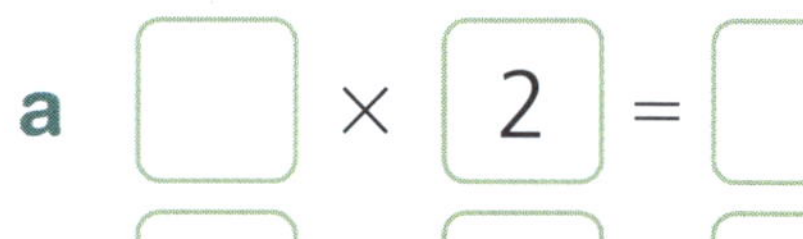

a $\square \times 2 = \square$

b $\square \times 4 = \square$

c $\square \times 8 = \square$

d $\square \times 16 = \square$

3 Complete:

a Mina and Sam each ate 6 ice creams.

How many did they eat altogether? $\square$

$\square \times \square = \square$

b Four plates each held five biscuits.

How many biscuits altogether? $\square$

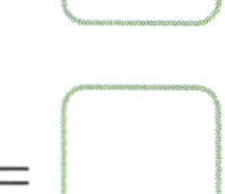

$\square \times \square = \square$

 ISBN 9780655708766

Count the sides.

Pattern: 5, 10, 15, ...
Rule: + 5

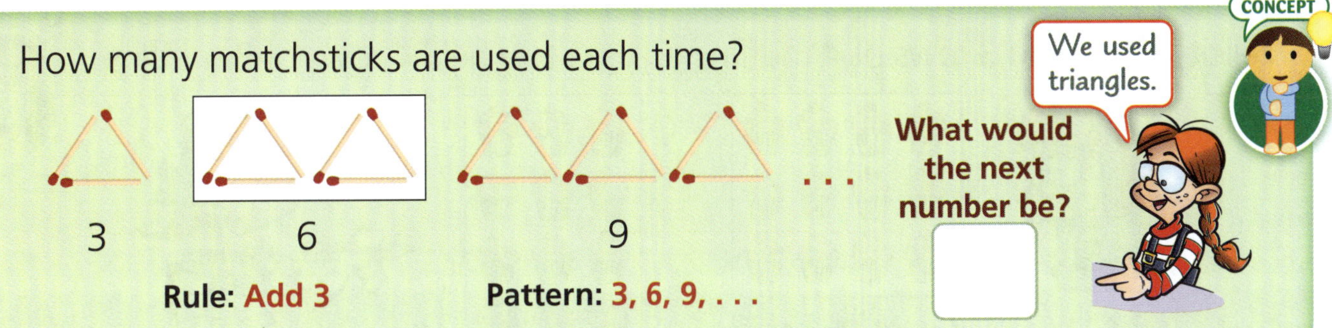

1 Count the number of matchsticks used each time, then write the rule.

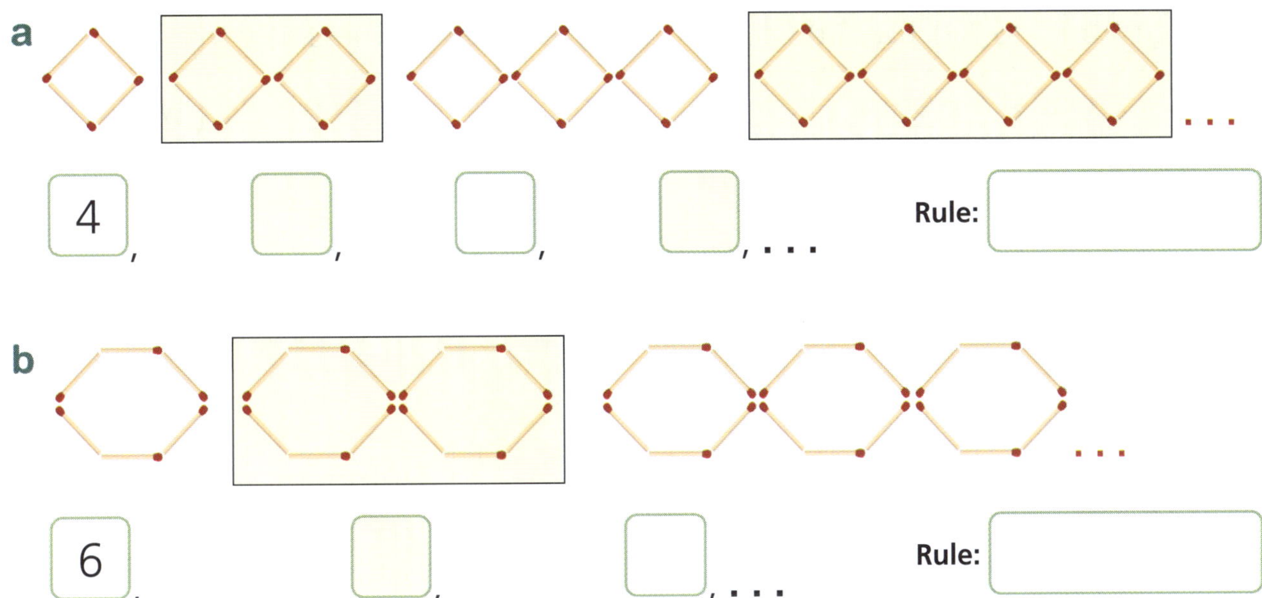

2 Continue the number pattern and write the rule.

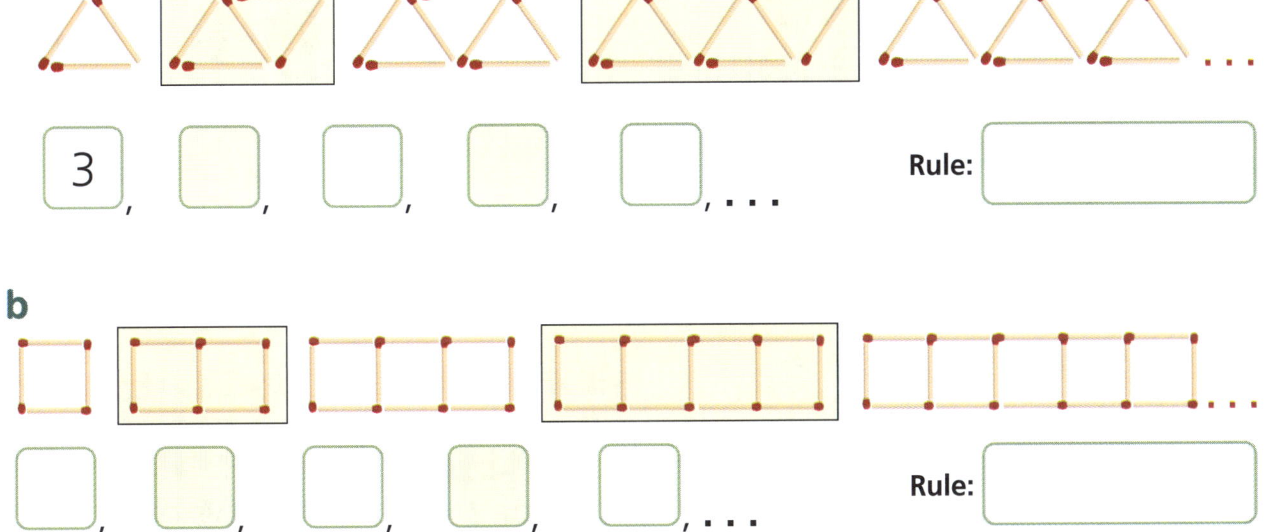

14A Using arrays

In arrays, objects are lined up into equal rows and columns.

CONCEPT

Felicity's tray held 3 rows of 4 muffins. Cailin's tray held 4 rows of 3 muffins.

3 × 4

3 rows of 4 = 12

4 rows of 3 = 12

4 × 3

Each muffin tray holds 12 muffins.
Felicity turned her tray and found the trays looked the same.

3 rows of 4 = 4 rows of 3 = 12

3 x 4 = 4 x 3 = 12

Here we are multiplying two numbers.

1 Describe each array and find the total.

a 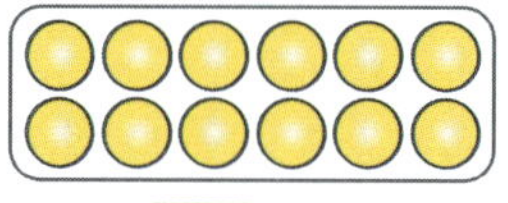 **2 × 6 =** ☐

☐ rows of ☐ = ☐

Number of sixes in 12 = ☐.

b 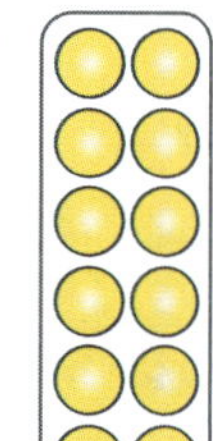 **6 × 2 =** ☐

☐ rows of ☐ = ☐

Number of twos in 12 = ☐.

c 2 rows of 6 is the same as ☐ rows of ☐. Total = ☐

2 a **4 × 2 =** ☐

☐ rows of ☐ = ☐

b **2 × 4 =** ☐

These are the same.

☐ rows of ☐ = ☐

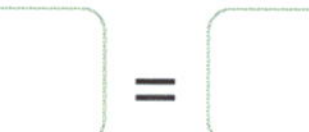

c 4 rows of 2 = 2 rows of ☐

d 2 × 4 = 4 × ☐ = ☐

ACTIVITY

Use counters to make arrays that are equal.

Describe what you have done.

3 rows of 2 = 6

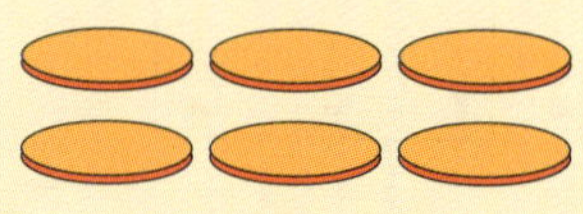

☐ rows of ☐ = ☐

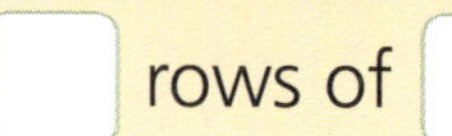

14B Using rows

4 rows of 3 = 12 We write 4 x 3 = 12
3 rows of 4 = 12 We write 3 x 4 = 12

CONCEPT

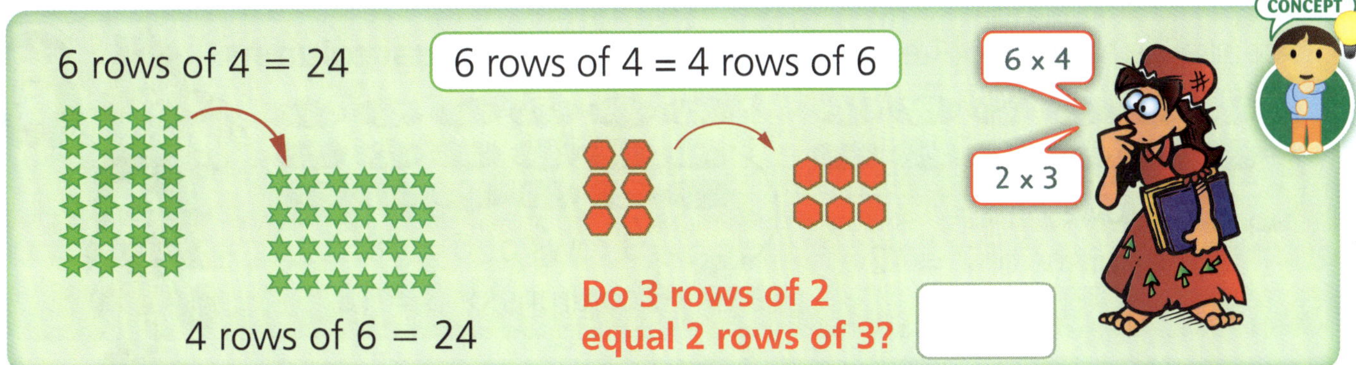

1 

We write 3 × 4.

How many are in 3 rows of 4? ☐

How many are in 4 rows of 3? ☐

True or false?
3 rows of 4 = 4 rows of 3 ☐

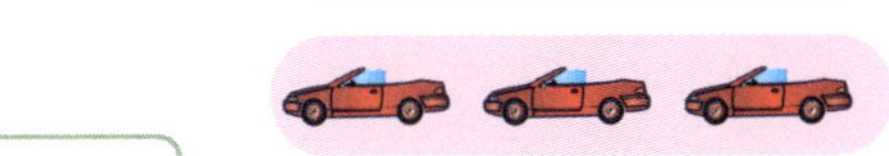

We write 4 × 3.

2 

We write 3 × 5.

How many are in 3 rows of 5? ☐

How many are in 5 rows of 3? ☐

True or false?
3 rows of 5 = 5 rows of 3 ☐

3

How many are in 4 rows of 10? ☐

How many are in 10 rows of 4? ☐

True or false?
4 rows of 10 = 10 rows of 4 ☐

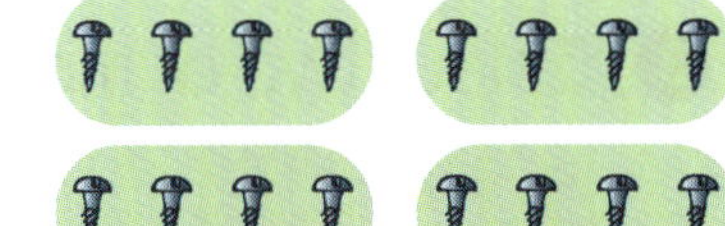
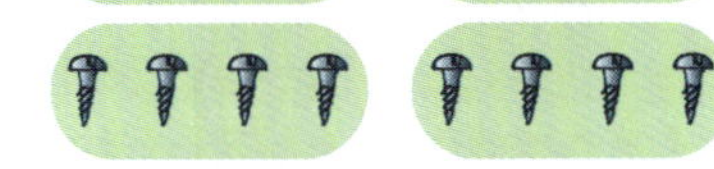

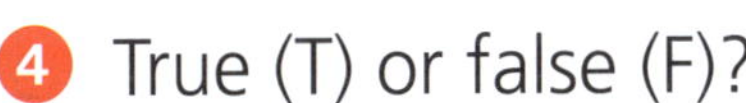

4 True (T) or false (F)?

a 2 rows of 8 = 8 rows of 2 ☐

b $2 \times 8 = 8 \times 2$ ☐

c 7 rows of 4 = 4 rows of 7 ☐

d $7 \times 4 = 4 \times 7$ ☐

 • *AUSTRALIAN SIGNPOST MATHS 2* • ISBN 9780655708766

14C Arrays

In arrays, objects are lined up into equal rows and equal columns.

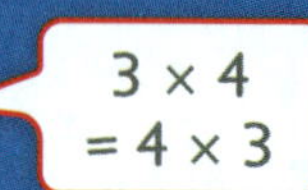

CONCEPT

An array is a group of items with **equal rows** and **equal columns**.

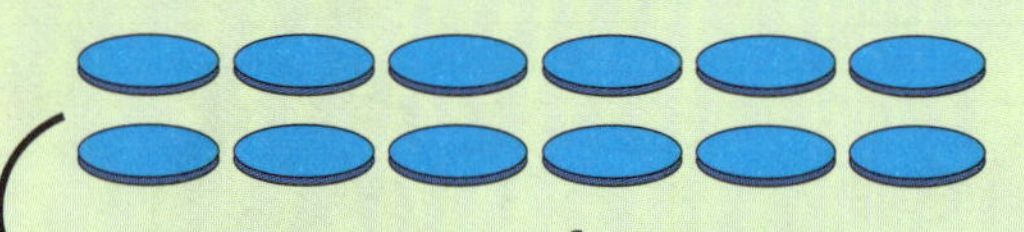

2 rows of 6 = 12
6 columns of 2 = 12

3 rows of 6 = 18
6 columns of 3 = 18

1 Draw and use counters to make these arrays.

a 3 rows of 2 = ☐ (3 x 2)

b 4 rows of 5 = ☐ (4 x 5)

c 2 rows of 4 = ☐ (2 x 4)

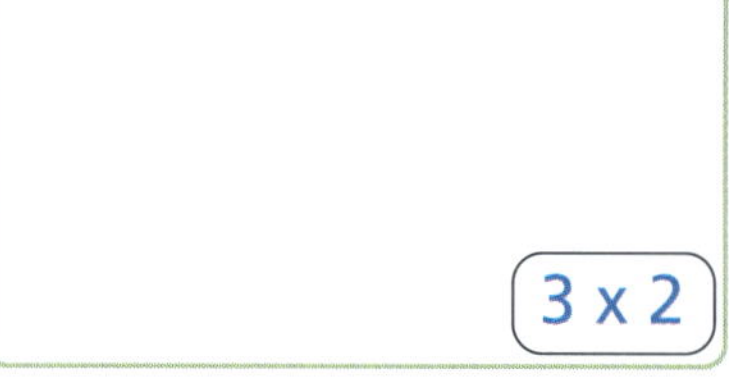

2 Draw two of your own arrays and describe them below.

a ☐
rows of ____ = ____
columns of ____ = ____

b ☐

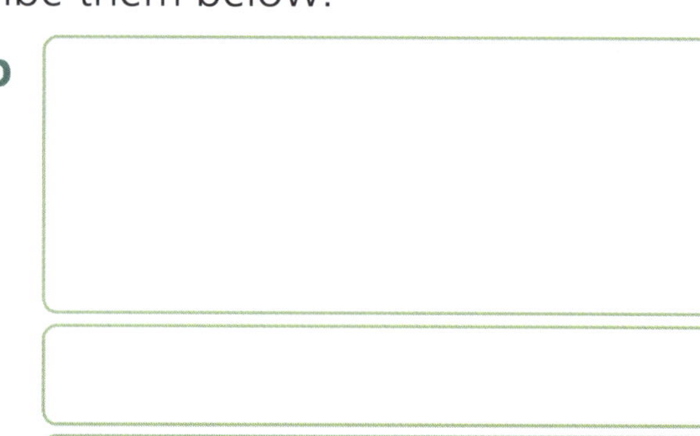

3 Colour two or more rectangles. Write two number sentences for each new array.

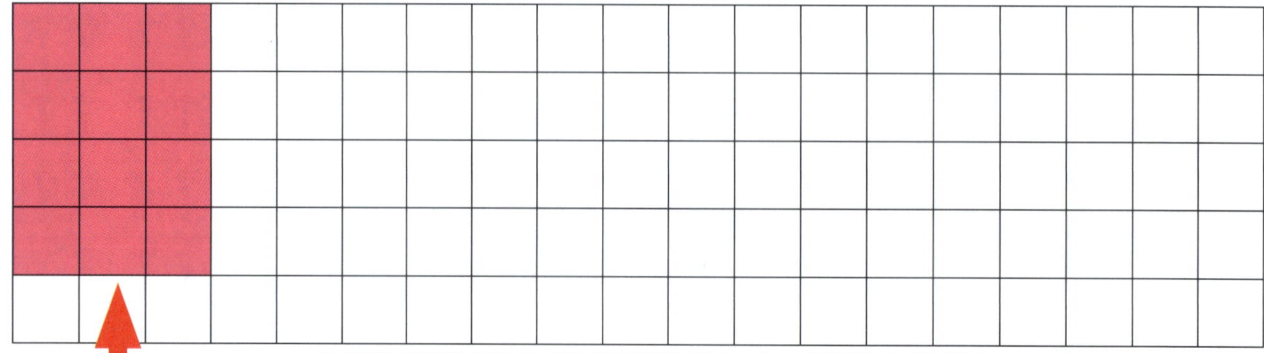

4 rows of 3 = 12
3 columns of 4

 ISBN 9780655708766

To find "how much", start with the highest value and count on.

\$1 … \$1.50 … \$1.70 … \$1.80

1 How much money?

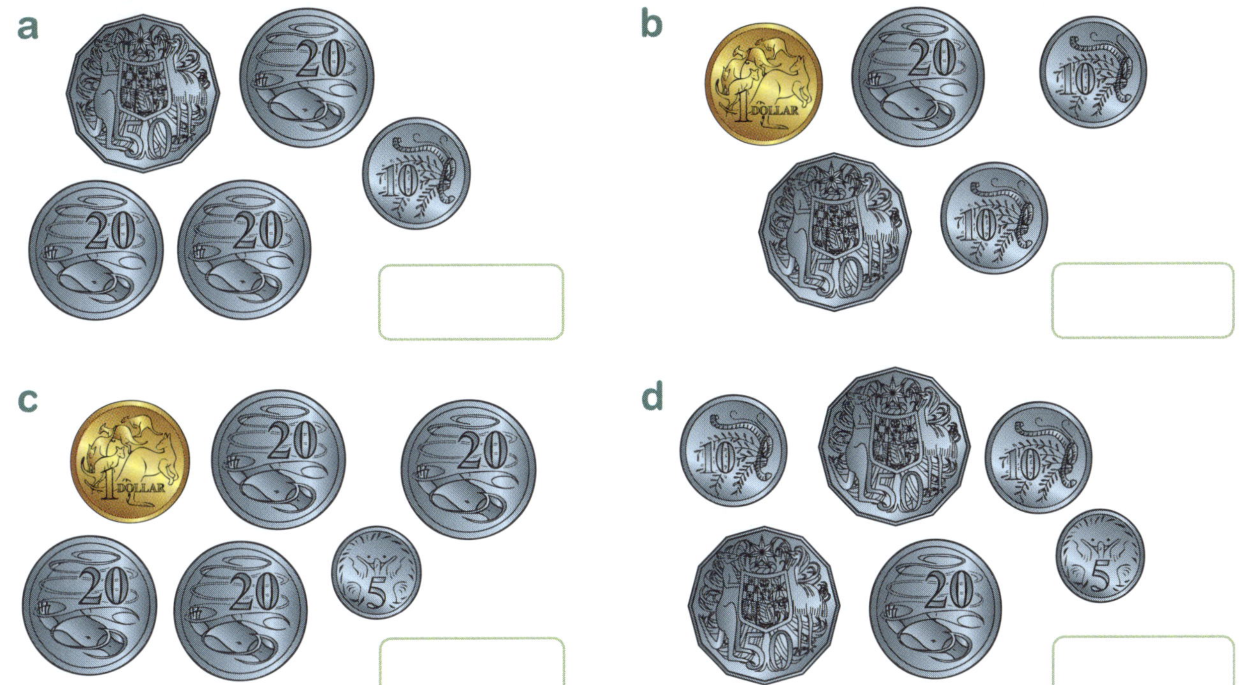

2 Colour the coins you would use to pay for each item.

 • *AUSTRALIAN SIGNPOST MATHS 2* • ISBN 9780655708766

15A Using skip counting

Can you skip count by 10s?
10, 20, 30, 40, 50, 60 ...

CONCEPT

Skip counting by 2s: 2, 4, 6, 8, 10, 12, 14, 16 ...

Skip counting by 5s: 5, 10, 15, 20, 25, 30, 35, 40 ...

Skip counting by 3s: 3, 6, 9, 12, 15, 18, 21, 24 ...

Learn to skip count by 2s, 3s, 5s and 10s.

1. **a** 3 groups of 2 ☐ **b** 6 groups of 2 ☐ **c** 8 groups of 2 ☐
   d 4 groups of 2 ☐ **e** 7 groups of 2 ☐ **f** 5 groups of 2 ☐

2. **a** 2 x 5 ☐ **b** 4 x 5 ☐ **c** 3 x 5 ☐ **d** 5 x 5 ☐
   e 8 x 5 ☐ **f** 6 x 5 ☐ **g** 1 x 5 ☐ **h** 7 x 5 ☐

3. **a** 3 x 3 ☐ **b** 2 x 3 ☐ **c** 5 x 3 ☐ **d** 7 x 3 ☐
   e 1 x 3 ☐ **f** 6 x 3 ☐ **g** 8 x 3 ☐ **h** 4 x 3 ☐

4. **a** 4 tens ☐ **b** 2 tens ☐ **c** 6 tens ☐ **d** 3 tens ☐
   e 7 tens ☐ **f** 5 tens ☐ **g** 8 tens ☐ **h** 9 tens ☐

5. Skip counting by 4s: **4, 8, 12, 16, 20, 24, 28, 32, 36, 40**

   a 4 groups of 4 ☐ **b** 2 columns of 4 ☐ **c** 3 rows of 4 ☐
   d 6 groups of 4 ☐ **e** 5 columns of 4 ☐ **f** 8 rows of 4 ☐

15B Using columns to multiply

We say 3 times 2 (3 x 2).

CONCEPT

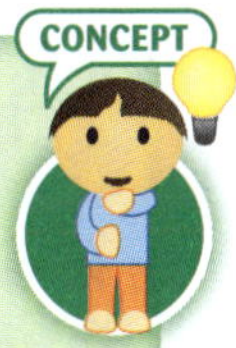

4 columns of 6
(4 × 6)
number of stars ☐ 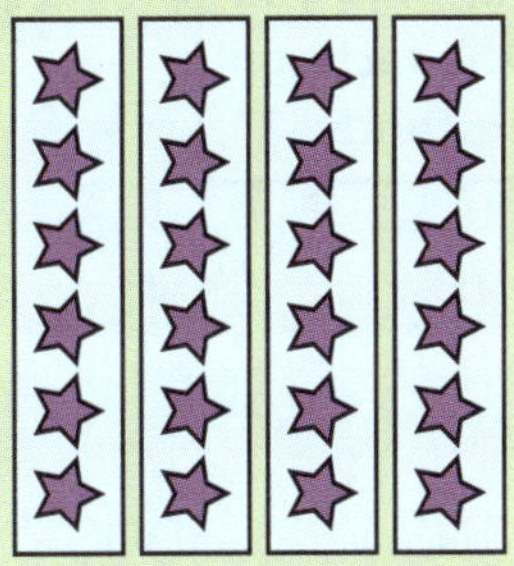

4 rows of 6
(4 × 6) 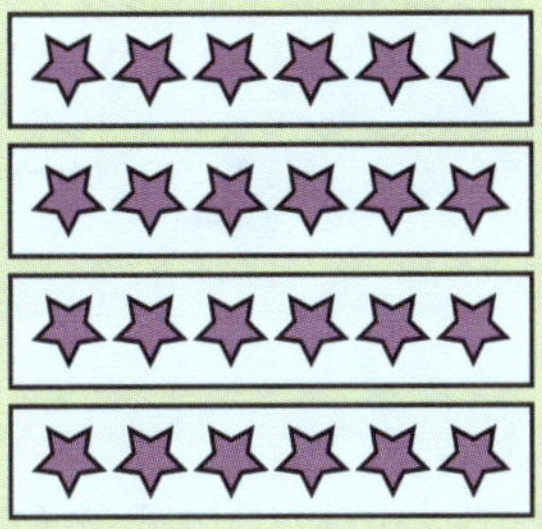
number of stars ☐

4 groups of 6
(4 × 6) 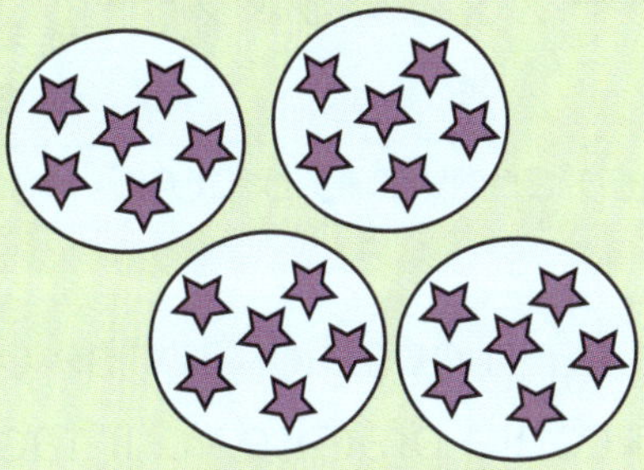
number of stars ☐

True (T) or false (F)? 4 columns of 6 = 4 rows of 6 = 4 groups of 6 ☐

1

a 3 columns of 4 (3 × 4) ☐

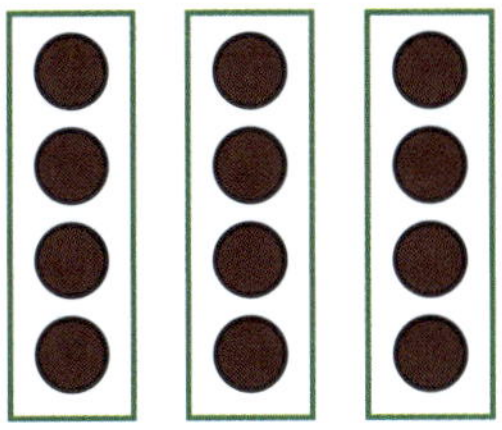

b 4 columns of 4 (4 × 4) ☐

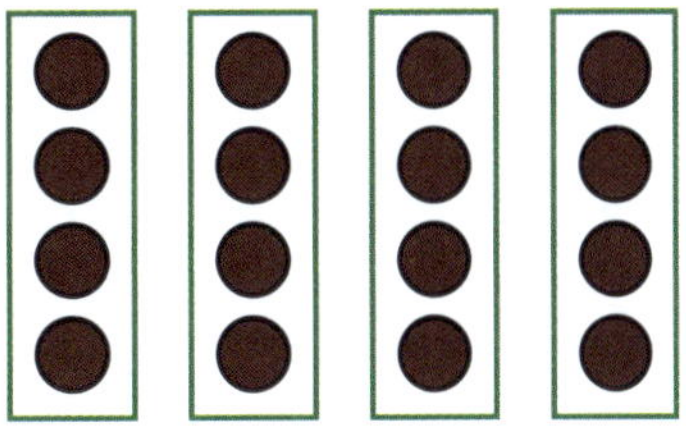

c 5 columns of 4 (5 × 4) ☐

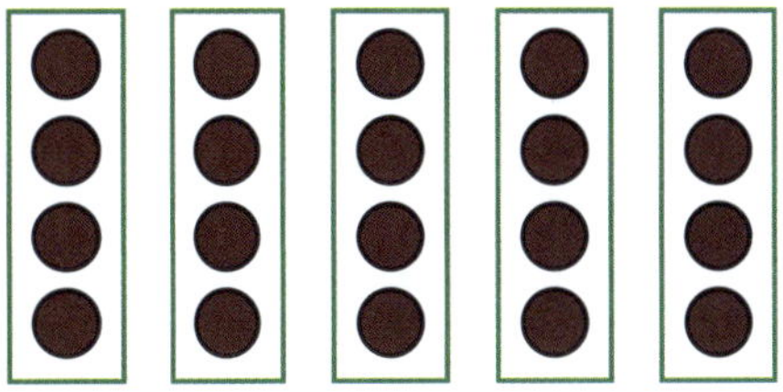

d 4 columns of 5 (4 × 5) ☐

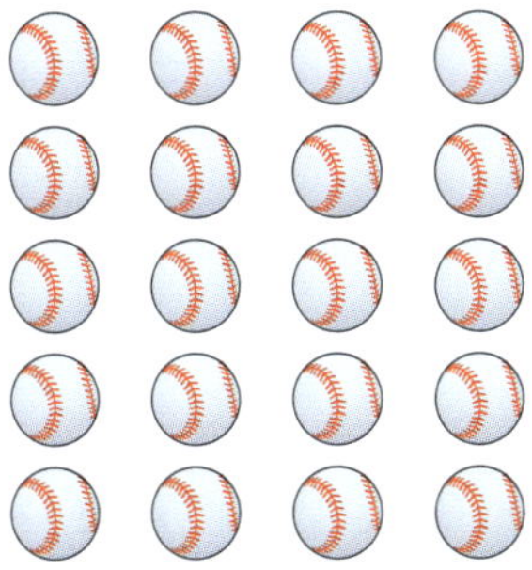

e 5 columns of 5 (5 × 5) ☐

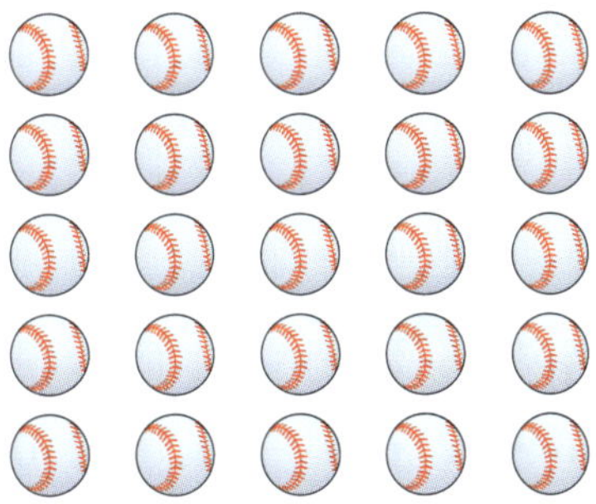

f 6 columns of 5 (6 × 5) ☐

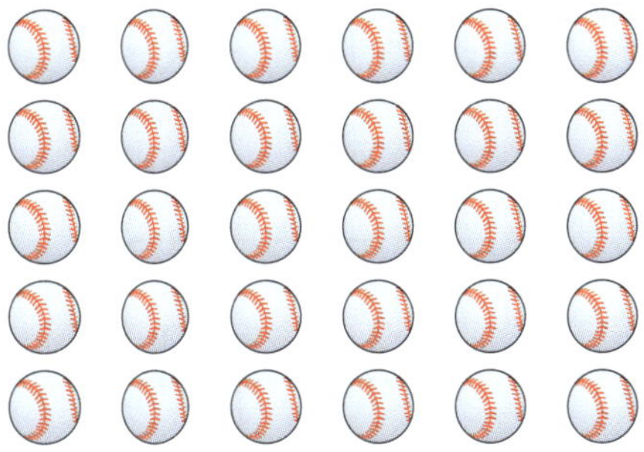

2

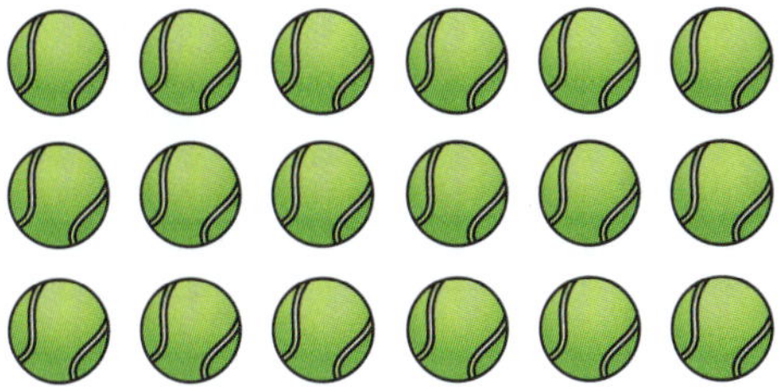

a How many columns of 3? ☐

b How many rows of 6? ☐

c How many groups of 2? ☐

d How many balls altogether? ☐

Skip count: 3, 6, 9, 12, 15 ...

x 2, x 10

3 x 2 means "3 groups of 2" or "3 rows of 2".

CONCEPT

2 threes is the same as 3 twos.

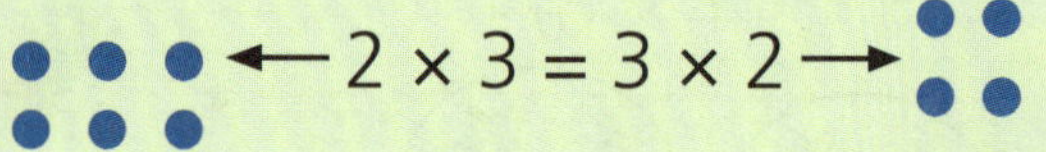

$2 \times 3 = 3 \times 2$

Each array has 6 dots.

Are you a tables champion?

Keep practising until you can recall all the facts on this page instantly.

1 Join each question to the correct answer using a pencil and ruler. You could practise your tables facts by rubbing out your answers and doing them again.

a

	x	
0 x 2		0
1 x 2		2
2 x 2		4
3 x 2		6
4 x 2		8
5 x 2		10
6 x 2		12
7 x 2		14
8 x 2		16
9 x 2		18
10 x 2		20
Scores:		

b

	x	
3 x 2		0
2 x 2		2
0 x 2		4
6 x 2		6
1 x 2		8
4 x 2		10
5 x 2		12
9 x 2		14
10 x 2		16
7 x 2		18
8 x 2		20
Scores:		

c

	x	
1 x 2		0
3 x 2		2
0 x 2		4
5 x 2		6
2 x 2		8
6 x 2		10
4 x 2		12
9 x 2		14
7 x 2		16
10 x 2		18
8 x 2		20
Scores:		

d

	x	
2 x 2		0
4 x 2		2
1 x 2		4
0 x 2		6
6 x 2		8
3 x 2		10
5 x 2		12
8 x 2		14
7 x 2		16
9 x 2		18
10 x 2		20
Scores:		

3 tens = 30
3 x 10 = 30

3 tens is the same as 10 threes.

e

	x	
0 x 10		0
1 x 10		10
2 x 10		20
3 x 10		30
4 x 10		40
5 x 10		50
6 x 10		60
7 x 10		70
8 x 10		80
9 x 10		90
10 x 10		100
Scores:		

f

	x	
3 x 10		0
2 x 10		10
0 x 10		20
5 x 10		30
1 x 10		40
4 x 10		50
8 x 10		60
6 x 10		70
10 x 10		80
9 x 10		90
7 x 10		100
Scores:		

g

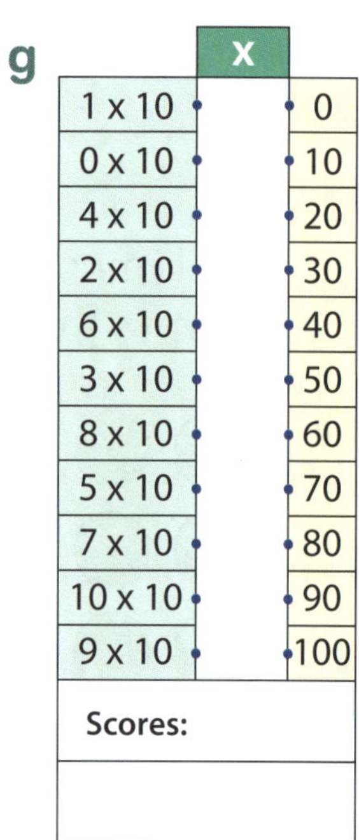

	x	
1 x 10		0
0 x 10		10
4 x 10		20
2 x 10		30
6 x 10		40
3 x 10		50
8 x 10		60
5 x 10		70
7 x 10		80
10 x 10		90
9 x 10		100
Scores:		

 ISBN 9780655708766

15D Balance scales

hefting

CONCEPT

Using balance scales is like hefting.

These scales are **balanced**.

One toy car balanced ☐ marbles.

Two toy cars would balance ☐ marbles.

Each marble must be the same weight.

1 Use marbles as a unit of measure to find the mass of each object.

Object	Estimate (guess)	Measure of mass
a ball	☐ marbles	☐ marbles
can of drink	☐ marbles	☐ marbles
a glass	☐ marbles	☐ marbles
a cup	☐ marbles	☐ marbles

The "mass" or "weight" of an object is "how heavy it is".

a Which is the heaviest object you measured? ☐

b Which is the lightest object you measured? ☐

c How much heavier is the heaviest object than the lightest object?

☐ marbles

d Why does each marble have to have the same mass?

☐

2 What other units could have been used in Question 1 to measure mass?

☐

 • *AUSTRALIAN SIGNPOST MATHS 2* • ISBN 9780655708766

16A Numbers to 150

CONCEPT

one hundred and seven

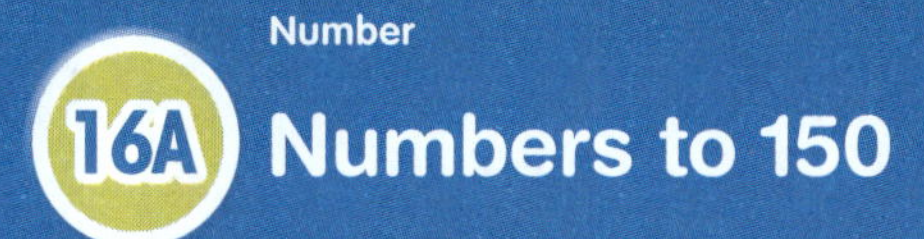

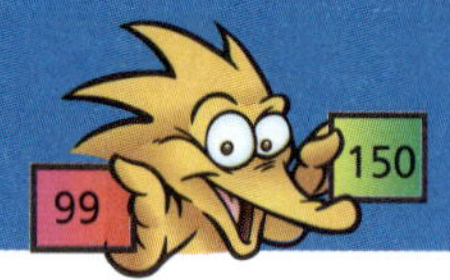

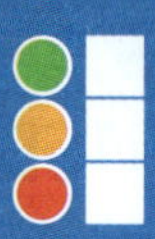

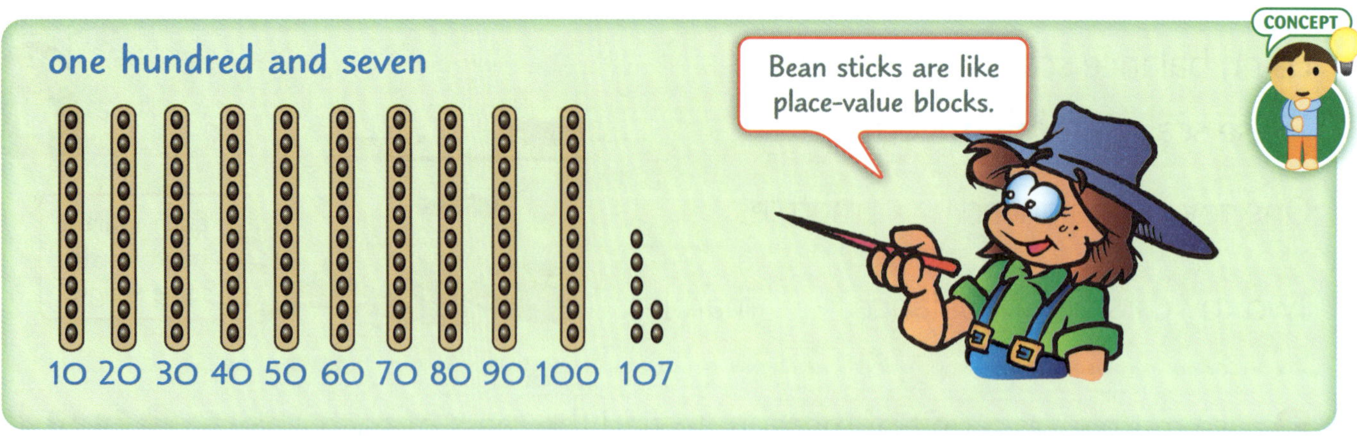

1 Write these numerals.

a

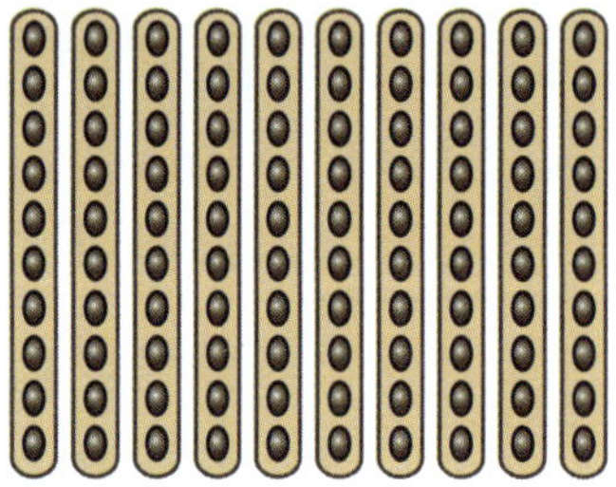

☐ hundreds ☐ tens ☐ ones

b

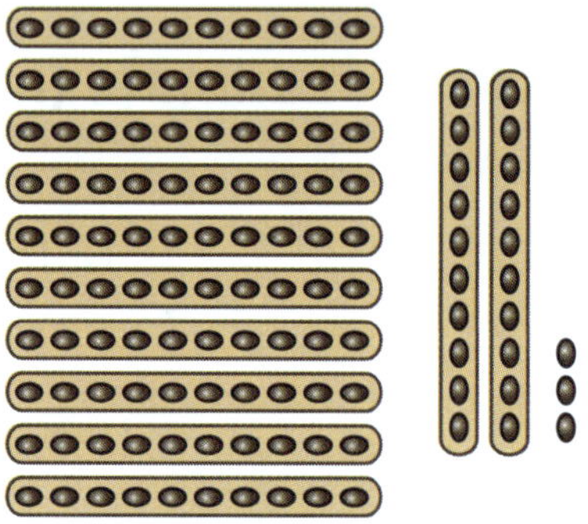

☐ hundreds ☐ tens ☐ ones

c

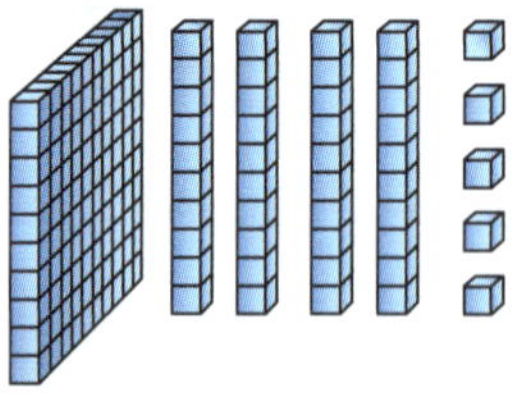

☐ hundreds ☐ tens ☐ ones

d

1 hundred and ....

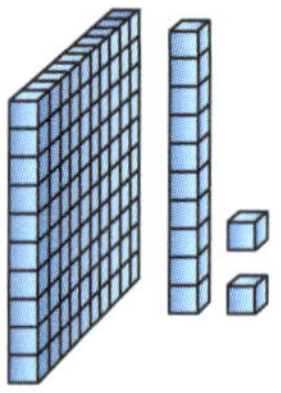

☐ hundreds ☐ tens ☐ ones

e

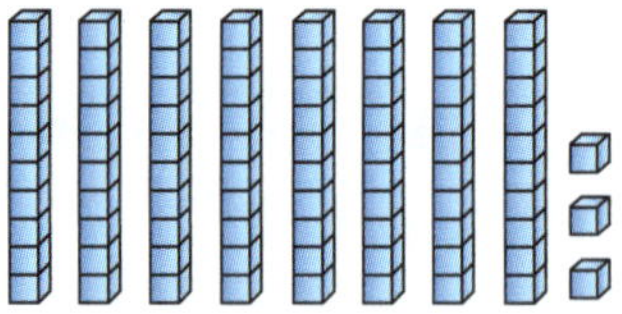

☐ hundreds ☐ tens ☐ ones

f

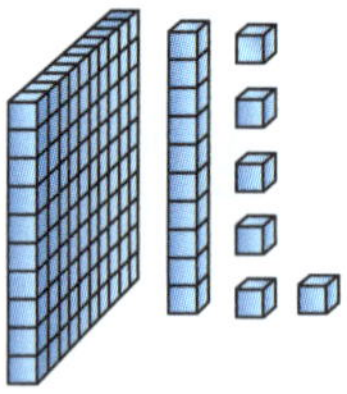

☐ hundreds ☐ tens ☐ ones

ACTIVITY

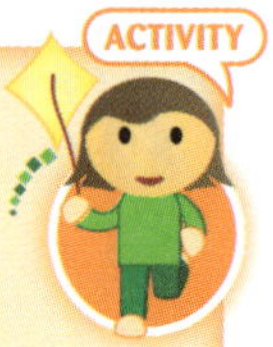

- Use place-value blocks to make these numbers.
  - 106
  - 98
  - 117
  - 123
  - 66
  - 100
- Explain your answers to a friend.

 • *AUSTRALIAN SIGNPOST MATHS 2* • ISBN 9780655708766

Numbers to 1000

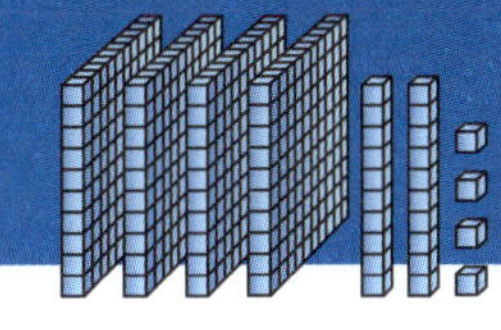

1 Complete each part.

a

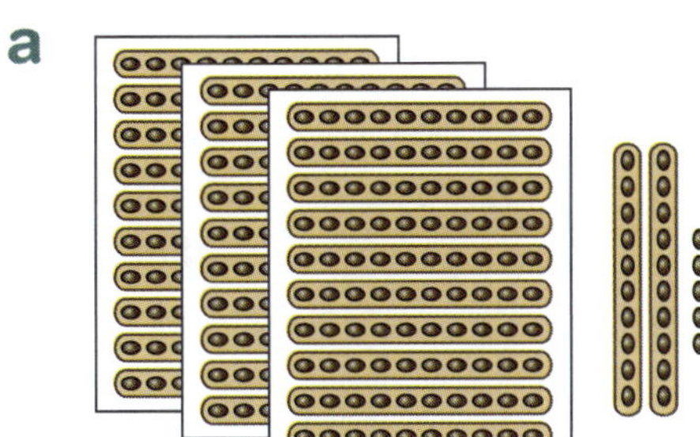
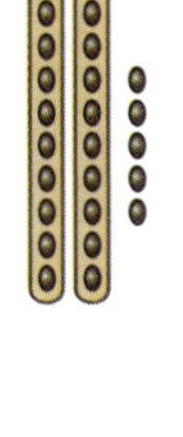

☐ hundreds + ☐ tens + ☐ ones

Hundreds	Tens	Ones
☐	☐	☐

= ☐

b

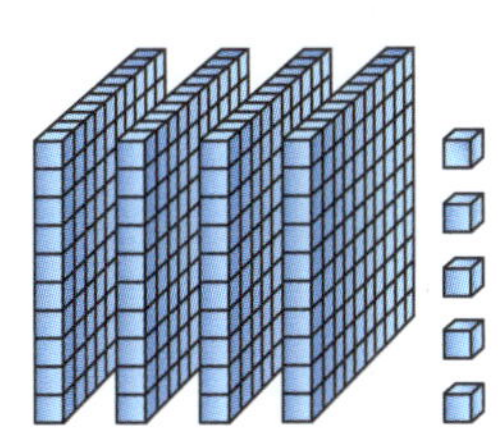

☐ hundreds + ☐ tens + ☐ ones

Hundreds	Tens	Ones
☐	☐	☐

= ☐

c

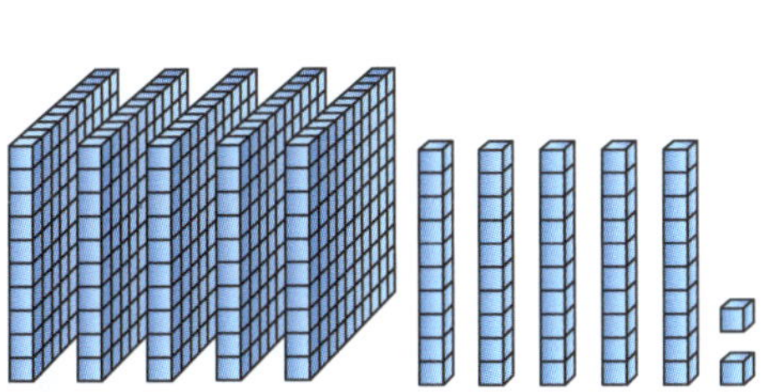

☐ hundreds + ☐ tens + ☐ ones

Hundreds	Tens	Ones
☐	☐	☐

= ☐

d

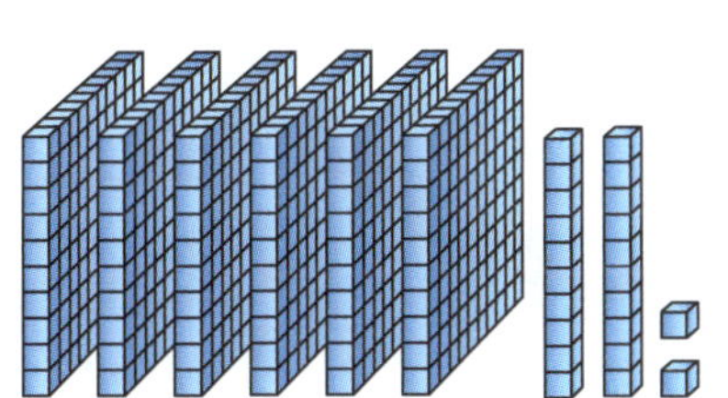

☐ hundreds + ☐ tens + ☐ ones

Hundreds	Tens	Ones
☐	☐	☐

= ☐

e

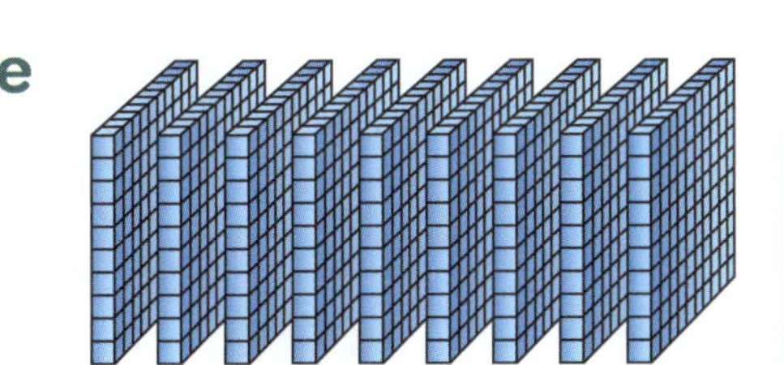

☐ hundreds + ☐ tens + ☐ ones

Hundreds	Tens	Ones
☐	☐	☐

= ☐

- Use place-value blocks to make these numbers.

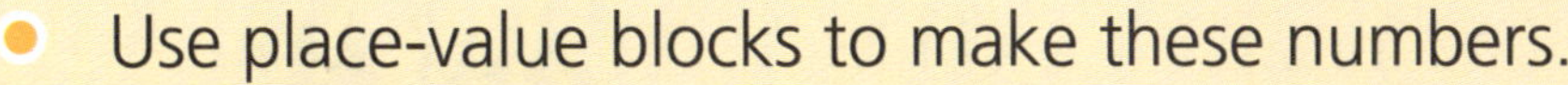

- 427 • 381 • 836 • 592 • 679 • 764

- Count large groups of objects by grouping in tens and hundreds. Estimate each number first, then check by grouping and counting.

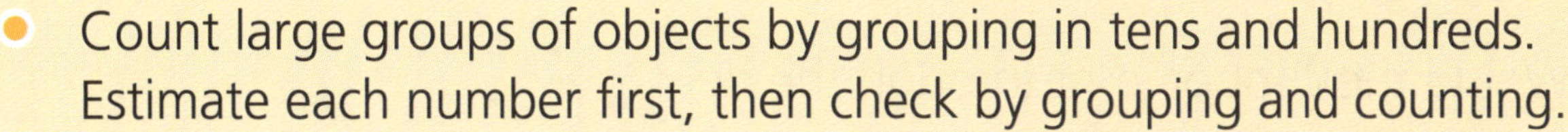

 • *AUSTRALIAN SIGNPOST MATHS 2* • ISBN 9780655708766

16C Informal units of length

ACTIVITY

Use parts of your body to measure objects. Compare your results with your partner's. Are the answers different? Discuss.

Length	Unit	Estimate	Measurement	Partner's measurement
Width of book	hand span			
Width of book	finger			
Width of window	hand span			

Using a standard informal unit

- Choose a standard length unit (such as an eraser).
- Mark this unit's lengths (1 eraser, 2 erasers, 3 erasers, …) along a ribbon or a piece of string.
- Use your ribbon or string to measure lengths.
- Record your results.

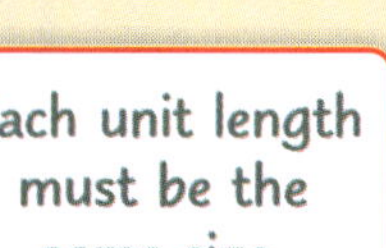

Length	Estimate	Measurement
Length of table	units	units
Width of door	units	units
Width of cupboard	units	units

Would the cupboard fit through the door?

 • *AUSTRALIAN SIGNPOST MATHS 2* • ISBN 9780655708766

16D Telling the story from data

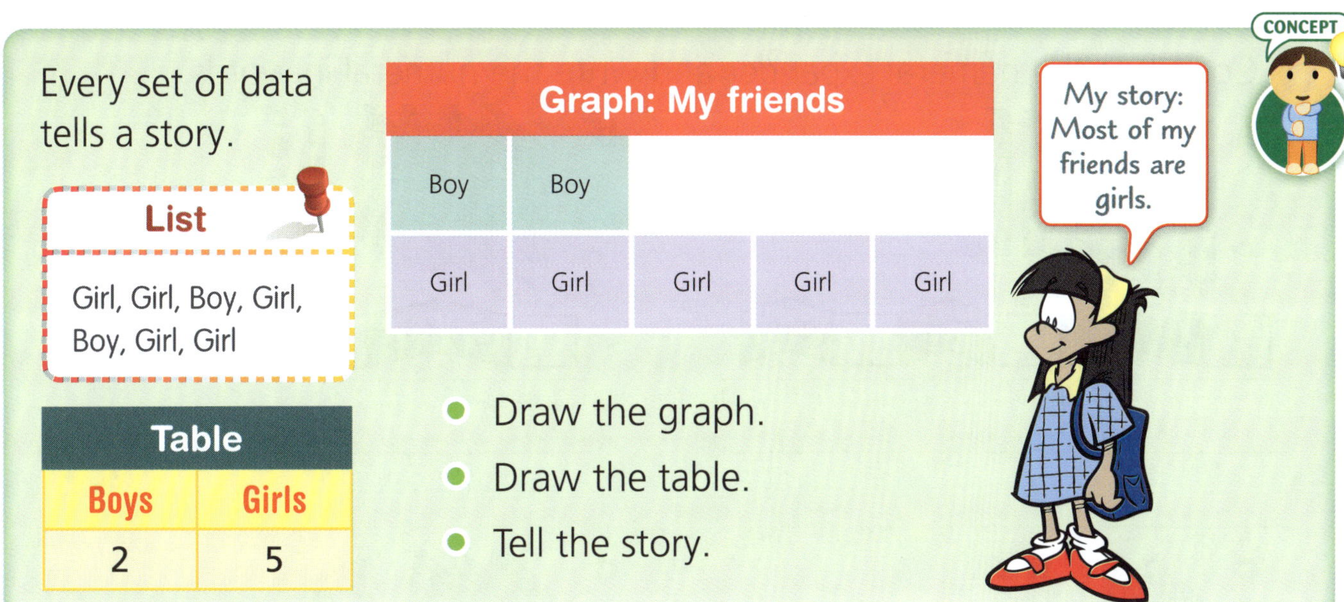

Complete the graph and table, then tell the story.

1. Children at the party.

List

Boy, Girl, Boy, Boy, Girl, Boy, Boy, Girl

Graph:

At the party	
Boys	Girls

Table:

Boys	
Girls	

Tell the story.

____

____

____

2. Buttons on shirts.

List

3, 1, 4, 4, 2, 9, 3, 6, 4, 2, 8, 2, 1, 9, 5

0 or 1 button	2 or 3 buttons	4 or 5 buttons	6 or 7 buttons	8 or 9 buttons

Numbers of buttons					
0 or 1					
2 or 3					
4 or 5					
6 or 7					
8 or 9					

Tell the story.

____

____

17A Numbers to 1000

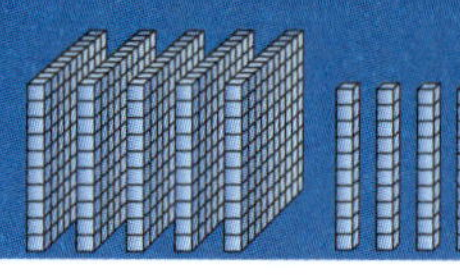

1 Complete the numeral expander and write the numeral in words.

a

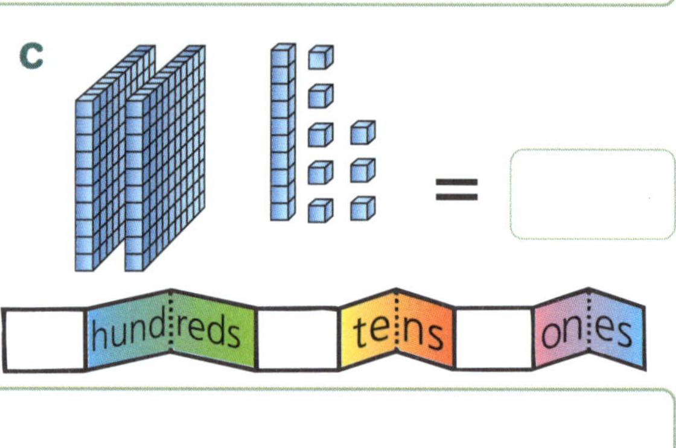

hundreds tens ones

b

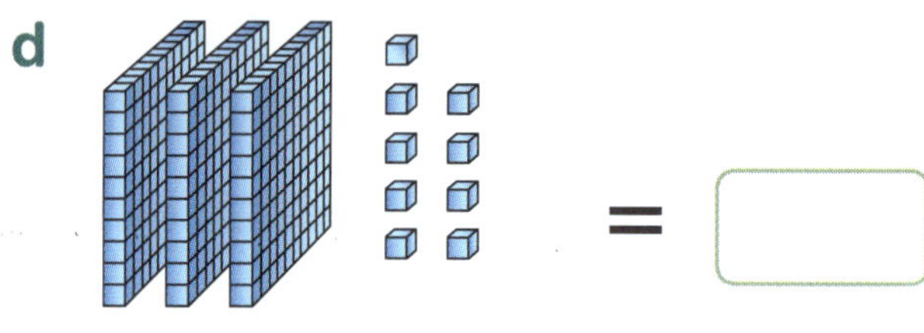

hundreds tens ones

c

hundreds tens ones

d

hundreds tens ones

2 Write the next number (the number one more than).

a 213 **b** 407 **c** 728 **d** 699

e 817 **f** 202 **g** 909 **h** 999

3 Write these numbers in expanded form as hundreds and ones and as tens and ones.

a 476 = ☐ hundreds ☐ ones **b** 591 = ☐ hundreds ☐ ones

c 476 = ☐ tens ☐ ones **d** 591 = ☐ tens ☐ ones

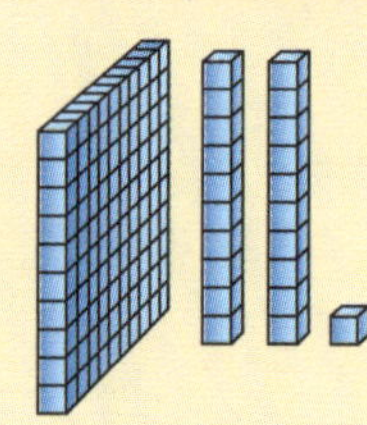

Use place-value blocks to model these numbers.

a 267 **b** 399 **c** 701

d 425 **e** 512 **f** 430

17B Numbers to 1000

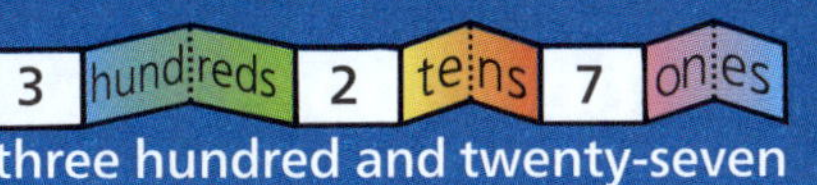

1 Complete each part.

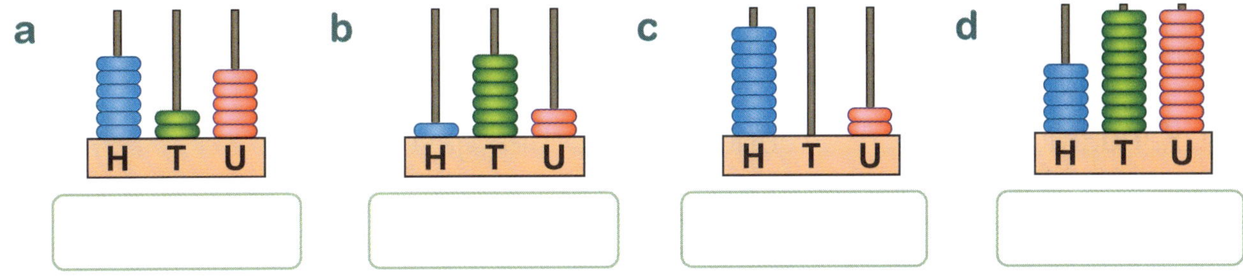

e

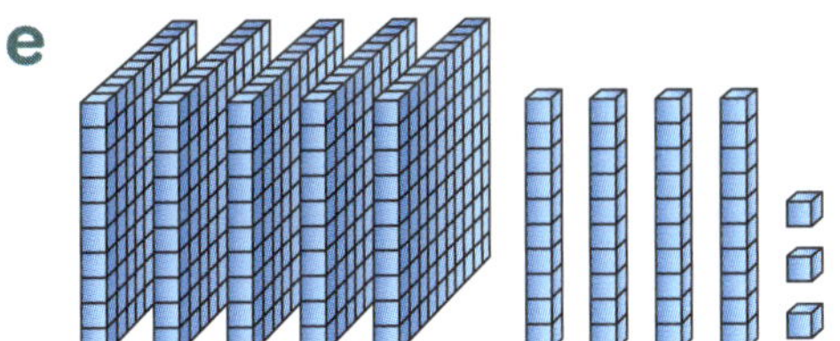

☐ hundreds + ☐ tens + ☐ ones

Hundreds	Tens	Ones
☐	☐	☐

= ☐

f

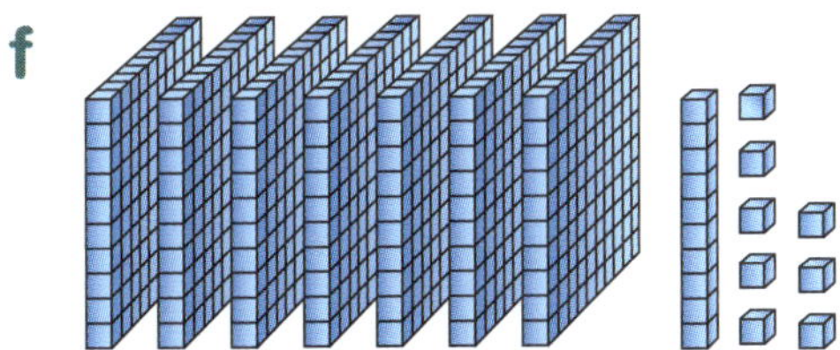

☐ hundreds + ☐ tens + ☐ ones

Hundreds	Tens	Ones
☐	☐	☐

= ☐

g

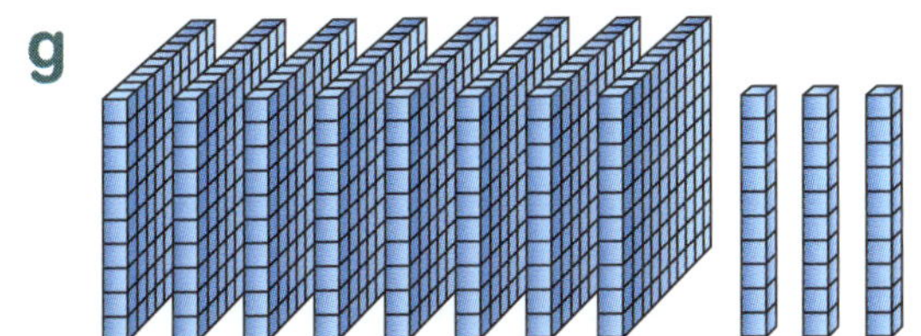

☐ hundreds + ☐ tens + ☐ ones

Hundreds	Tens	Ones
☐	☐	☐

= ☐

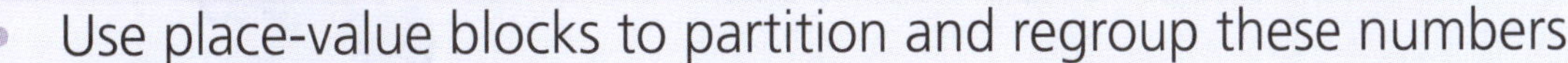

- Use place-value blocks to partition and regroup these numbers.
- Explain your answers to a friend.
  For example, 500: 5 hundreds, 50 tens, 500 ones.
  - 800
  - 300
  - 700
  - 400
  - 265

17C Inverse operations

CONCEPT

Adding 5 is the opposite of taking away 5.

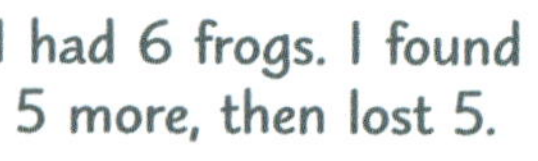

1 Rand had 10 balls. He found 6 more, then gave 6 away. How many does he have now?

$10 + 6 - 6 = \square$

2 Sarah had 12 stickers. She gave away 5, then was given 5 more. How many does she have now?

$\square - \square + \square = \square$

3 Perrin could see 12 dogs. Another 4 dogs came, then 4 left. How many can he see now?

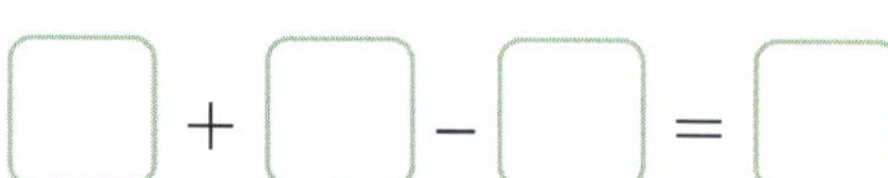

$\square + \square - \square = \square$

4 **a** $12 + 3 - 3 = \square$ **b** $14 + 5 - 5 = \square$ **c** $13 + 5 - 5 = \square$

d $17 + 7 - 7 = \square$ **e** $9 + 11 - 11 = \square$ **f** $7 + 12 - 12 = \square$

g $23 - 8 + 8 = \square$ **h** $15 - 6 + 6 = \square$ **i** $21 - 4 + 4 = \square$

ACTIVITY

Create your own number stories and sentences where the addition and subtraction undo each other.

    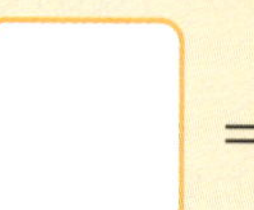 = 

 • *AUSTRALIAN SIGNPOST MATHS 2* • ISBN 9780655708766

Informal units of length

The pencil is 4 ovals long.

1 Find the lengths of these pictures using the ones block as a unit of length.

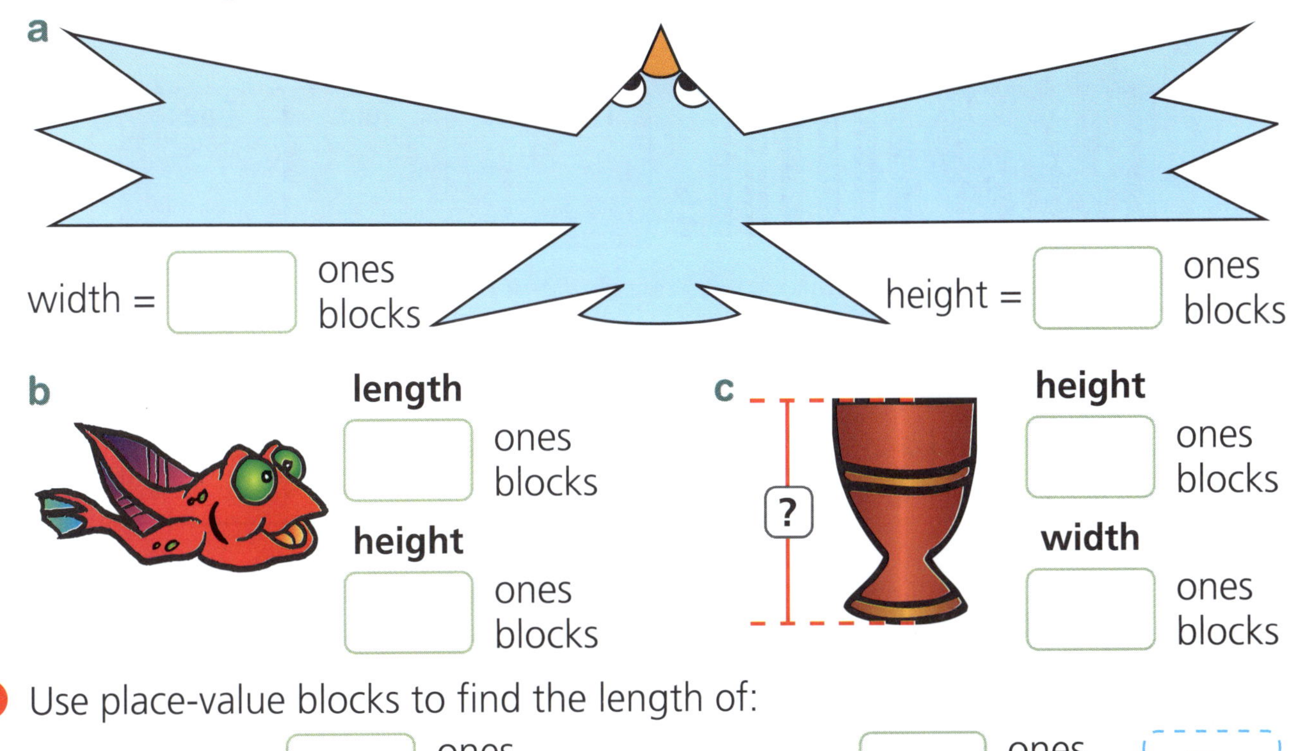

a width = ☐ ones blocks height = ☐ ones blocks

b **length** ☐ ones blocks
height ☐ ones blocks

c **height** ☐ ones blocks
width ☐ ones blocks

2 Use place-value blocks to find the length of:

a this page	☐ ones blocks	**b** your finger	☐ ones blocks	Give answers to the nearest ones block.
c a pencil	☐ ones blocks	**d** a pencil case	☐ ones blocks	
e a lunch box	☐ ones blocks	**f** a hand span	☐ ones blocks	

g Circle the longest object. Underline the shortest object.

 • *AUSTRALIAN SIGNPOST MATHS 2* • ISBN 9780655708766

18A Numbers to 1000

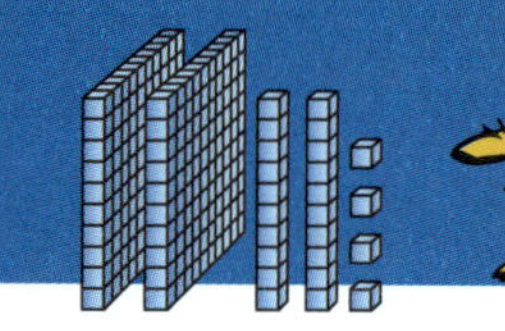

CONCEPT

To make large numbers, count the place-value blocks as you go.

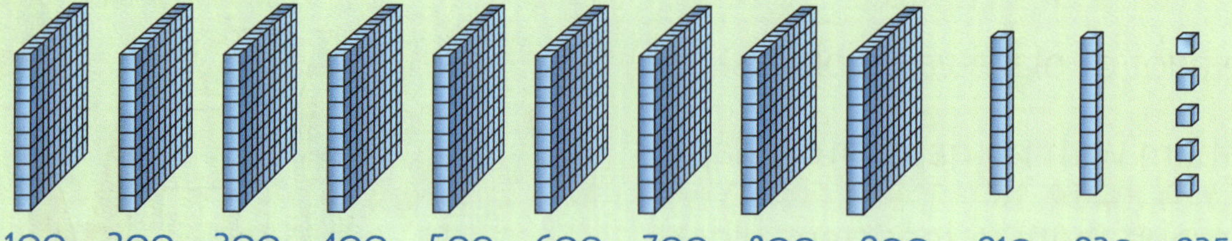

100 ...200 ...300 ...400 ...500 ...600 ...700 ...800 ...900 ...910 ...920 ...925

9 hundreds + 2 tens + 5 ones = 925

Hundreds	Tens	Ones
IIIIIIIII	II	IIIII
9	2	5

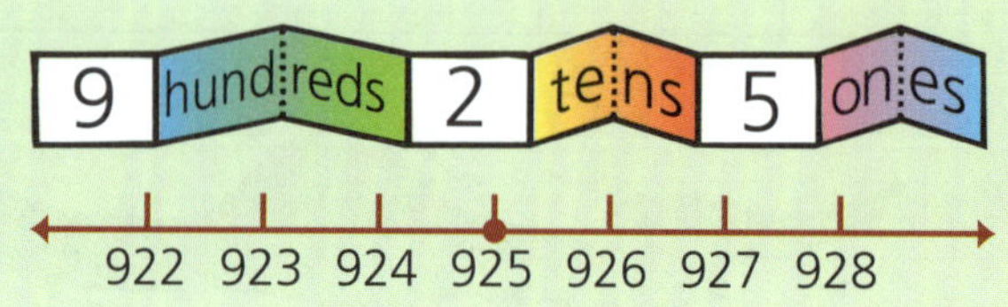

1 Complete each part.

a

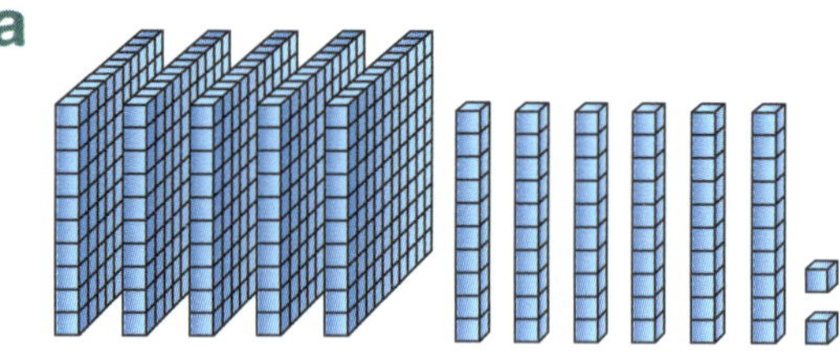

☐ hundreds + ☐ tens + ☐ ones

Hundreds	Tens	Ones
☐	☐	☐

= ☐

b

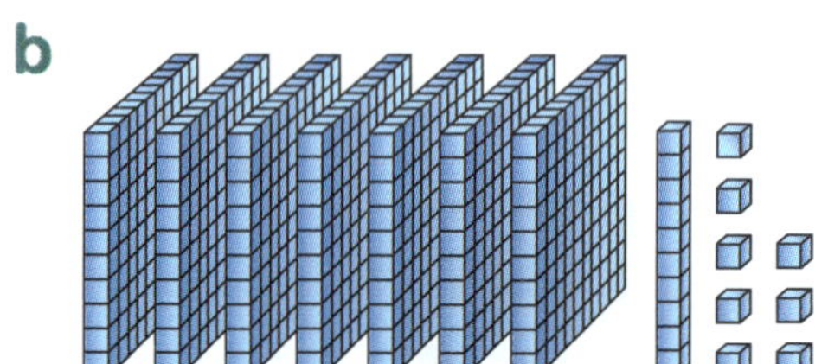

☐ hundreds + ☐ tens + ☐ ones

Hundreds	Tens	Ones
☐	☐	☐

= ☐

c

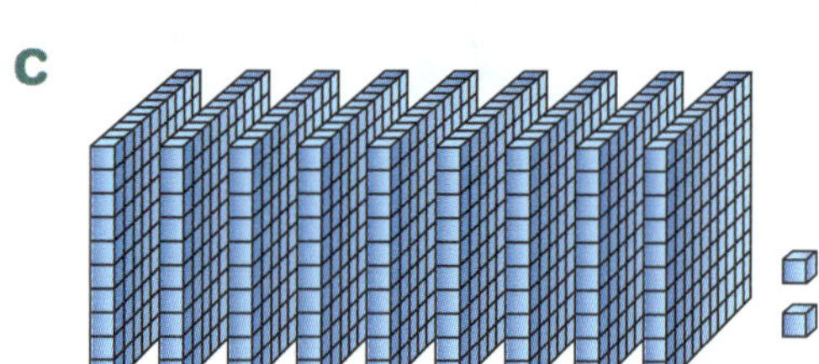

☐ hundreds + ☐ tens + ☐ ones

Hundreds	Tens	Ones
☐	☐	☐

= ☐

ACTIVITY

Model the numbers **703**, **906**, **658**, **812** and **543** using place-value blocks. Write these numbers in order from smallest to largest.

8 hundreds 0 tens 8 ones

805 806 807 808 809 810

1. Write true (T) or false (F) for each statement.

a 124 is less than 130. ☐ **b** 297 is more than 421. ☐

c 333 is more than 309. ☐ **d** 598 is less than 700. ☐

e 888 is less than 808. ☐ **f** 995 is less than 959. ☐

2. Write the missing numbers for each answer box on the number line.

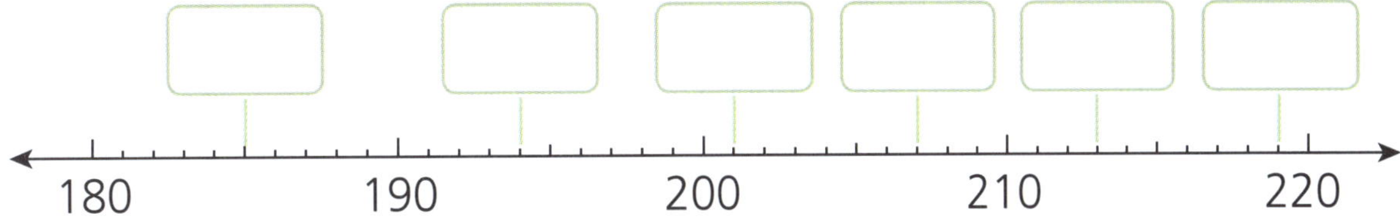

3.

Read each numeral first.

Circle 8 hundred and 8. Tick 8 hundred and eighteen.
Underline 8 hundred and eighty-one.
Order the numbers from smallest to largest.

4. Use colour to match each puzzle piece with a gap on the puzzle.

81		83		85				89	
				95				99	
	102	103					108		110
	112			115					120

Puzzle pieces: 87, 97 | 104, 113, 114 | 107, 116, 117 | 84, 93, 94 | 105, 106 | 90, 100 | 82, 91, 92 | 101, 111 | 86, 96 | 109, 118, 119 | 88, 98

18C Number patterns

4, 14, 24, ...

If you read down a column, you are saying an "add 10" pattern.

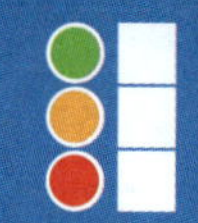

1 On the number chart:

a count by twos to fifty.

b count by fives to fifty and circle each number counted.

c count by tens to one hundred and colour each number counted.

d What number is before and after:

☐ 57 ☐ ?

☐ 70 ☐ ?

1	2	3	4	5	6	7	8	9	10
11	12	13	14	15	16	17	18	19	20
21	22	23	24	25	26	27	28	29	30
31	32	33	34	35	36	37	38	39	40
41	42	43	44	45	46	47	48	49	50
51	52	53	54	55	56	57	58	59	60
61	62	63	64	65	66	67	68	69	70
71	72	73	74	75	76	77	78	79	80
81	82	83	84	85	86	87	88	89	90
91	92	93	94	95	96	97	98	99	100

2 Complete the number patterns and describe them.

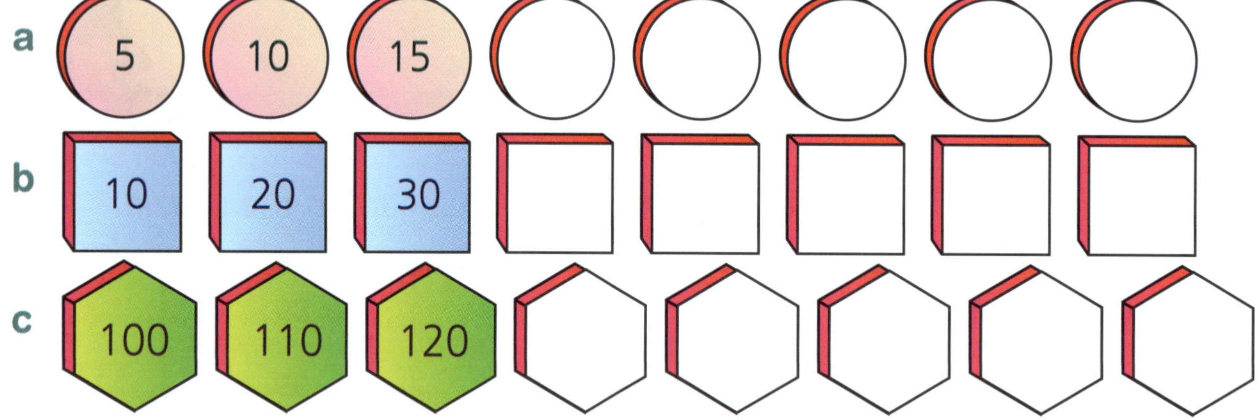

3 Write the **largest** number possible using these digits.

a 2, 1 ☐ b 6, 9 ☐ c 7, 5 ☐

4 Write the **smallest** number possible using these digits.

a 1, 2 ☐ b 8, 7 ☐ c 4, 8 ☐

d 4, 1, 2 ☐ e 6, 9, 1 ☐ f 3, 8, 2 ☐

 • *AUSTRALIAN SIGNPOST MATHS 2* • ISBN 9780655708766

18D Gathering data

||||| = $\cancel{||||}$ or $\cancel{||||}$

1. Rachel recorded the girls (**G**) and the boys (**B**) arriving at her party. This is the list she made. Use tally marks to fill in the table.

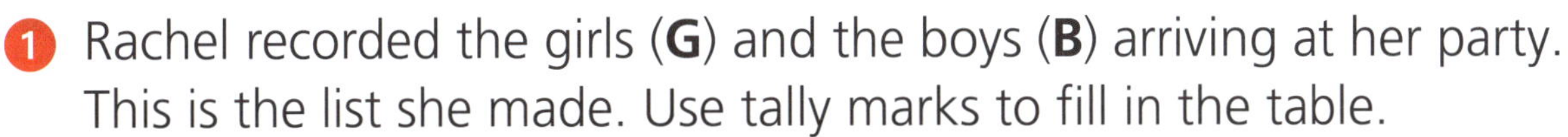

	Tally	Number
Girls		
Boys		

Make a graph to show how many boys and girls came to the party by colouring one picture for each person.

Friends at the party

2. a Write true (T) or false (F) next to each number sentence.

1 + 1 = 8 F	7 + 1 = 8	2 + 2 = 5	3 + 3 = 6
1 + 5 = 6	2 + 5 = 9	2 + 3 = 5	5 + 1 = 6
2 + 1 = 3	4 + 4 = 2	8 + 2 = 9	7 + 5 = 8
4 + 5 = 6	8 + 0 = 8	0 + 9 = 9	2 + 5 = 7

Test results

True False

b Complete the table and draw a graph by colouring boxes.

	Tally	Number
True		
False		

c How many questions were there altogether?

Number lines

12 + ☐ = 18

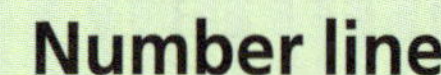

Number line

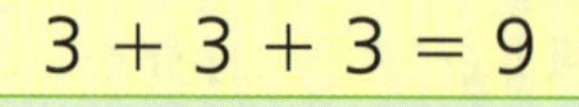

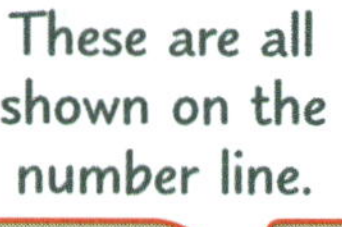

3 + 3 + 3 = 9

3 groups of 3 = 9

3 × 3 = 9

3 threes = 9

1 Write a number sentence to match each number line.

a 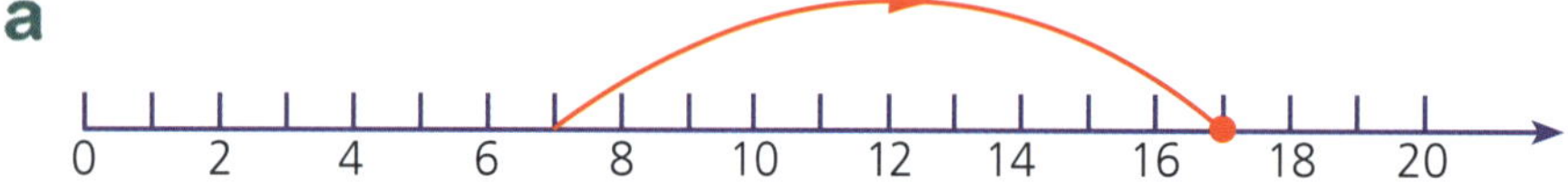

7 + ☐ = 17

b 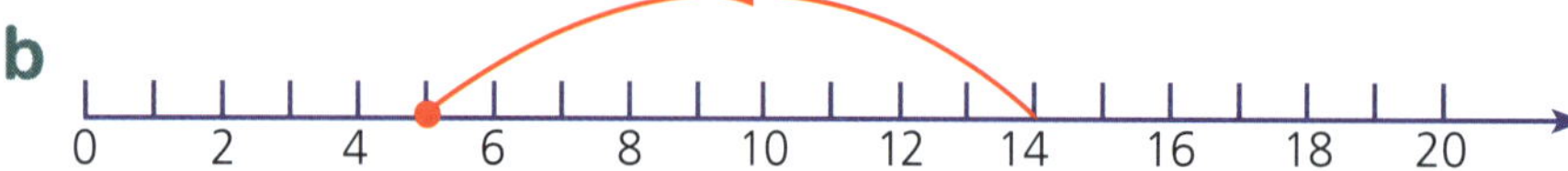

14 − ☐ = 5

c 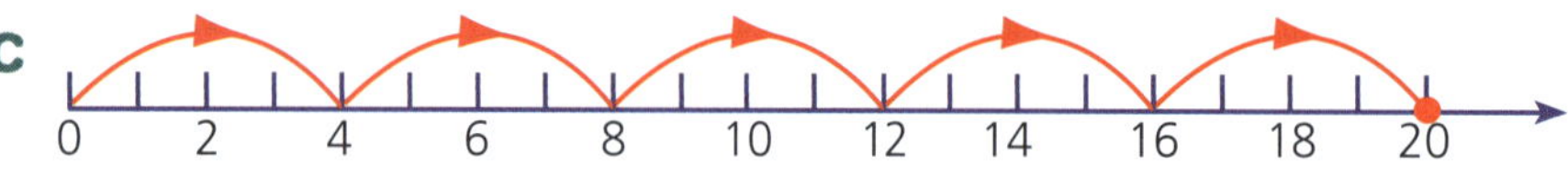

☐ × 4 = 20

d 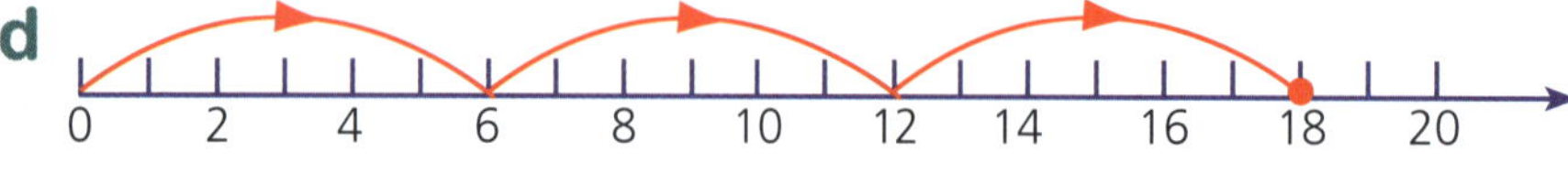

3 × ☐ = 18

e 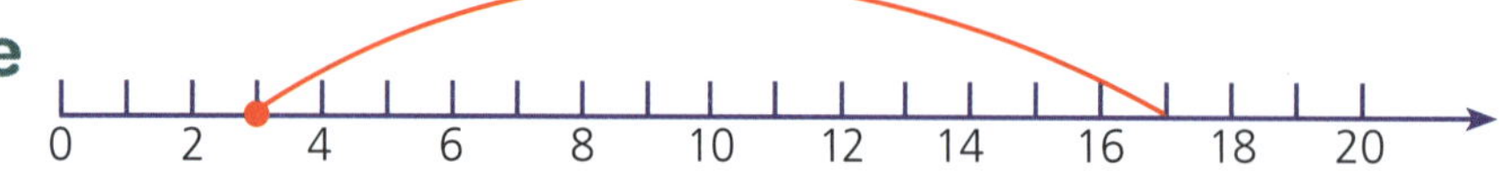

17 − ☐ = 3

f 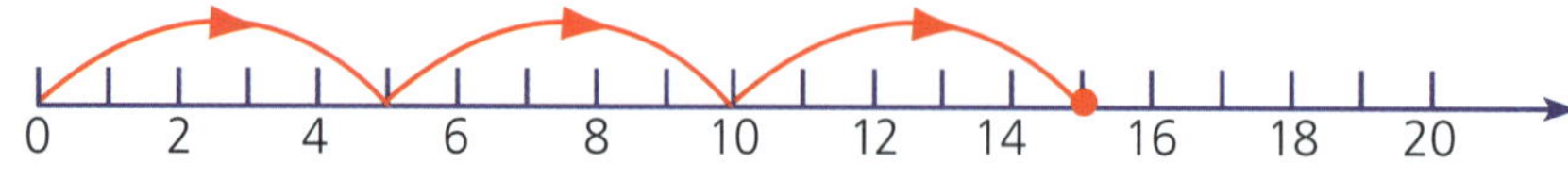

☐ × ☐ = 15

2 Make up two number sentences and show each on a number line.

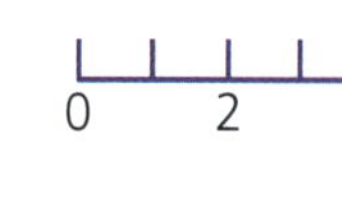

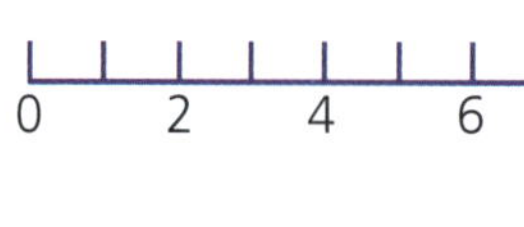

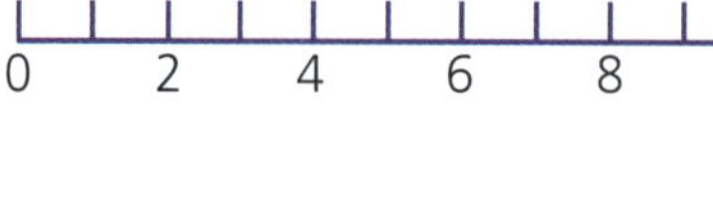

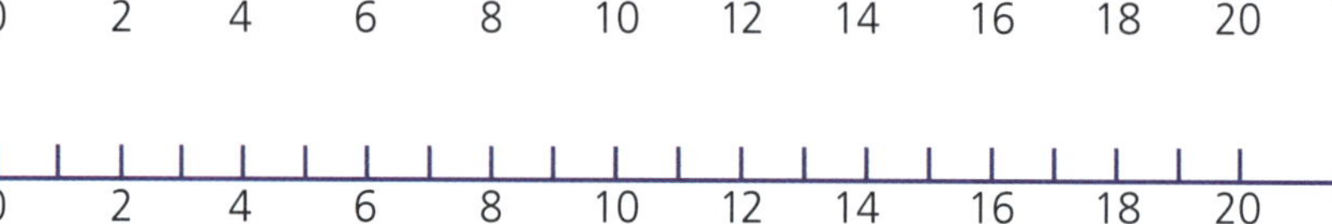

Related problems

12 + 8 = 20
so
12 + 18 = 30

9 + 21 = 30
so
19 + 21 = 40

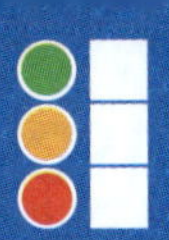

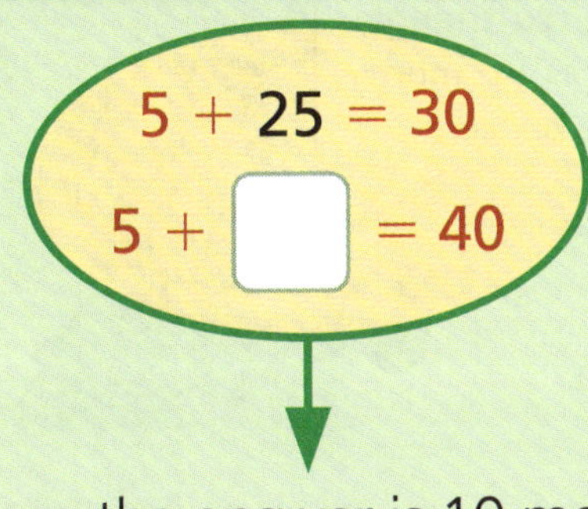

Since the answer is 10 more, we must have added 10 more.

5 + 35 = 40

The more we add, the larger the answer will be.

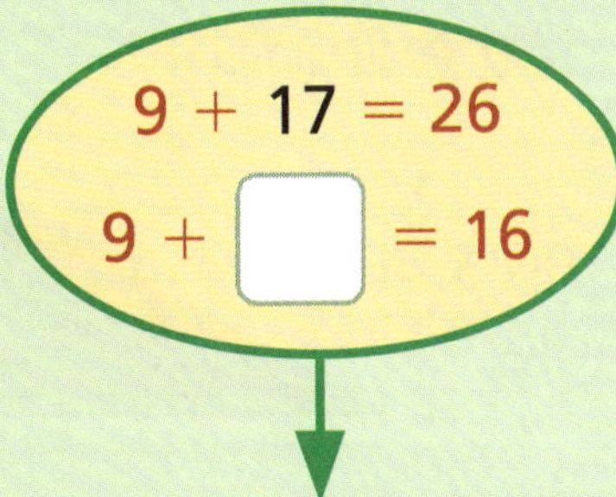

Since the answer is 10 less, we must have added 10 less.

9 + 7 = 16

The less we add, the smaller the answer will be.

CONCEPT

1 Use the first number sentence to work out the other two answers.

a 4 + 8 = 12 so 4 + 18 = ☐ and 4 + 28 = ☐

b 7 + 6 = 13 so 7 + 16 = ☐ and 7 + 26 = ☐

c 8 + 7 = 15 so 8 + 17 = ☐ and 8 + 27 = ☐

d 4 + 6 = 10 so 4 + 16 = ☐ and 4 + 26 = ☐

e 6 + 7 = 13 so 6 + 17 = ☐ and 6 + 27 = ☐

f 17 + 9 = 26 so 17 + 19 = ☐ and 17 + 29 = ☐

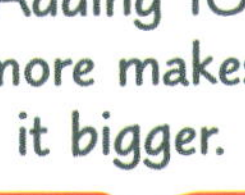

2 Use the first number sentence to work out the other answer.

a 9 + 3 = 12 so 9 + ☐ = 22

b 4 + 8 = 12 so 4 + ☐ = 22

c 8 + 6 = 14 so 8 + ☐ = 24

d 4 + 9 = 13 so 4 + ☐ = 23

e 6 + 19 = 25 so 6 + ☐ = 35

f 13 + 18 = 31 so 13 + ☐ = 21

g 5 + 19 = 24 so 5 + ☐ = 14

h 8 + 19 = 27 so 8 + ☐ = 17

19C Comparing areas

CONCEPT

Area is the measure of the amount of surface.

The red triangle has more area than the yellow triangle.

1 For each pair of shapes, circle the shape that has more area.

a  

b 

c  

2 For each group of shapes, circle the largest area and colour the smallest area.

a 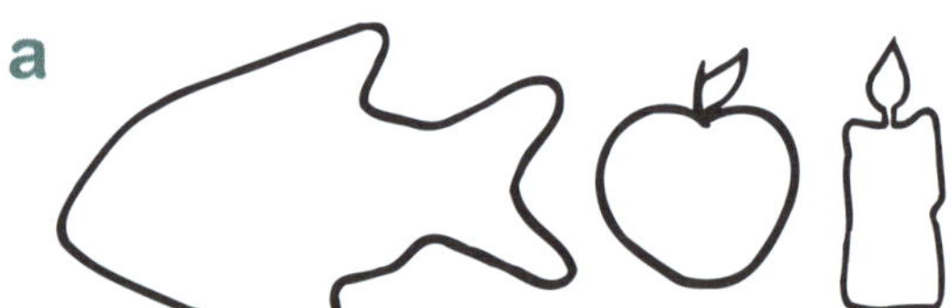 

b 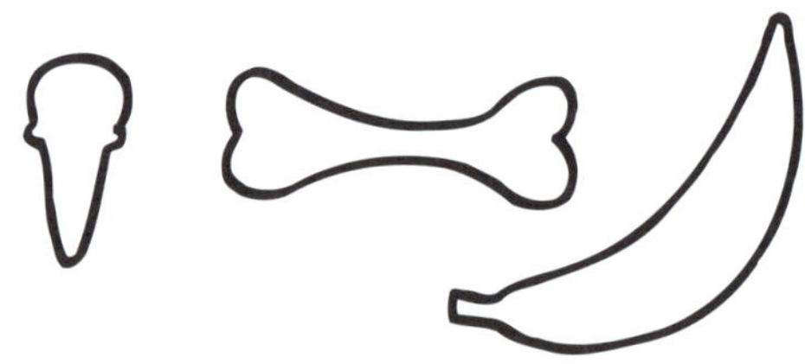

ACTIVITY

Use sheets of newspaper to find the larger area. Count how many sheets it takes to cover one area, then compare this with the next area.

You will need:

- newspaper

- sticky tape

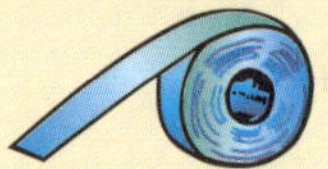

- scissors

First area	Second area	Compare
Door	Window	
Desk	Gate	
Computer	Television	

Explain the reasoning you used to find your answers.

Area

1 Record the area of these patterns. (They have no gaps or overlaps.)

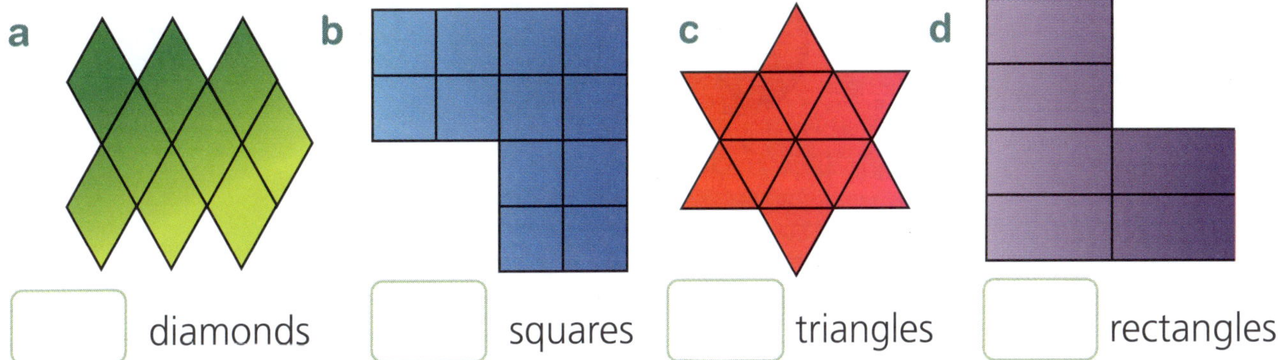

a ☐ diamonds b ☐ squares c ☐ triangles d ☐ rectangles

2 Shape **A** has 3 rows of 3 (or 3 columns of 3). Describe the area of shape:

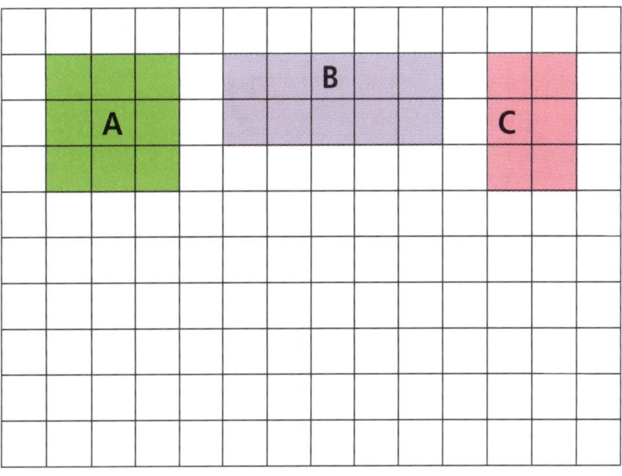

a **B** ☐

b **C** ☐

Draw a shape with:

c 4 columns of 3. Label it with a **D**.

d 2 rows of 2. Label it with an **E**.

Which shape has:

e the largest area? ☐

f the smallest area? ☐

3 a Estimate which letter has the largest area. How many ones place-value blocks are needed to cover each letter?

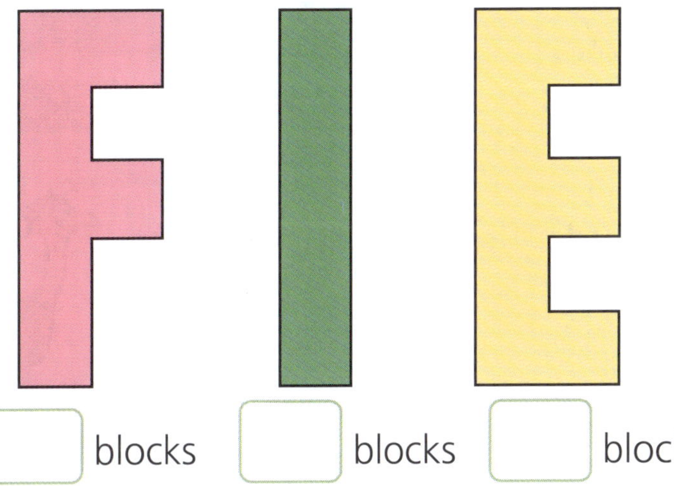

☐ blocks ☐ blocks ☐ blocks

b Which letter has the largest area? ☐

c Which letter has the smallest area? ☐

d Which letter has an area smaller than F? ☐

e Which letter has an area larger than F? ☐

Draw the repeated unit on each shape.

20A Australian money

1 Write the value of each coin.

2 Match each banknote to the correct label.

$20
twenty dollars

$50
fifty dollars

$100
one hundred dollars

$10
ten dollars

$5
five dollars

3 Write the value of the banknotes in order from smallest to largest.

 • *AUSTRALIAN SIGNPOST MATHS 2* • ISBN 9780655708766

20B Symmetry

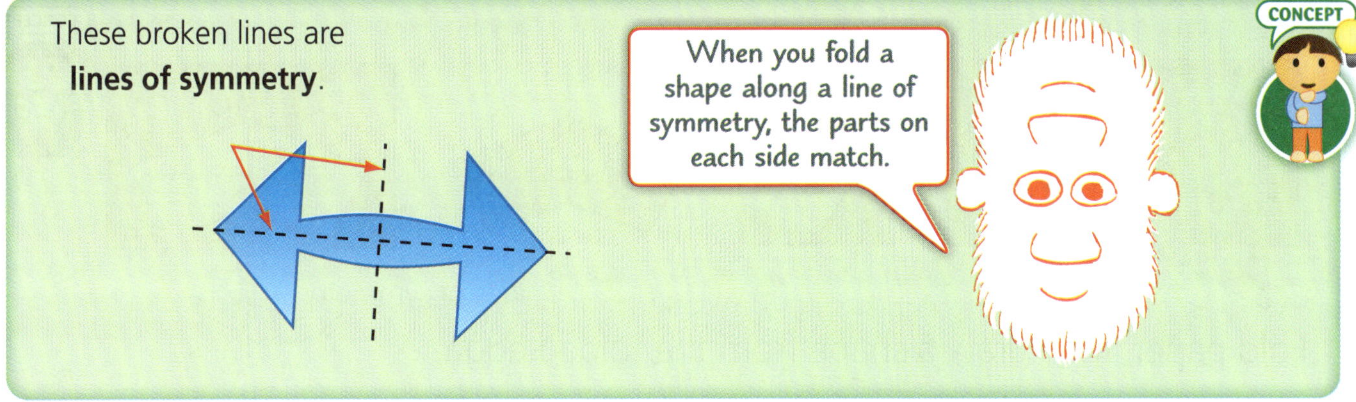

1. Use a ruler to draw a line of symmetry on each picture.

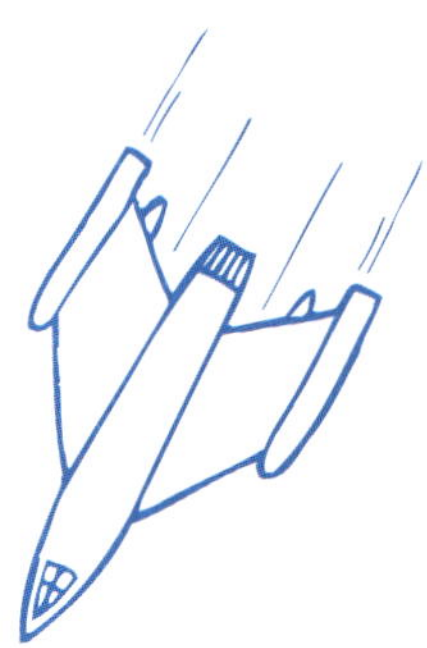

Slide back the edge of this page so that it matches the pictures on page 81 underneath. What do you see?

2. Draw lines of symmetry on each letter.

3. Draw lines of symmetry on each shape.

- Use block shapes to make symmetrical designs.
- Paint a piece of paper. While the paint is still wet, fold the paper onto itself to make a symmetrical painting. Discuss the results.

20C Symmetry

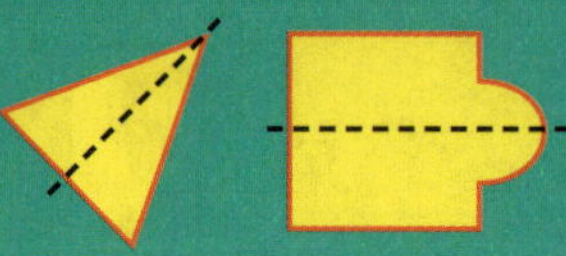

CONCEPT

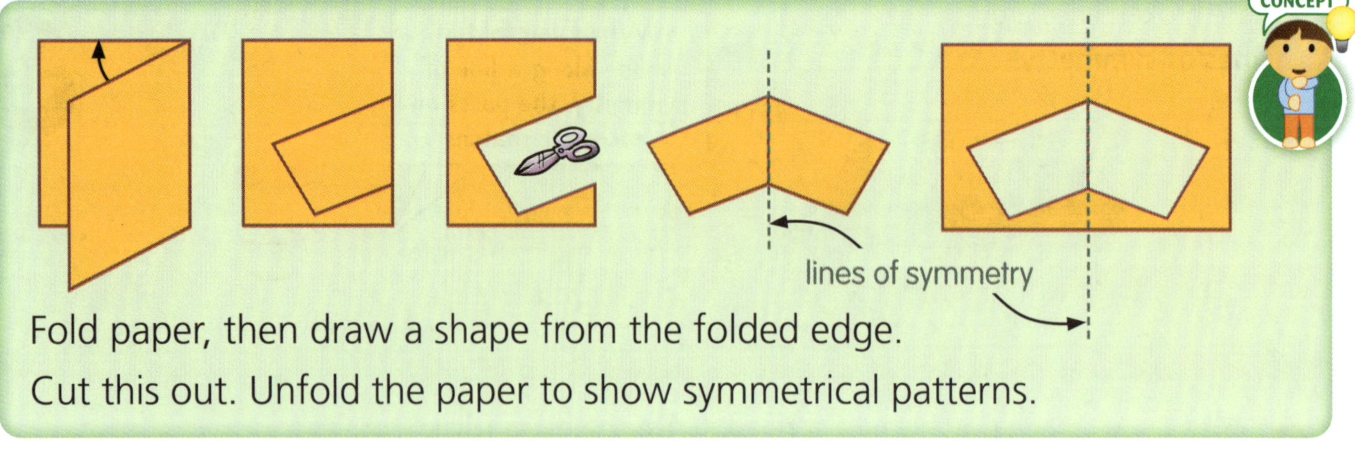

Fold paper, then draw a shape from the folded edge.
Cut this out. Unfold the paper to show symmetrical patterns.

1. Draw a line of symmetry for each.

When you fold a shape along a line of symmetry, the parts on each side match.

two lines of symmetry

2. Circle the shapes where a line of symmetry is shown correctly.

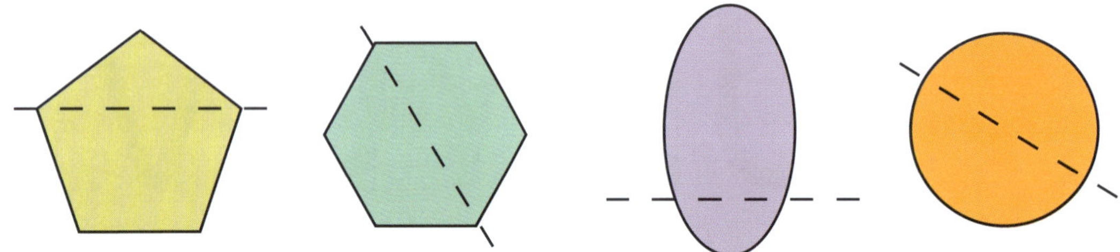

3. Draw each line of symmetry. Use pattern blocks to make these designs.

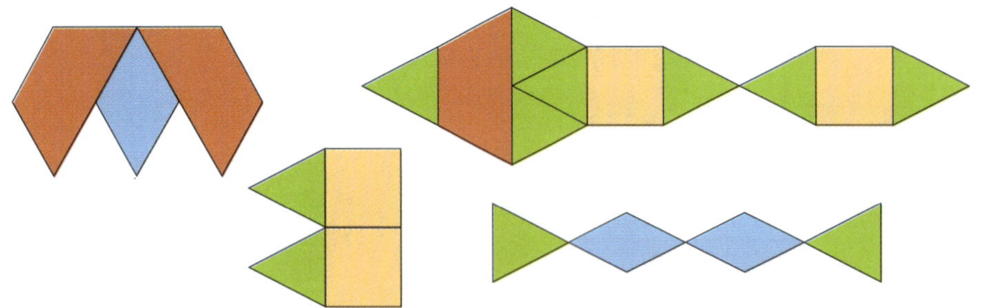

Slide back the edge of page 82 to show the edge of this page beside it. Discuss the result.

ACTIVITY

- Make symmetrical designs using paper folding, pattern blocks, drawing, computer software or by folding paper that has wet paint (or ink blots) on it.

20D Symmetry in our world

Do you think I'm symmetrical?

CONCEPT

In our world, there are many things that are almost symmetrical. Talk about some of these things.

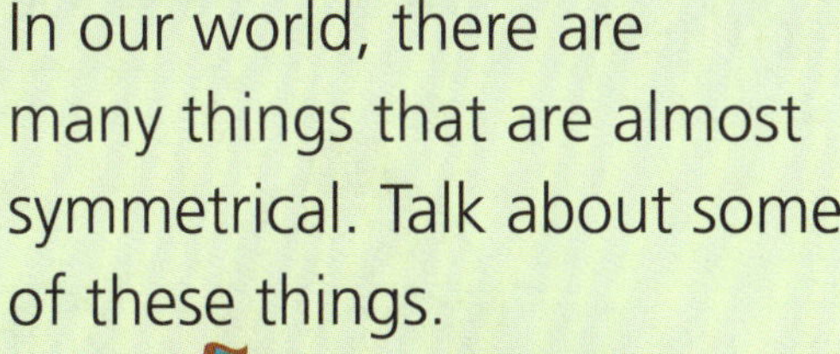

Draw the other half of each picture.

1. Draw every line of symmetry.

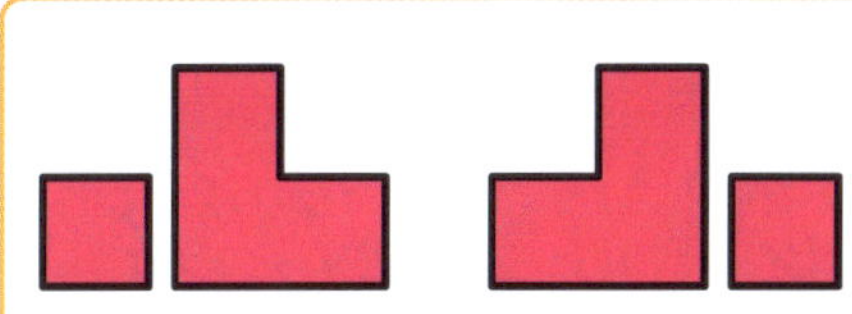

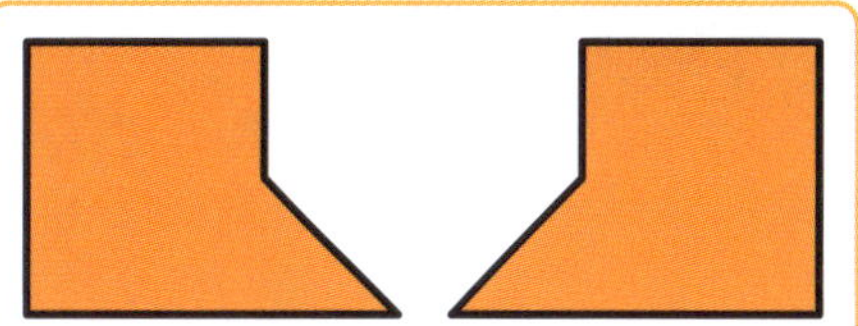

2. Draw the other half to make each picture symmetrical.

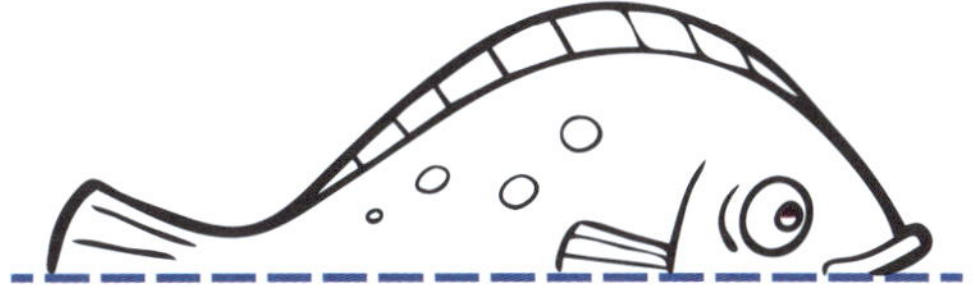

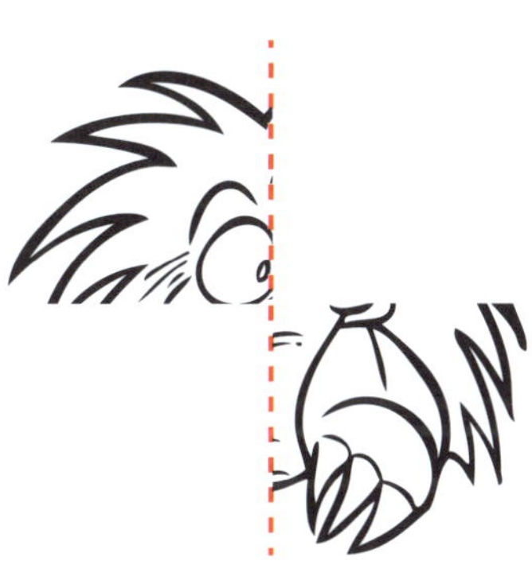

3. Which of **flip**, **slide** or **turn** always makes a symmetrical picture (when put together with its original)? ______

ACTIVITY

- Use block shapes to make symmetrical patterns.

 • *AUSTRALIAN SIGNPOST MATHS 2* • ISBN 9780655708766

21A Value of coins

$1 = 100c

1 Colour the coins you would use to pay for each item.

a

b

c

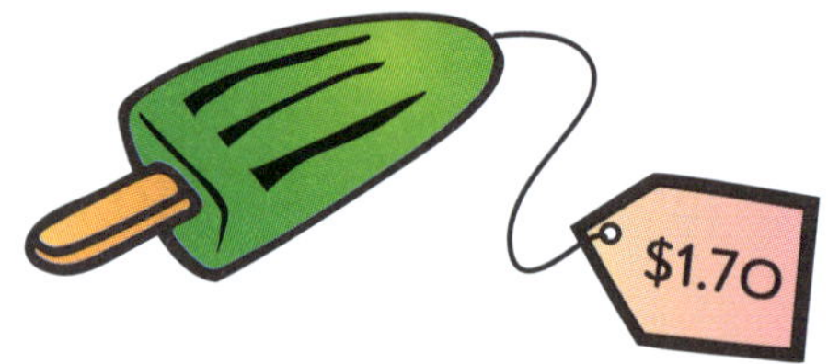

d

e

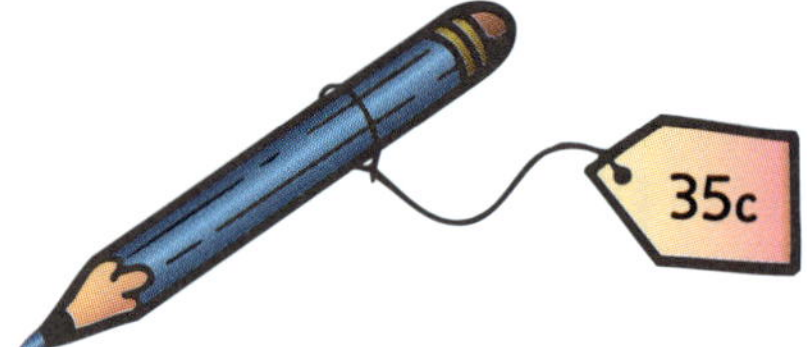

INVESTIGATION

2 Write the **value** of each coin in order.

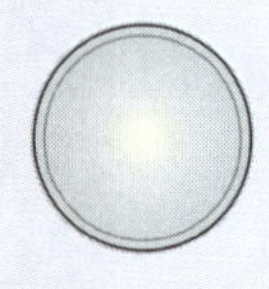
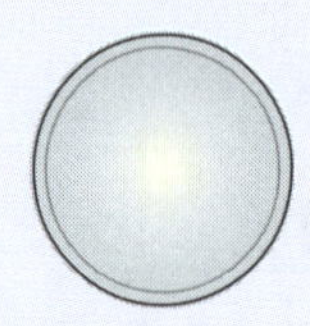
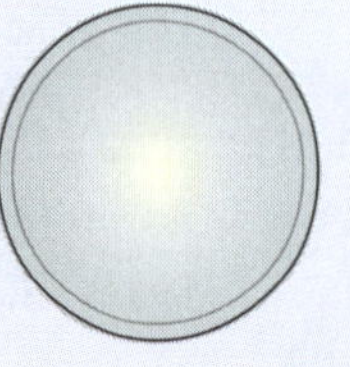
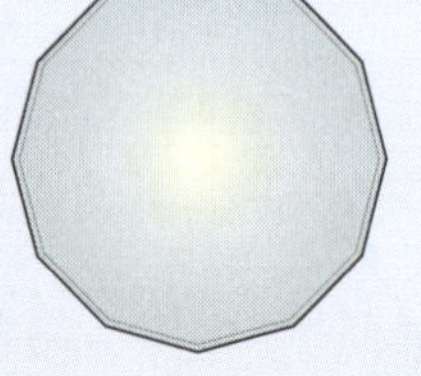

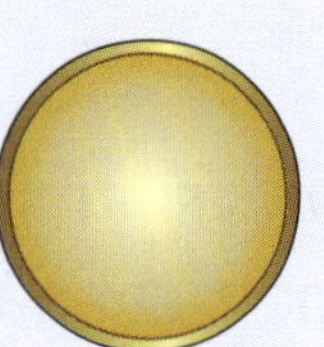

List the coins in order of height.

 ISBN 9780655708766

21B Value of coins

1 Colour the coins you would use to pay for each item.

a

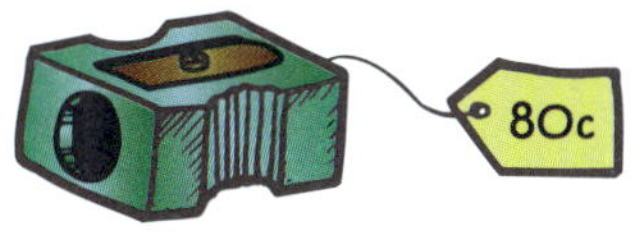

b

c

d

2 Use skip counting to find each total.

a          cents

b         cents

3 Write the value of each group of coins.

a

b

c

21C Numbers

237 = 2 hundreds, 3 tens and 7 ones
or 23 tens and 7 ones

1. 100 cents make a dollar. Write the number of 10 cent coins in:

   a $1 ☐ b $2 ☐ c $3 ☐ d $4 ☐

   100 cents make a dollar. Write the number of 50 cent coins in:

   e $1 ☐ f $2 ☐ g $3 ☐ h $4 ☐

2. How many groups of 100 are in each number?

   a 328 ☐ b 740 ☐ c 237 ☐ d 1000 ☐

   e 534 ☐ f 198 ☐ g 671 ☐ h 928 ☐

3. Write these numbers as tens and ones (518 = 51 tens and 8 ones).

   a 100 = ☐ tens ☐ ones b 135 = ☐ tens ☐ ones

   c 456 = ☐ tens ☐ ones d 309 = ☐ tens ☐ ones

   e 294 = ☐ tens ☐ ones f 673 = ☐ tens ☐ ones

4. How many groups of 10 are in each number?

   a 100 ☐ b 130 ☐ c 456 ☐ d 221 ☐

   e 345 ☐ f 510 ☐ g 329 ☐ h 107 ☐

5. Estimate to the nearest 100, the number of marbles that are in this collection. Check by grouping and counting. ☐

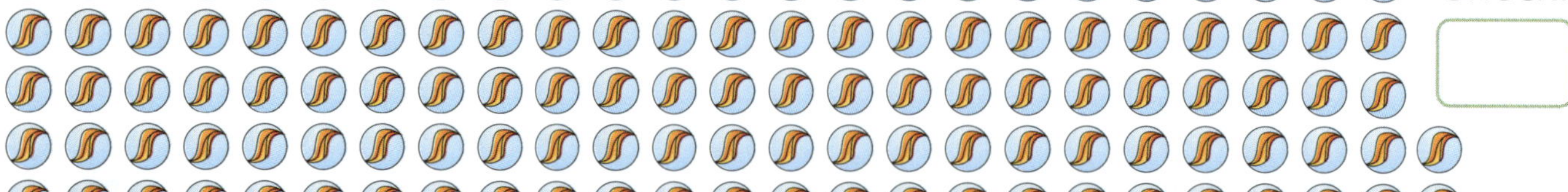

Check: ☐

21D Area using informal units

Which cover has the greater area?

We can use ones blocks as a uniform unit to compare areas.

We can record areas using drawings, numerals and uniform units of measurement.

Why do you think square shapes are best for measuring area?

1 Use the square informal unit (ones block) to find the area of each shape.

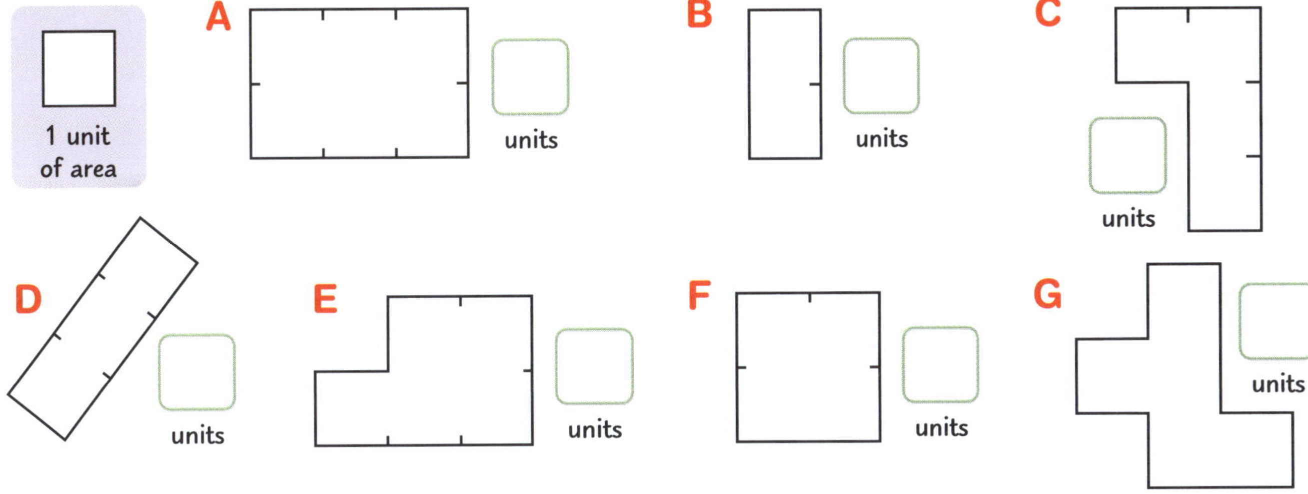

a Which shape has the smallest area? 

b Which shape has the largest area? 

c Which shape has the same area as F? 

d Which shape has the same area as E?

e Which shape has double the area of D?

2 Draw a shape with an area of 8 square units on this grid.

3 Choose the unit you would use, (A) **ones block**, (B) **a page from this book** or (C) **a page from a newspaper** if you wanted to measure the area of:

a the top of your desk

b the top of a mobile phone

c the top of a lunch box

d a large window in a classroom 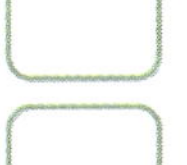

 • *AUSTRALIAN SIGNPOST MATHS 2* • ISBN 9780655708766

22A Amounts to $2

1 How much money is in each moneybox?

a

b

CONCEPT

$1 + 20c + 5c = $1.25

To find "how much", start with the highest coin and count on.

c

d

e

2 What is the value of each set of coins?

a

b

c

d

INVESTIGATION

- Use coins or play money to make 50c in as many ways as you can.
  My number of ways = ☐.
- Use coins to make amounts chosen by your partner.

 • *AUSTRALIAN SIGNPOST MATHS 2* • ISBN 9780655708766

22B Using groups

2 groups of 6
2 x 6

CONCEPT

We can use counters or blocks to model problems.

I had 20 stars. I put 5 on each card.
How many cards did I use?

20
5

Get well soon.

Answer: I used 4 cards.

Circle rows of 5 stars.

1 Draw circles to show these groups and rows.

a groups of 3 balls

How many balls? ☐

How many groups? ☐

How many balls in each group? ☐

b rows of 6 flowers

How many flowers? ☐

How many rows? ☐

How many flowers in each row? ☐

c groups of 5 fish

How many fish? ☐

How many groups? ☐

How many fish in each group? ☐

d groups of 2 coins

How many coins? ☐

How many groups? ☐

How many coins in each group? ☐

e groups of 4 stars

How many stars? ☐

How many groups? ☐

How many stars in each group? ☐

f rows of 5 coins

How many coins? ☐

How many rows? ☐

How many coins in each row? ☐

INVESTIGATION

Use 24 counters. How many students can be given:

a 2 counters? ☐ **b** 3 counters? ☐

c 4 counters? ☐ **d** 6 counters? ☐

24 is 12 twos, 8 threes, ☐ fours, ☐ sixes.

 • *AUSTRALIAN SIGNPOST MATHS 2* • ISBN 9780655708766

Prisms and cylinders

1 Write **prism** or **cylinder** under each object.

a b c d e

2 Use the words **flat surface**, **curved surface**, **slides** and **rolls** to describe each object.

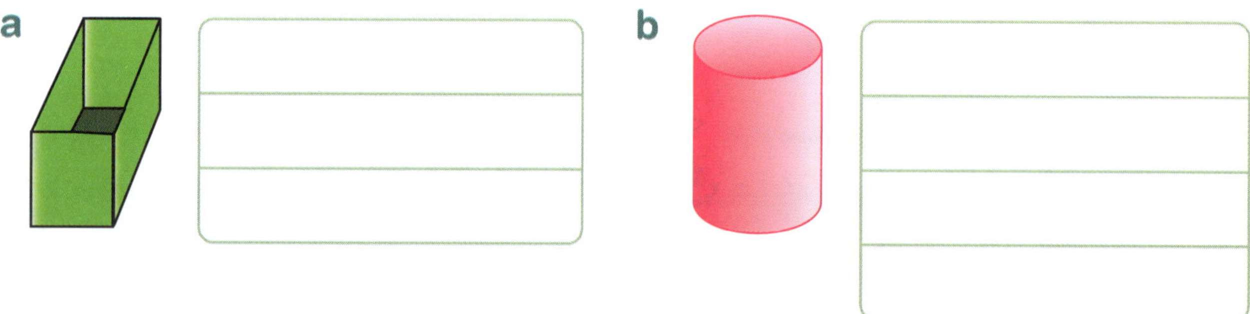

3 Write the shape names of the flat surfaces on each object.

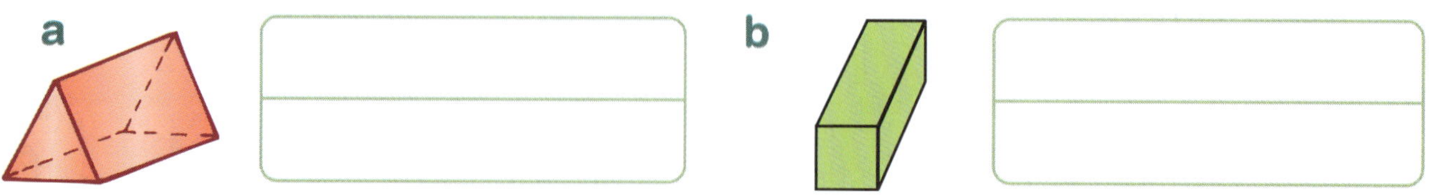

Use plasticine or playdough to make models of prisms and cylinders.

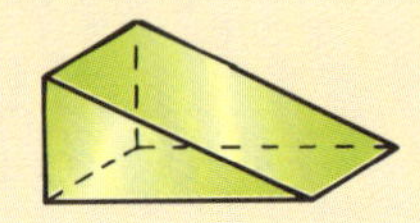

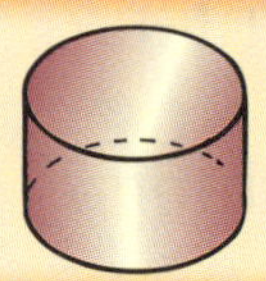

 ISBN 9780655708766

22D 3D objects

1 Match each item with one of the 3D objects. Write the name of each 3D object below it.

2 Draw a picture of the 3D object. How many surfaces does it have?

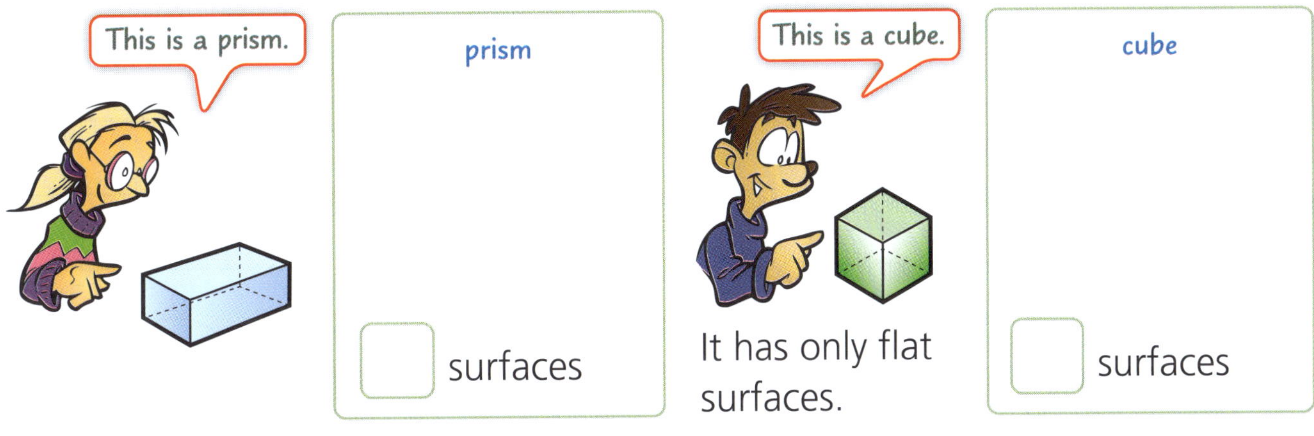

It has only flat surfaces.

3 Complete the pattern of cylinders and cones.

INVESTIGATION

Use plasticine or playdough to make a model of a:

- sphere
- cylinder
- cone
- prism

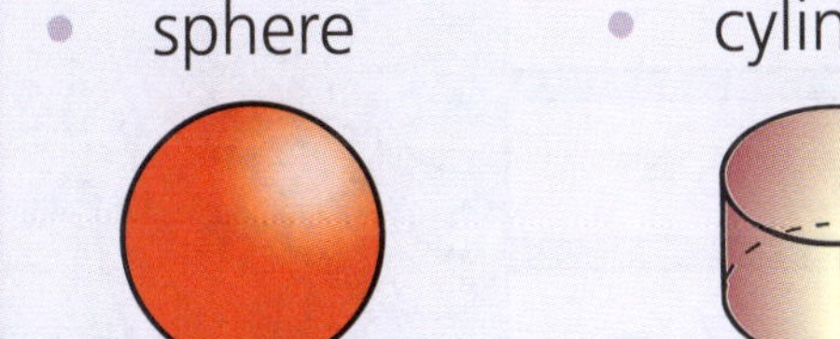
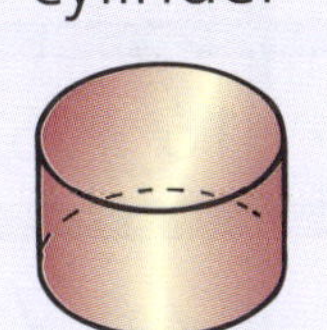
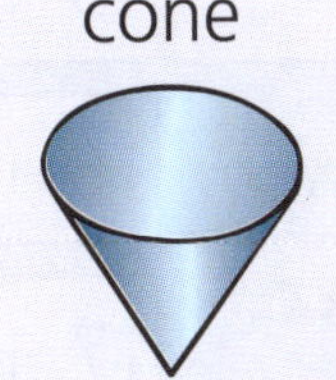
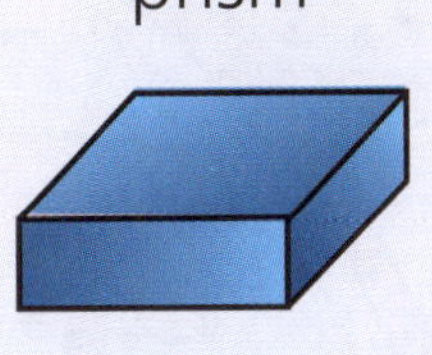

Build a model of a cube using toothpicks. Use Blu Tack, plasticine or playdough to hold the parts together.

23A Building to the next 10

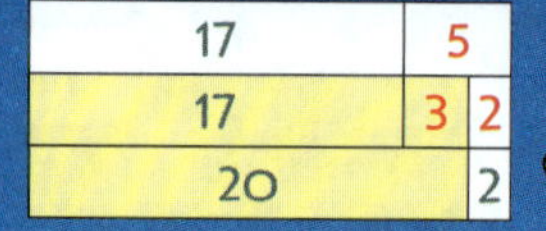

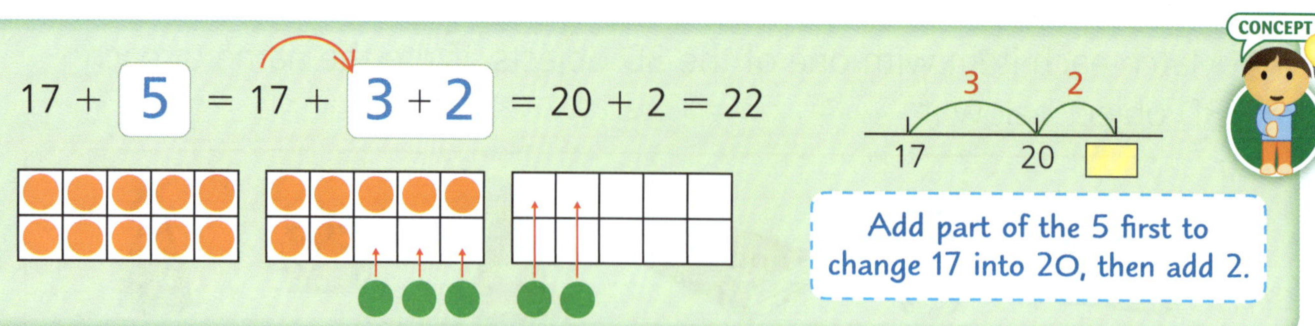

1 Use the ten frames to build to the next 10.

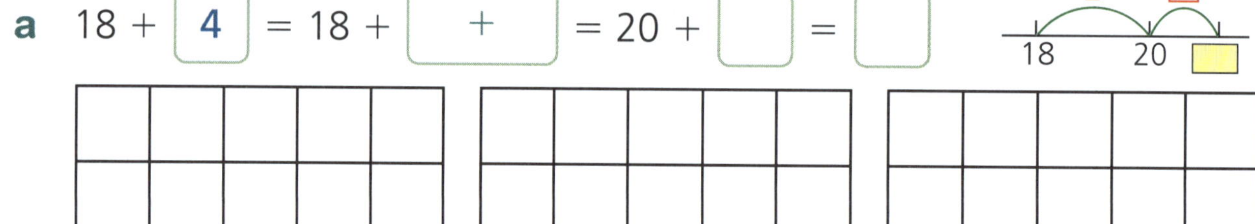

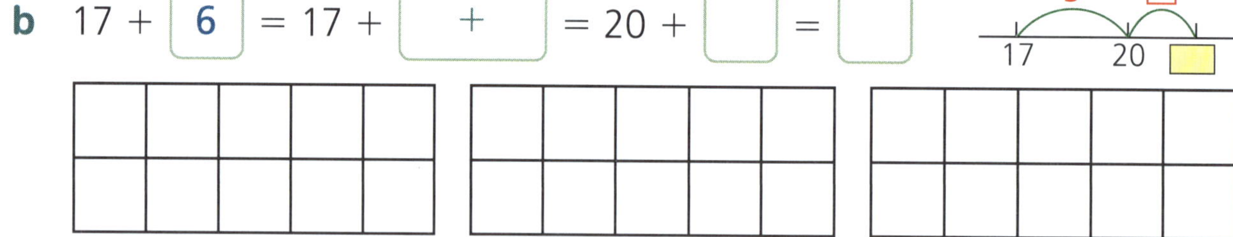

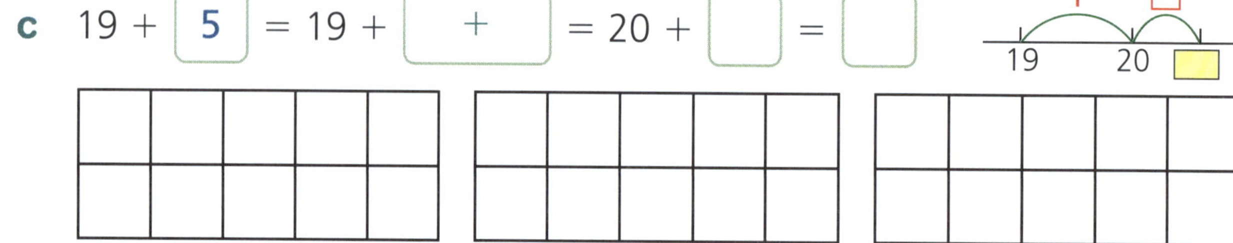

Use ten frames to make up questions of your own.

2 Help Banjo find the answers using the "build to the next 10" strategy.

 • *AUSTRALIAN SIGNPOST MATHS 2* • ISBN 9780655708766

23B Building to the next 10

65 + 7
= 65 + [5 + 2]

65 —5→ 70 —2→ [ ]

1 **a** 37 + 6 = 37 + 3 + [ ]
= [40 +]
= [ ]

b 25 + 7 = 25 + 5 + [ ]
= [30 +]
= [ ]

c 44 + 8 = 44 + 6 + [ ]
= [50 +]
= [ ]

d 73 + 9 = 73 + 7 + [ ]
= [80 +]
= [ ]

2 **a** 56 + 5 = 56 + 4 + [ ]
= [+]
= [ ]

b 69 + 4 = 69 + 1 + [ ]
= [+]
= [ ]

c 38 + 6 = 38 + 2 + [ ]
= [+]
= [ ]

d 84 + 8 = 84 + 6 + [ ]
= [+]
= [ ]

3 Try to do these in your head.

Ask: What is needed to reach the next 10?

a 38 + 3 = [ ]
b 54 + 7 = [ ]
c 77 + 8 = [ ]
d 29 + 5 = [ ]
e 46 + 9 = [ ]
f 55 + 7 = [ ]
g 35 + 5 = [ ]
h 89 + 4 = [ ]

23C Angles

We use a small square to show a right angle.

CONCEPT

This is a right angle.

An angle is made when 2 straight lines meet.

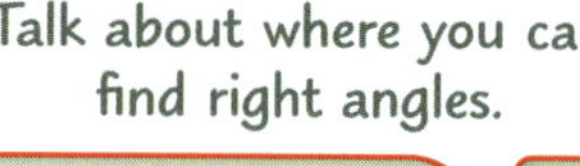

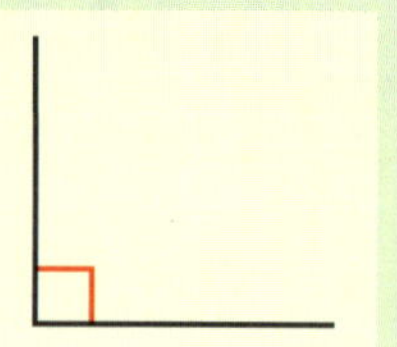

A right angle is made by the hands of a clock at 3 o'clock.

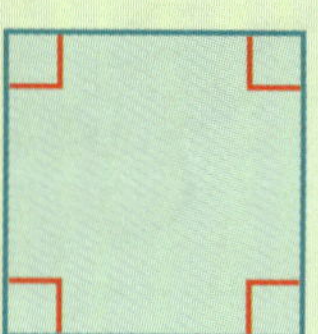

There are four right angles on a square.

1. Trace over the angle made by the hands on each clock.
   Is each angle **greater than**, **less than** or **equal to** a right angle?

a 

b 

c 

d 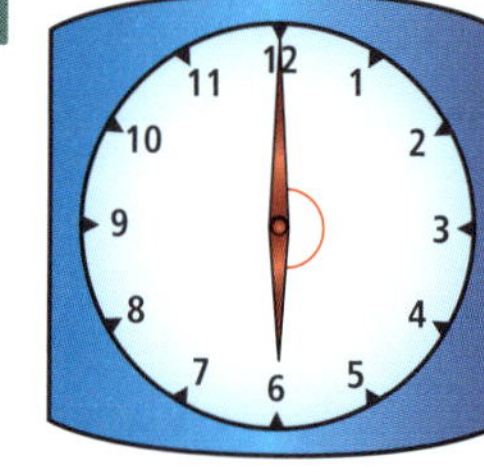

2. **a** Make a small square on each right angle in these shapes.

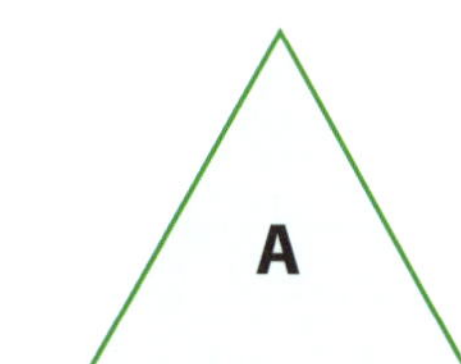

A

B

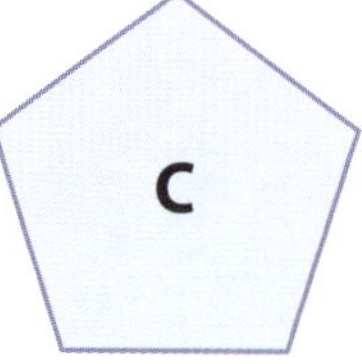

C

D

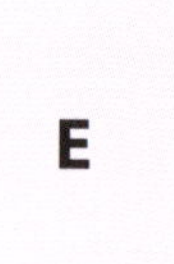

E

b Draw a blue dot in the angles that are less than a right angle.

c Draw a red dot in the angles that are greater than a right angle.

d Which shape has all angles less than a right angle?

e Which shapes have only right angles?

f Which shapes have all angles greater than a right angle?

This paper has 4 angles.

 ISBN 9780655708766

23D Using column graphs

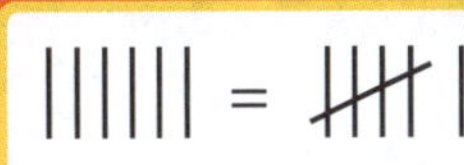

CONCEPT

Table

Test results

	Tally	Number
True	卌 ||||	9
False	卌 ||	7

We gathered this data on page 73 and we drew a picture graph like this.

Picture graph

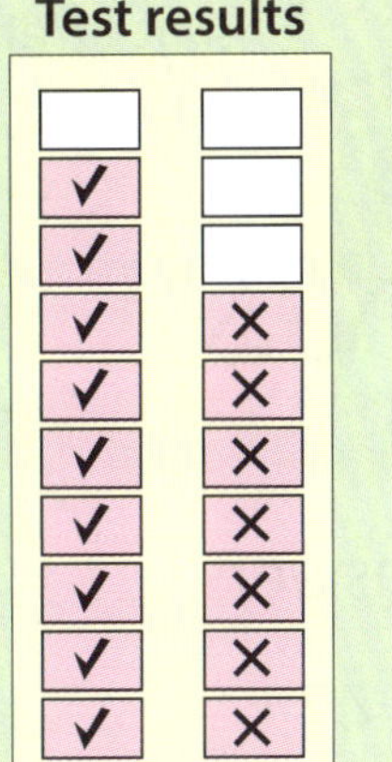

Column graph

A column graph can stand up straight or be on its side.

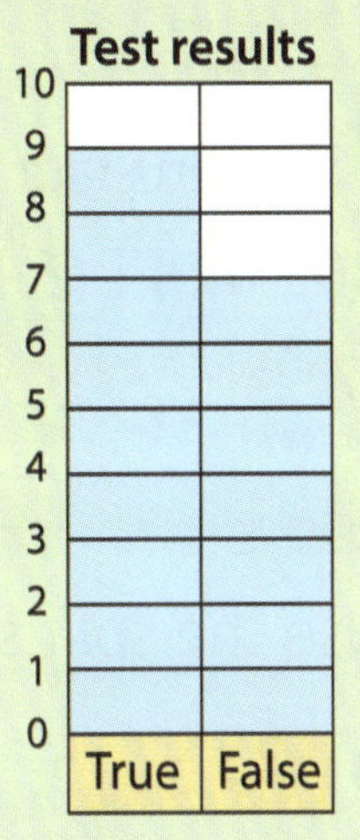

Test results

True
False
0 1 2 3 4 5 6 7 8 9 10

- We join the boxes and put numbers (a scale) on one side to make a column graph.

1 We all played Uno yesterday and then drew a graph of the results.

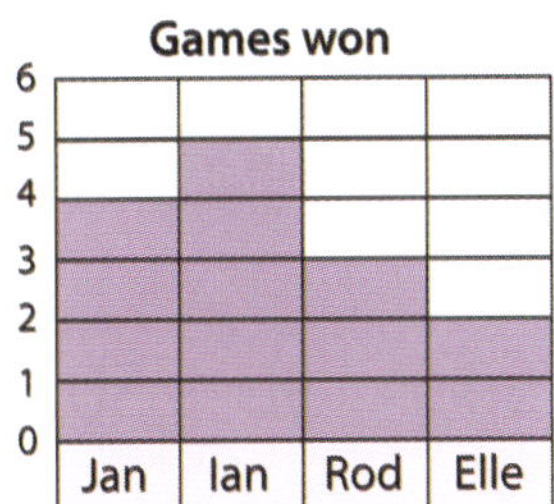

a Who won the most games?

b Who won four games?

c How many games were played?

2 I asked my friends to choose between soccer and tennis.

Choices made by my friends

Soccer
Tennis
0 1 2 3 4 5 6 7 8 9 10

a How many friends chose tennis?

b How many more chose soccer than tennis?

c How many friends made a choice?

3 Draw a column graph of our test scores.

Scores:

3, 5, 7, 10, 9 4, 3, 6, 8, 8, 10, 8, 7, 9, 4, 5, 5, 9, 9, 8

Score	Tally	No.
3 or 4		
5 or 6		
7 or 8		
9 or 10		

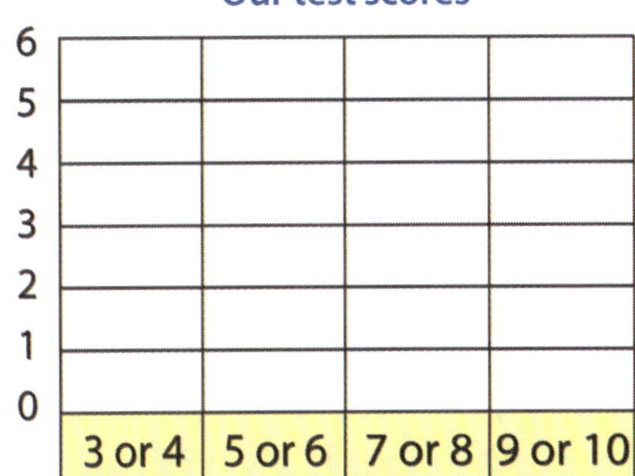

 • *AUSTRALIAN SIGNPOST MATHS 2* • ISBN 9780655708766

24A Split strategy (addition)

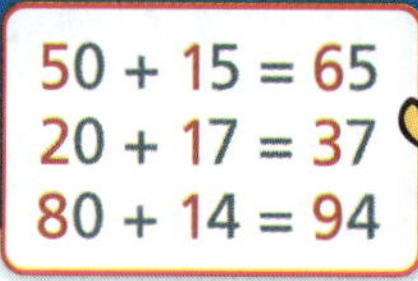

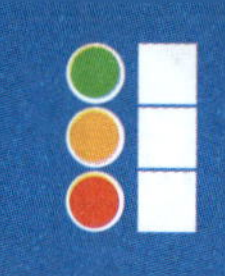

CONCEPT

Add the tens, add the ones.

32 = 30 + 2

= (30 + 40) + (2 + 5) Add tens.

= 77 Add ones.

This is the split strategy.

28 = 20 + 8
57 = 50 + 7

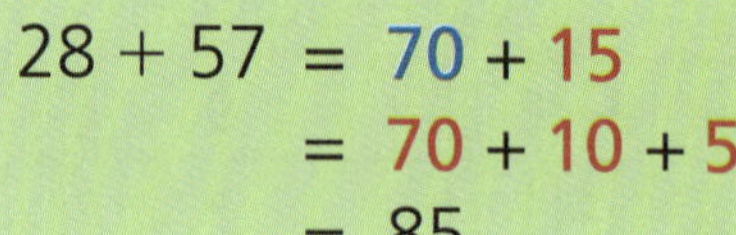

1 Use the split strategy to find the answers.

a 23 + 15
= (20 + 10) + (3 + 5)
= ☐

b 32 + 47
= (30 + 40) + (2 + 7)
= ☐

c 16 + 71
= (10 + 70) + (6 + 1)
= ☐

d 52 + 24
= ☐ + ☐
= ☐

e 81 + 15
= ☐ + ☐
= ☐

f 45 + 54
= ☐ + ☐
= ☐

2 Use the split strategy. (Remember that 70 + 11 = 81.)

a 57 + 24 = 50 + 20 + 7 + 4
= 70 + 11
= ☐

b 38 + 59 = 30 + 50 + 8 + 9
= 80 + 17
= ☐

c 28 + 25 = ☐ + ☐ + ☐ + ☐
= ☐ + ☐
= ☐

d 46 + 38 = ☐ + ☐ + ☐ + ☐
= ☐ + ☐
= ☐

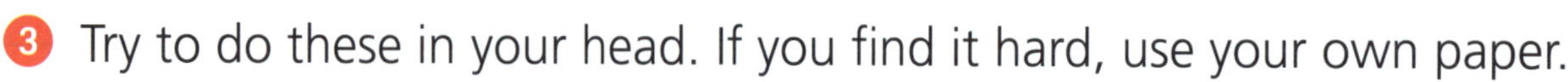

a 32 + 64 = ☐
b 33 + 44 = ☐
c 74 + 16 = ☐
d 52 + 28 = ☐
e 17 + 37 = ☐
f 38 + 16 = ☐

24B Split strategy (addition)

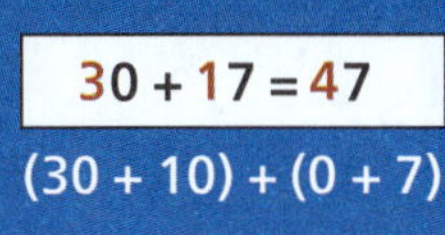

1 a $48 + 6 = 40 + 8 + 6$
$= 40 + 14$
$= 40 + 10 + 4$
= ☐

b $56 + 9 = 50 + 6 + 9$
$= 50 + 15$
$= 50 + 10 + 5$
= ☐

c $35 + 16 = 30 + 5 + 10 + 6$
$= (30 + 10) + (5 + 6)$
$= 40 + 11$
= ☐

d $16 + 57 = 10 + 6 + 50 + 7$
$= (10 + 50) + (6 + 7)$
$= 60 + 13$
= ☐

2 a $16 + 67 = (10 + 60) + (6 + 7)$
= ☐ + ☐
= ☐

b $39 + 35 = (30 + 30) + (9 + 5)$
= ☐ + ☐
= ☐

c $64 + 26 = (60 + 20) + (4 + 6)$
= ☐ + ☐
= ☐

d $52 + 29 = (50 + 20) + (2 + 9)$
= ☐ + ☐
= ☐

3 a $43 + 29 =$ 60 + 12
= ☐

b $37 + 56 =$ ☐ + ☐
= ☐

c $74 + 26 =$ ☐ + ☐
= ☐

d $42 + 39 =$ ☐ + ☐
= ☐

4 a $44 + 38 =$ ☐

b $57 + 17 =$ ☐

c $68 + 15 =$ ☐

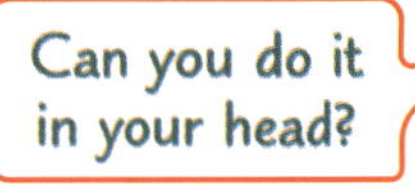

24C Ordering masses

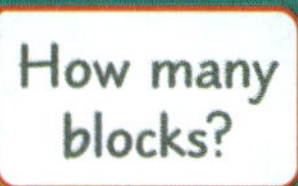

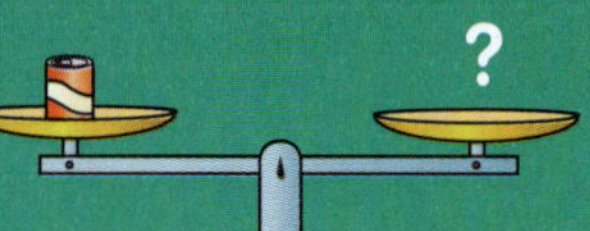

1 a Handle (heft) three objects like these and estimate which one is the lightest and which one is the heaviest.

b Order the objects from lightest to heaviest.

______ (lightest), ______, ______ (heaviest)

c Use blocks and a balance scale to find the mass of each object.

Object	Mass
	blocks
	blocks
	blocks

d Write a sentence about the masses of the three objects.

______

______

2 Choose other sets of three objects and compare them in the same way. Record your results.

Object	Mass
	marbles
	marbles
	marbles

Object	Mass

______

______

______

______

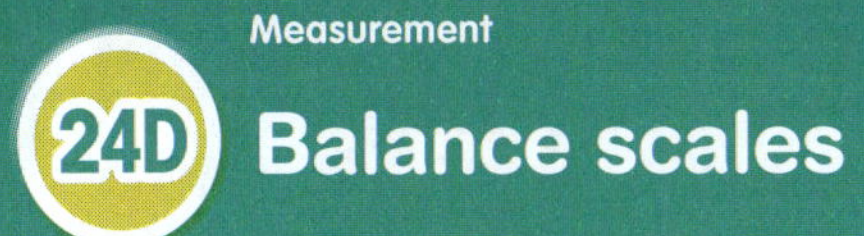

24D Balance scales

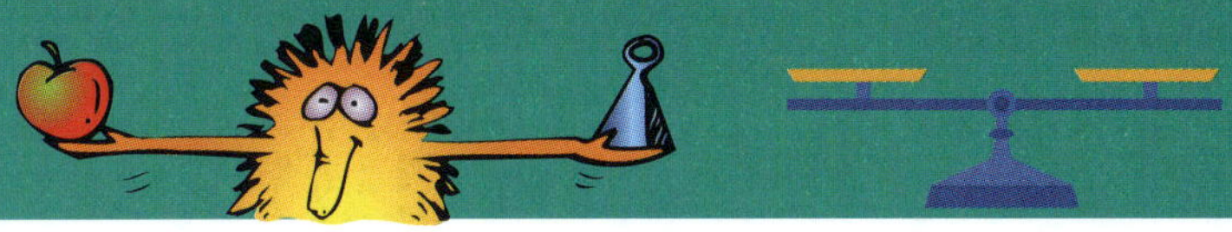

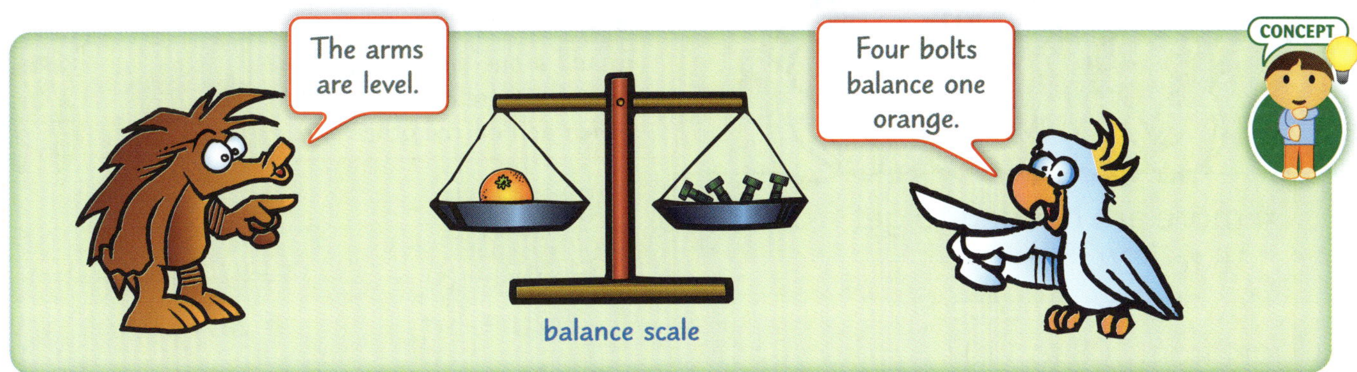

ACTIVITY

1. Use a balance scale to find answers to these.

   a 2 marbles balance ☐ craft sticks.

   b 1 ball balances ☐ marbles.

   c 8 pens balance ☐ marbles.

   d 4 pens balance ☐ craft sticks.

   e 1 tennis ball balances ☐ marbles.

   f 5 marbles balance ☐ blocks.

2. a Choose a unit to use and balance some plasticine. Change the shape of the plasticine and weigh it again. What did you find?

   ____

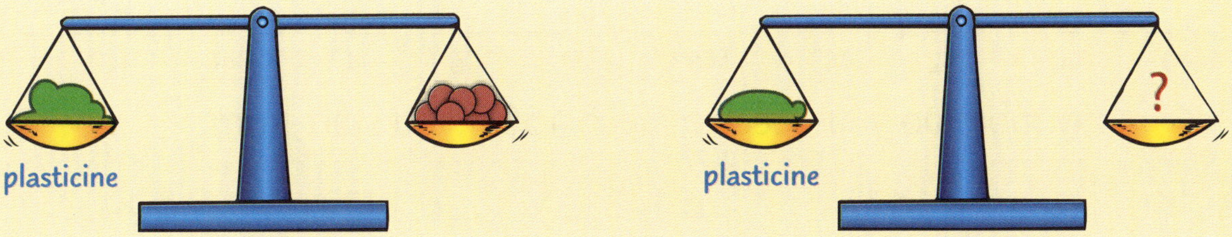

   plasticine

   plasticine ?

   b Choose a different unit to weigh the plasticine. Do you think you will need more of these units? ☐ Weigh the plasticine. What did you discover?

   ____

   ____

 • *AUSTRALIAN SIGNPOST MATHS 2* • ISBN 9780655708766

25A Building to the next 10

Multiples of 10 end in zero.
10, 20, 30 …
or 80, 130, 250, 870 …

CONCEPT

To add a one-digit number, use part of it to reach the next ten, then add on the other part.

4 more are needed to get from 116 to 120.

How many are needed to get from 108 to 110? ☐

101	102	103	104	105	106	107	108	109	110
111	112	113	114	115	116	117	118	119	120
121	122	123	124	125	126	127	128	129	130

How many are needed to get from 126 to 130? ☐

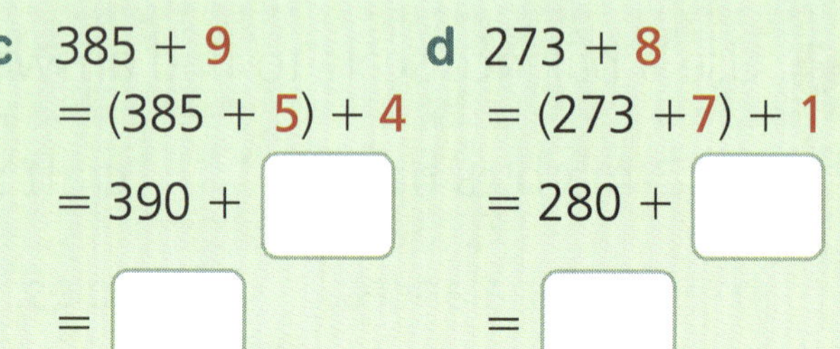

a 17 + 8
= (17 + 3) + 5
= 20 + 5
= 25

b 79 + 5
= (79 + 1) + 4
= 80 + 4
= 84

c 385 + 9
= (385 + 5) + 4
= 390 + ☐
= ☐

d 273 + 8
= (273 + 7) + 1
= 280 + ☐
= ☐

1

71	72	73	74	75	76	77	78	79	80

How many more do you need to get to 80 if you start from:

a 78? ☐ **b** 76? ☐ **c** 79? ☐ **d** 75? ☐ **e** 77? ☐

2

271	272	273	274	275	276	277	278	279	280

How many more do you need to get to 280 if you start from:

a 279? ☐ **b** 277? ☐ **c** 275? ☐ **d** 274? ☐ **e** 278? ☐

3

140 141 142 143 144 145 146 147 148 149 150

How many more do you need to reach 150 if you start from:

a 146? ☐ **b** 147? ☐ **c** 148? ☐ **d** 143? ☐ **e** 145? ☐

4 257 + 8 = (257 + 3) + 5 = 260 + 5 = 265

Use this method to answer these questions.

a 278 + 4 ☐ **b** 279 + 3 ☐ **c** 277 + 5 ☐

d 274 + 8 ☐ **e** 277 + 7 ☐ **f** 279 + 6 ☐

g 186 + 7 ☐ **h** 349 + 6 ☐ **i** 418 + 9 ☐

25B Repeated subtraction

How many tins can I fill?

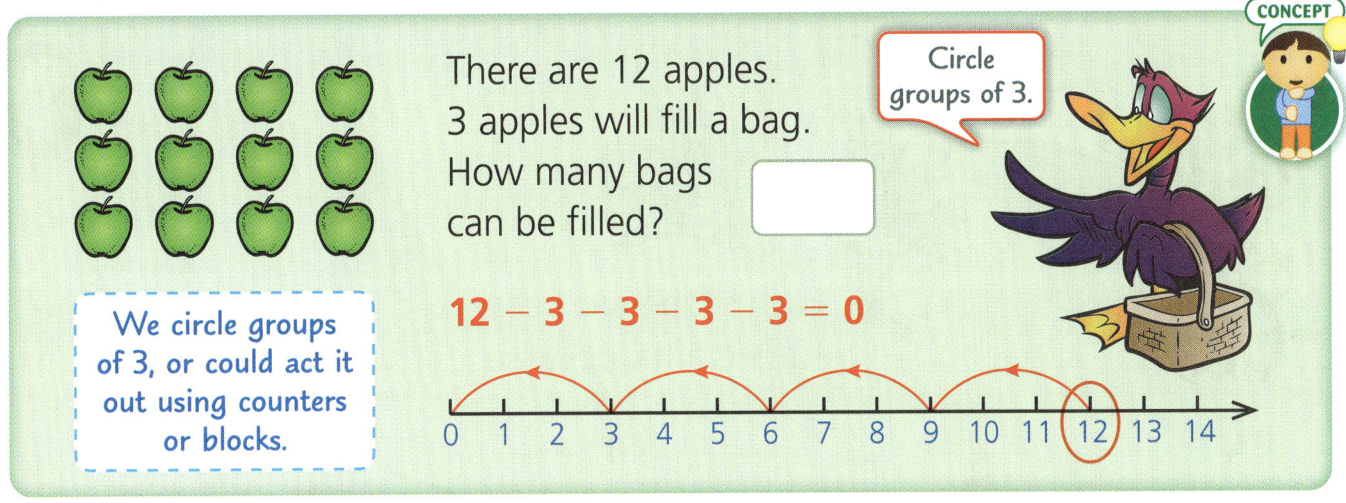

There are 12 apples.
3 apples will fill a bag.
How many bags can be filled? ☐

$12 - 3 - 3 - 3 - 3 = 0$

1 We have 12 apples. Write the number of students that can be given:

a 2 apples ☐ **b** 4 apples ☐ **c** 6 apples ☐

2

We have 16 balls.
How many children can be given:

a 4 balls? ☐ **b** 8 balls? ☐

c 2 balls? ☐ **d** 1 ball? ☐

3

We have 15 birds.
How many people can be given:

a 5 birds? ☐ **b** 3 birds? ☐

c 4 birds? ☐ with ☐ birds left over

d 6 birds? ☐ with ☐ birds left over

4

We have 20 lollies to share.
How many children can be given:

a 2 lollies? ☐ **b** 4 lollies? ☐

c 5 lollies? ☐ **d** 10 lollies? ☐

e 6 lollies? ☐ with ☐ lollies left over

25C Turning a shape

A

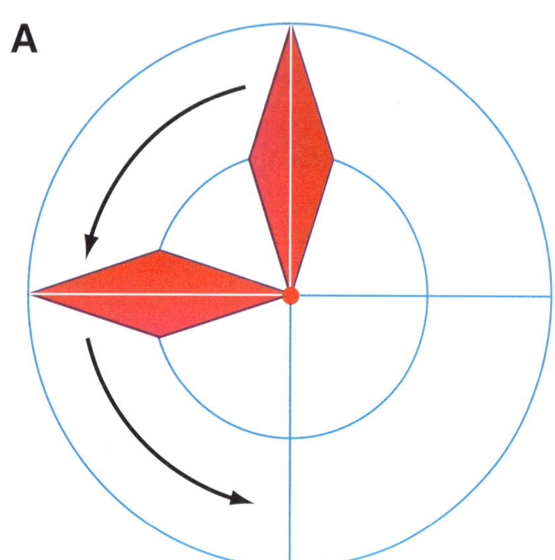

B

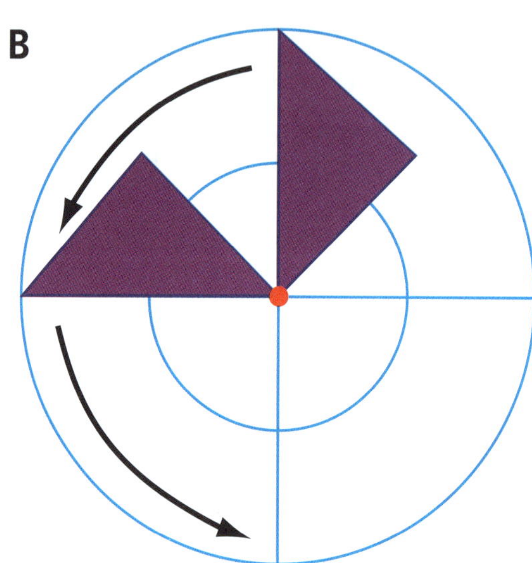

1. In picture **A** above, a pattern block has been traced, then turned, and then traced and turned again. Complete the pattern.
   - **a** Does the shape change as it turns? [ ]
   - **b** Does the shape turn around a point? [ ]

2. Complete pattern **B**.

ACTIVITY

- Play **Simon says**, giving directions using the words shown here.
- Write the directions.

[ ]

[ ]

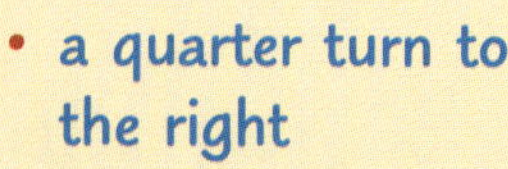

- a quarter turn to the right
- a quarter turn to the left
- 3 steps forward
- 3 steps backwards

Turning shapes

If the minute hand makes a three-quarter turn, it will be pointing to the 9.

1

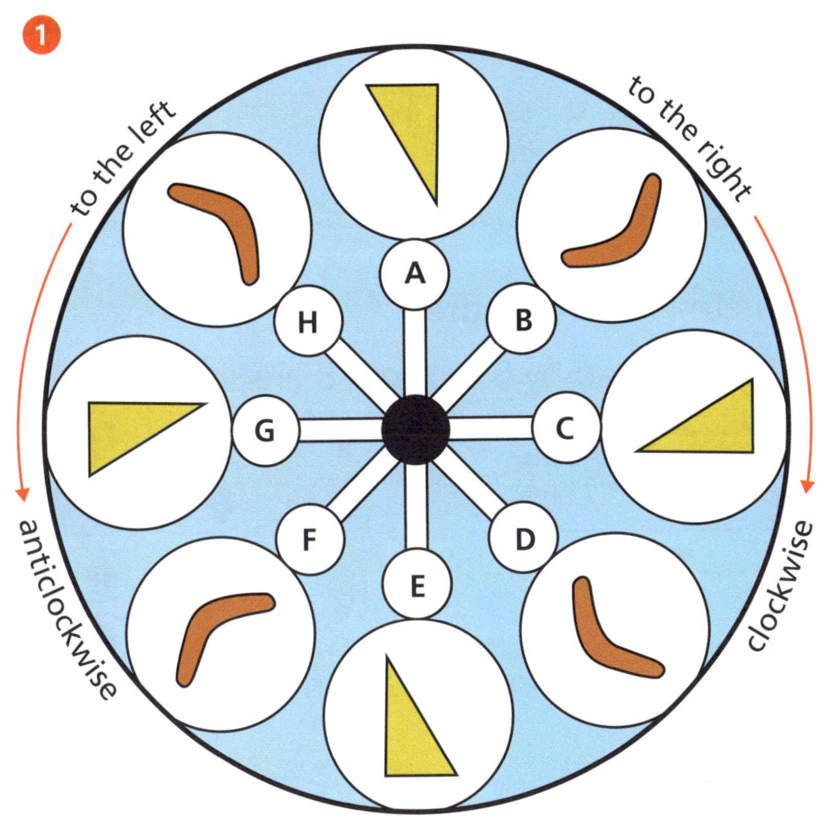

a When **A** turns a quarter turn to the right, it becomes shape ☐.

b When **A** turns a quarter turn to the left, it becomes shape ☐.

c When **A** turns a half turn to the right, it becomes shape ☐.

d When **B** turns a half turn to the right, it becomes shape ☐.

e When **B** turns a quarter turn to the right, it becomes shape ☐.

Using pattern blocks

ACTIVITY

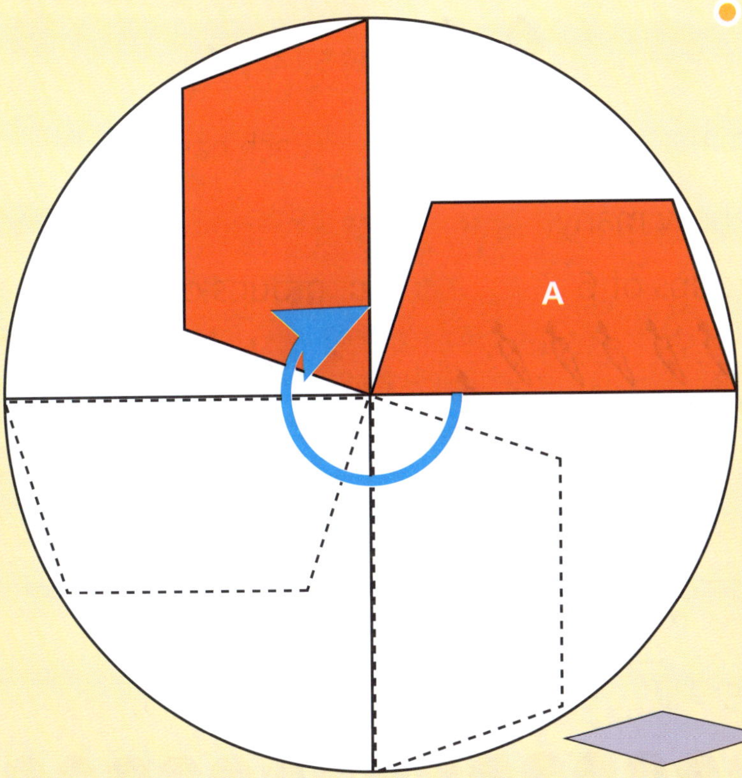

A

- Use a pattern block to finish this pattern. Turn it around the centre and trace the block.
- Make other turning patterns using the pattern blocks.

26A Division sign

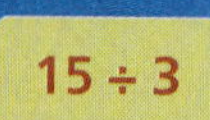

"15 shared by 3"
or
"How many 3s are in 15?"

÷ means **shared among**
means **in groups of**
means **divided by**

$15 \div 3 = $ 5

1. Use these pictures and counters to find **one share** if:

a 16 are shared by 4

$16 \div 4 = $ ☐

Each has ☐.

b 15 are shared by 5

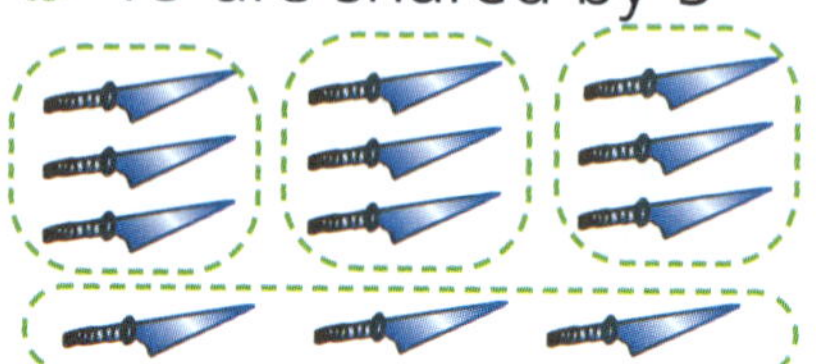

$15 \div 5 = $ ☐

Each has ☐.

c 18 are shared by 9

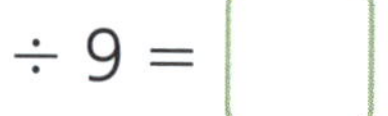

$18 \div 9 = $ ☐

Each has ☐.

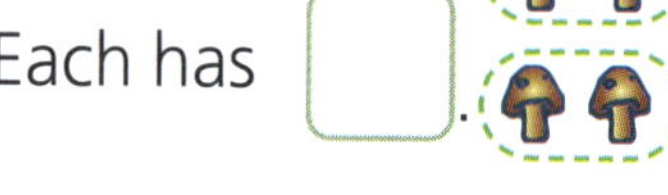

d 12 are shared by 3

$12 \div 3 = $ ☐

Each has ☐.

e 20 are shared by 4

$20 \div 4 = $ ☐

Each has ☐.

f 12 are shared by 4

$12 \div 4 = $ ☐

Each has ☐.

2. Use these pictures to find out how many:

a groups of 2

$8 \div 2 = $ ☐

☐ groups

b groups of 6

$12 \div 6 = $ ☐

☐ groups

c groups of 3

$21 \div 3 = $ ☐

☐ groups

d groups of 5 circles $25 \div 5 = $ ☐ There are ☐ groups of 5.

26B Division as repeated subtraction

CONCEPT

÷ means **shared among**
means **in groups of**
means **divided by**

÷ is the opposite of X.

You could use counters.

How many groups of 3 are in 18?

18 ÷ 3 = 6

1

Do these by subtracting equal groups.

a How many groups of 2 in 24?
24 ÷ 2 = ☐

b How many groups of 4 in 24?
24 ÷ 4= ☐

c How many groups of 8 in 24?
24 ÷ 8 = ☐

d How many groups of 3 in 24?
24 ÷ 3 = ☐

e How many groups of 6 in 24?
24 ÷ 6 = ☐

f How many groups of 12 in 24?
24 ÷ 12 = ☐

2

groups of 7 = ☐ 28 ÷ 7 = ☐

There are ☐ groups of 7 stars.

3

18 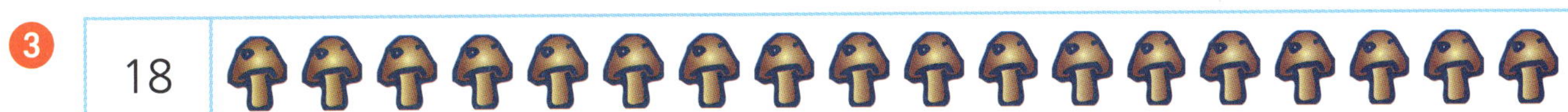

a How many groups of 3 in 18? ☐ 18 ÷ 3 = ☐

b How many groups of 6 in 18? ☐ 18 ÷ 6 = ☐

c How many groups of 2 in 18? ☐ 18 ÷ 2 = ☐

Estimate before you calculate.

 • *AUSTRALIAN SIGNPOST MATHS 2* • ISBN 9780655708766

26C Division as repeated subtraction

CONCEPT

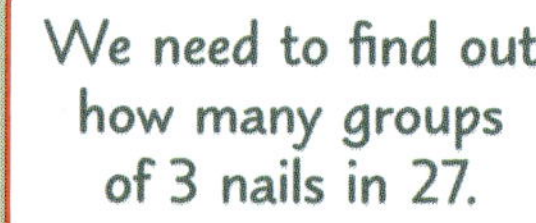

$27 \div 3 = 9$

Do these by subtracting equal groups.

1           

a How many groups of 2 kites are in 10? ☐ $10 \div 2 =$ ☐

b How many groups of 5 kites are in 10? ☐ $10 \div 5 =$ ☐

2  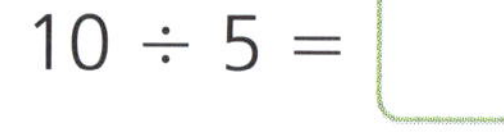  

a How many groups of 6 cars are in 12? ☐ $12 \div 6 =$ ☐

b How many groups of 4 cars are in 12? ☐ $12 \div 4 =$ ☐

3               

a How many groups of 2 balls are in 14? ☐ $14 \div 2 =$ ☐

b How many groups of 7 balls are in 14? ☐ $14 \div 7 =$ ☐

INVESTIGATION

4 Start with 36 counters. Use repeated subtraction for these.

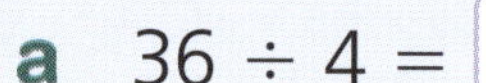

a $36 \div 4 =$ ☐ b $36 \div 9 =$ ☐ c $36 \div 12 =$ ☐

d $36 \div 3 =$ ☐ e $36 \div 6 =$ ☐ f $36 \div 1 =$ ☐

g $36 \div 2 =$ ☐ h $36 \div 18 =$ ☐ i $36 \div 36 =$ ☐

 ISBN 9780655708766

26D Making graphs

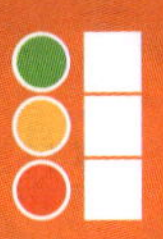

Without counting, estimate which group is largest.

1. Complete this table to record the animals in the picture. (Cross out each animal as you put its tally mark in the table.)

Animals seen	Tally	Number
Birds		
Kangaroos		
Wombats		

2. On the graph, draw one picture for each animal.

Animals seen		
Birds	Kangaroos	Wombats

a Which group is the smallest?

b How many more birds are there than wombats?

c What is the difference between the number of kangaroos and the number of birds?

d Draw a horizontal column graph using this data.

Animals seen				
Birds				
Kangaroos				
Wombats				

3. Draw a table showing the people in your classroom. Circle the category you predict will be largest.

Boys	
Girls	
Adults	

27A Jump strategy (addition)

38 + 6
= 38 + 2 + 4

38 + 6 Start at 38 and jump to 40.

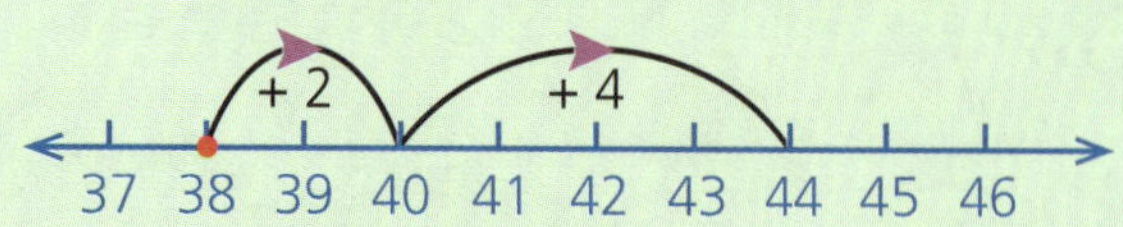

$$\begin{array}{r} 38 \\ +\ 6 \\ \hline 44 \end{array}$$

We use only part of the number line.

CONCEPT

1 Use the jump strategy to find the answers.

a 38 + 4 = ☐

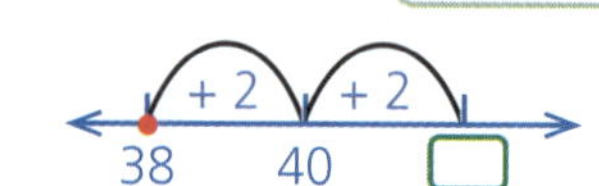

b 58 + 5 = ☐

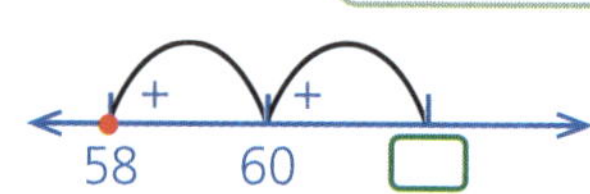

c 47 + 6 = ☐

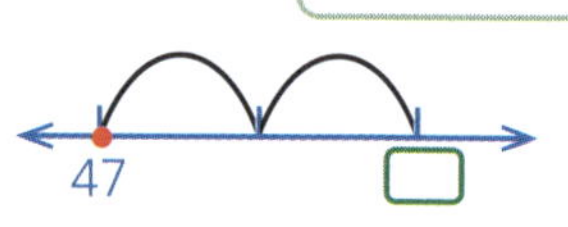

d 37 + 8 = ☐

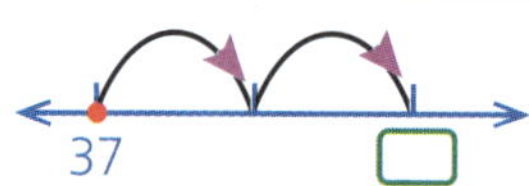

e 57 + 9 = ☐

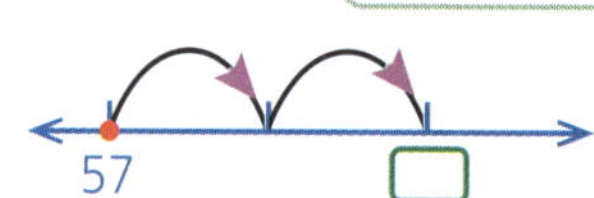

f 88 + 7 = ☐

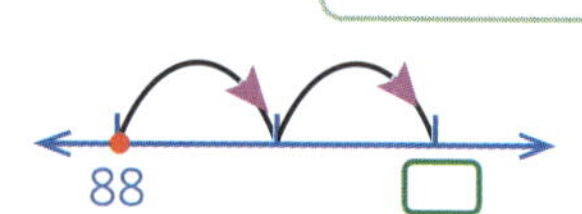

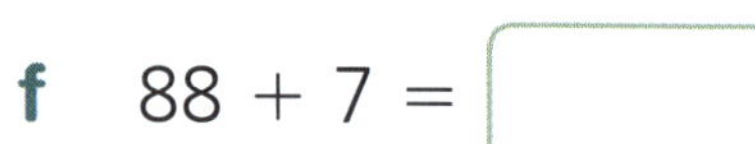

37 + 24 Start at 37 and count on. **or**

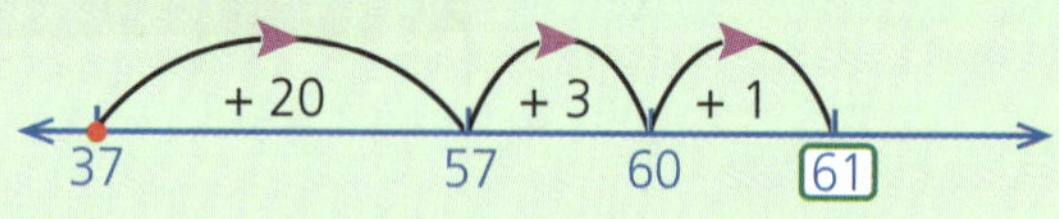

- We don't need marks on the line.
- We jump the tens, then the ones.

37 + 24
= 37 + 20 + 4
= 57 + 3 + 1
= 61

$$\begin{array}{r} 37 \\ +\ 24 \\ \hline 61 \end{array}$$

CONCEPT

2 Use the jump strategy to find the answers.

a 46 + 21 = ☐

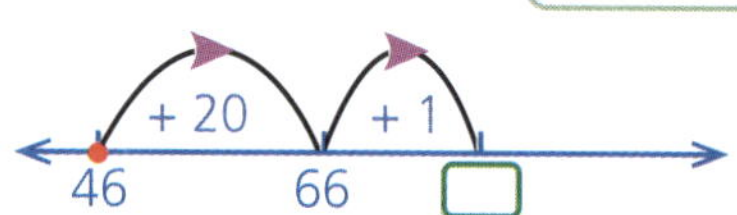

b 39 + 23 = ☐

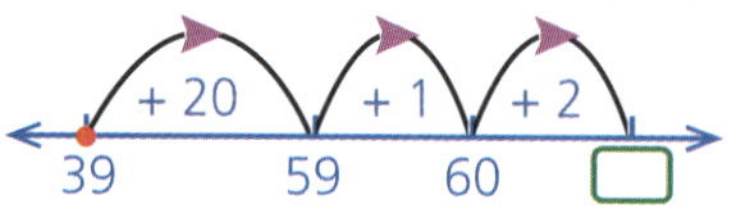

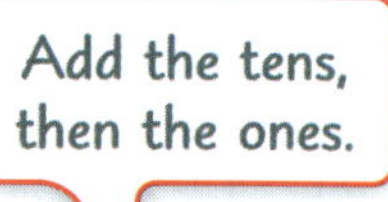

c 58 + 14 = ☐

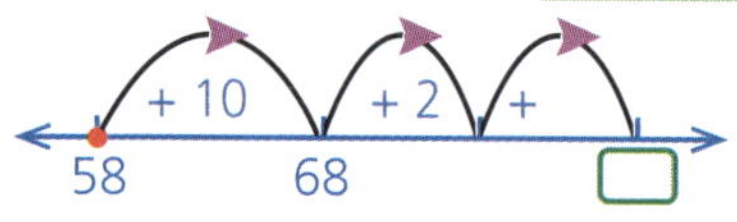

d 67 + 13 = ☐

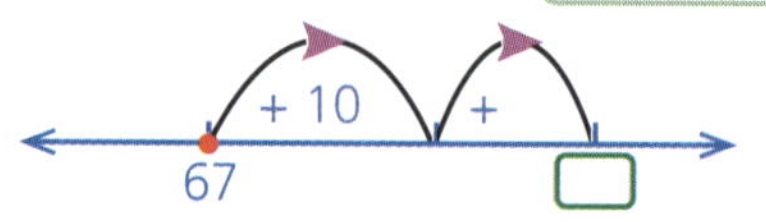

e 55 + 27 = ☐

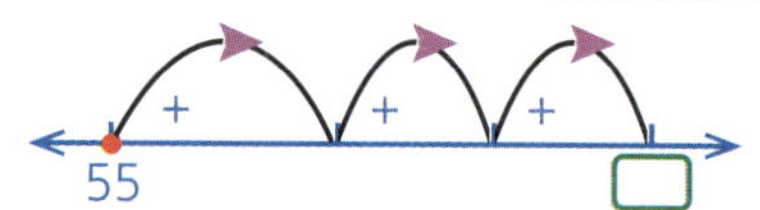

f 79 + 28 = ☐

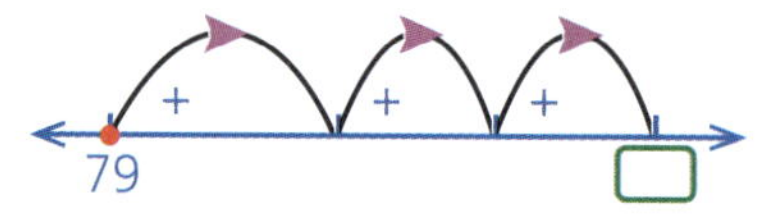

 • *AUSTRALIAN SIGNPOST MATHS 2* • ISBN 9780655708766

27B Jump strategy (subtraction)

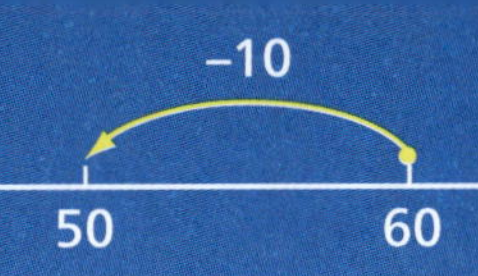

63 – 24 Start at 63 and jump back.

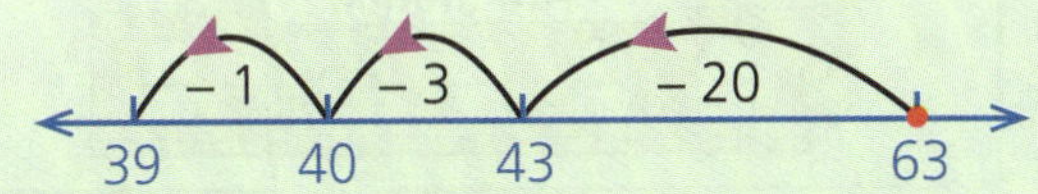

- We don't need marks on the line.
- We jump the tens, then the ones.

63 – 24 = 39

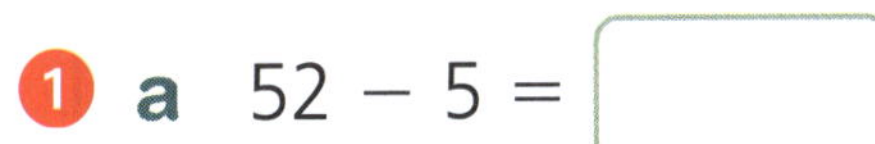

Use the jump strategy to find the answers.

1 **a** 52 – 5 = ☐ **b** 31 – 6 = ☐ **c** 93 – 4 = ☐

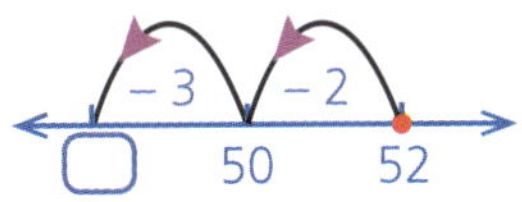

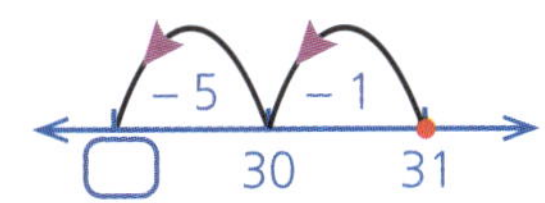

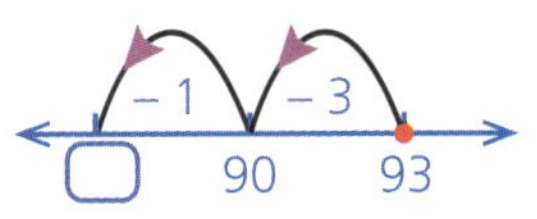

d 37 – 8 = ☐ **e** 57 – 9 = ☐ **f** 88 – 9 = ☐

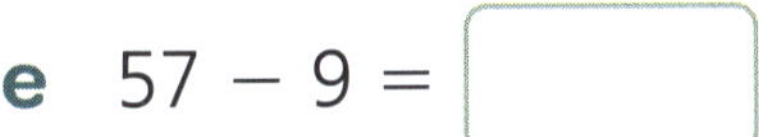

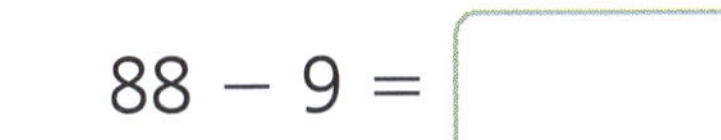

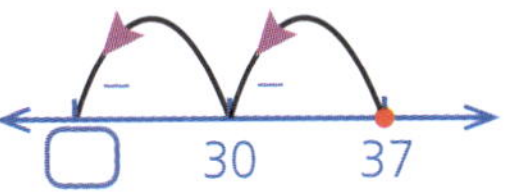

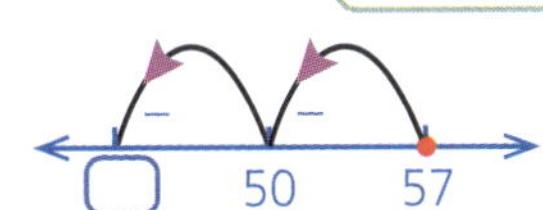

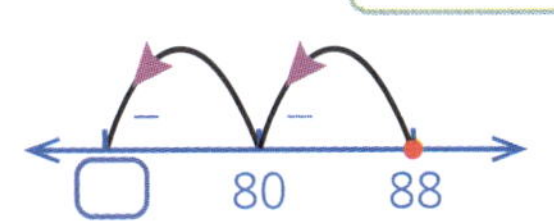

2 **a** 43 – 14 = ☐ **b** 64 – 25 = ☐

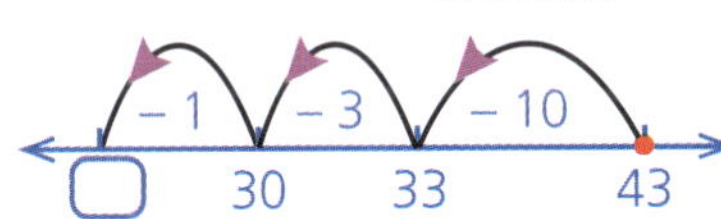

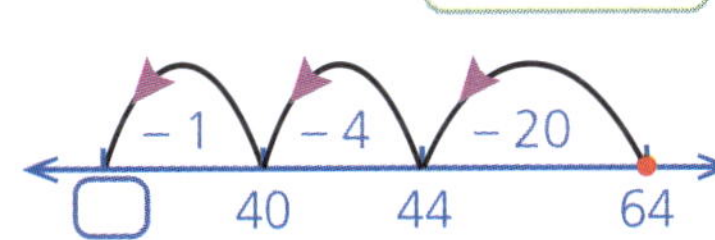

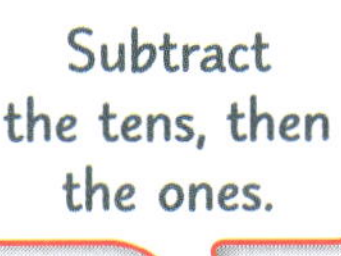

c 71 – 33 = ☐ **d** 82 – 57 = ☐

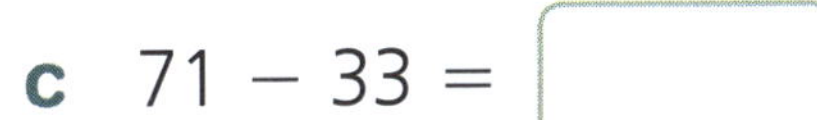

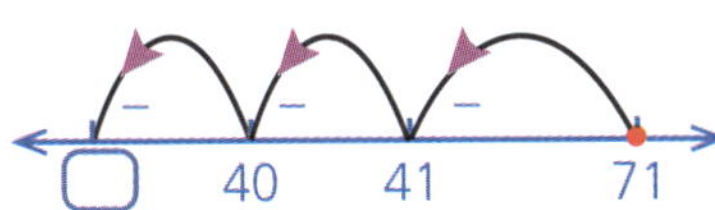

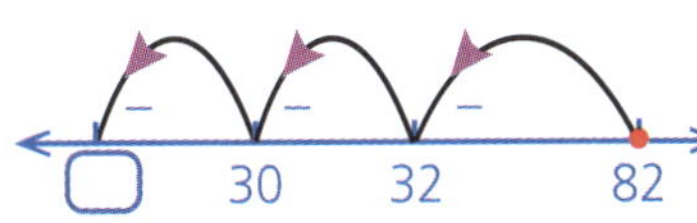

e 92 – 46 = ☐ **f** 55 – 38 = ☐

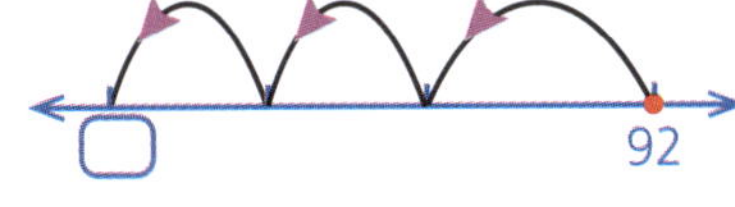

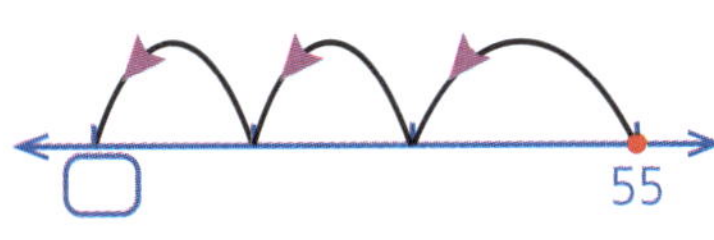

3 Can you do these in your head? If not, use a number line.

a 72 – 37 = ☐ **b** 96 – 29 = ☐ **c** 64 – 46 = ☐

d 85 – 27 = ☐ **e** 31 – 17 = ☐ **f** 42 – 23 = ☐

27C Giving directions

Go left.
Go right.
Go straight ahead.

1

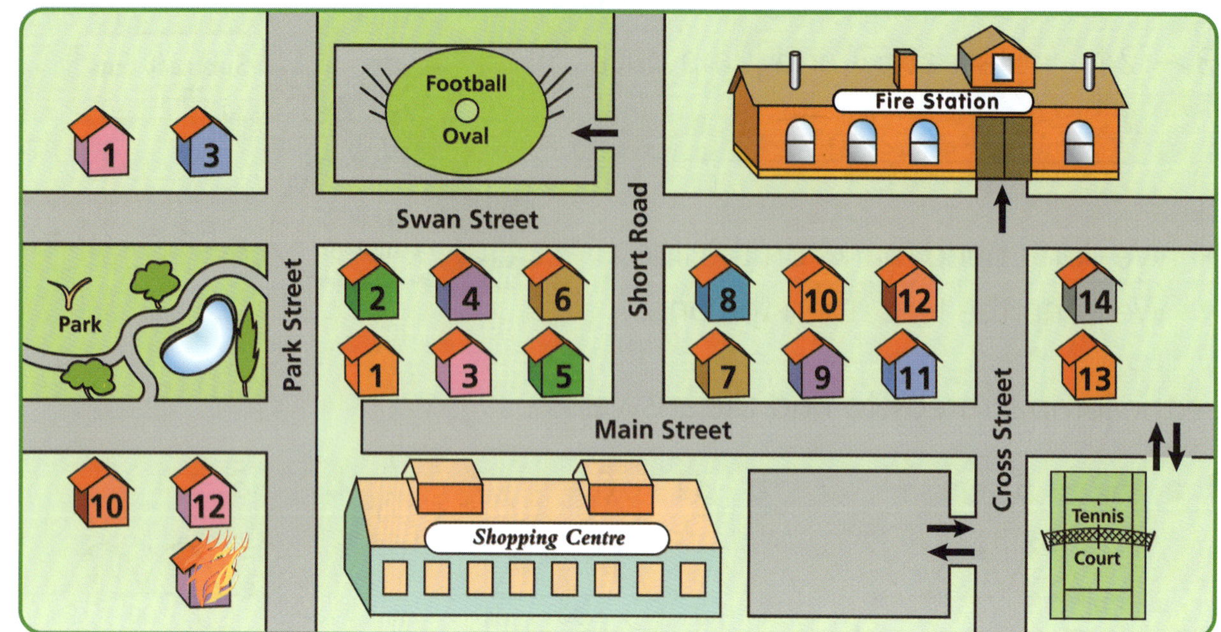

a Trace the shortest route from the fire station to the burning house. Write instructions.

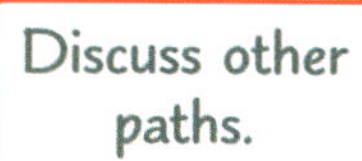

b Write instructions for getting from 11 Main Street to the football oval.

FUN SPOT

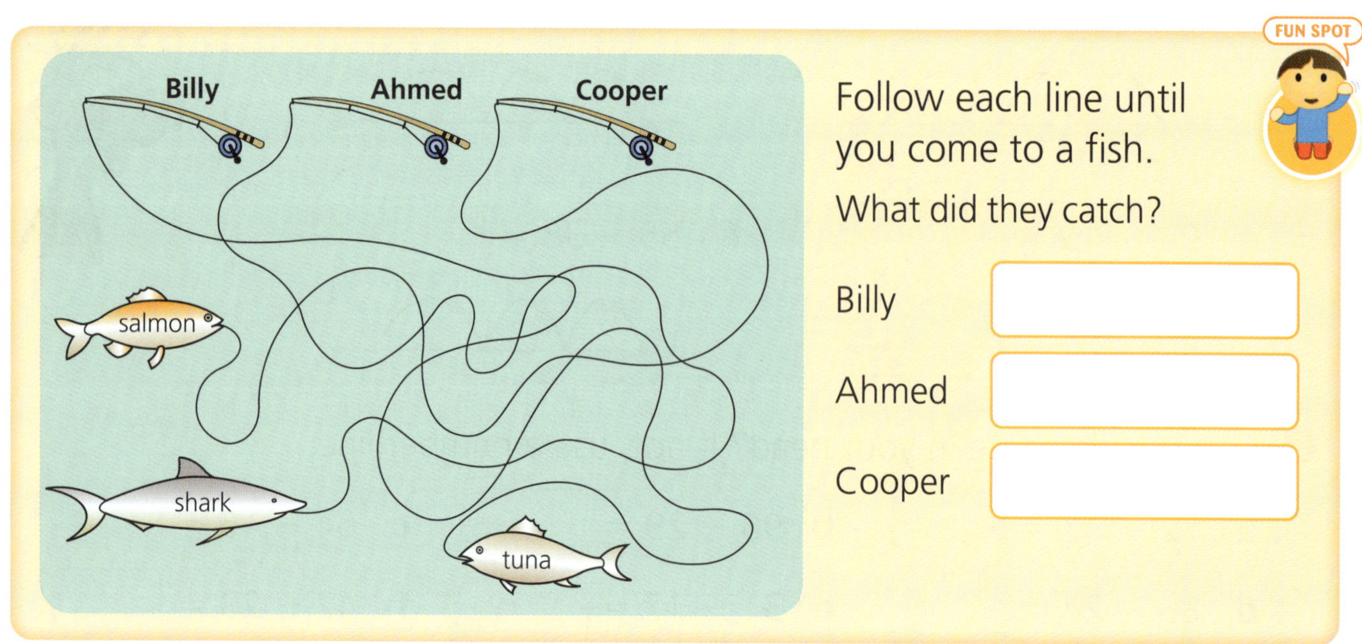

Follow each line until you come to a fish.
What did they catch?

Billy

Ahmed

Cooper

27D Gather and organise data

Tally marks

Tallies are usually placed in groups of 5. The fifth mark is usually drawn across the other four marks.

卌 卌 = 10

1. Make up a question and write 4 answers. Ask 15 students in your class to make a choice.

Write your question here.

4 possible choices:

2. Show the answers given by 15 students. Put your 4 possible choices in the left column. Trace one tally mark in black for each student.

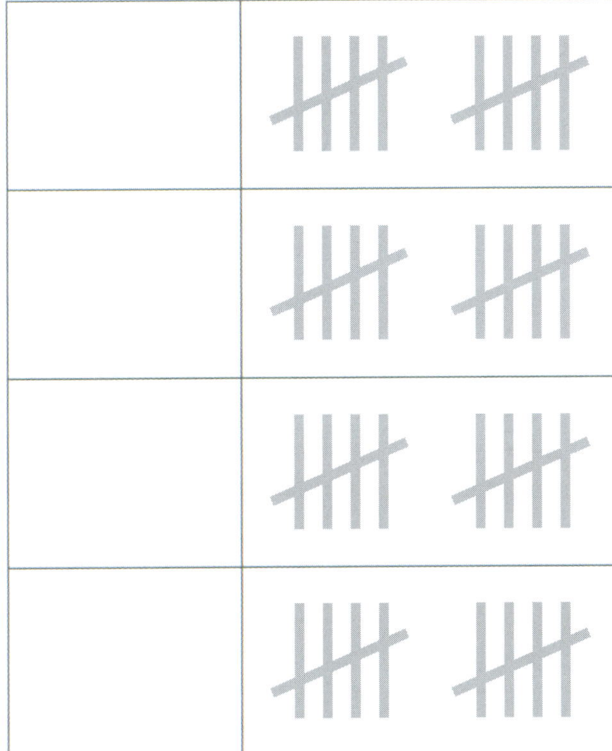

3. Make a picture graph on the right. Put your 4 possible choices in the spaces at the bottom of the graph. Use the information in the table to colour a face for each student who chose that answer.

28A Jump strategy

$47 + 10 = 57$ $67 - 10 = 57$
$47 + 20 = 67$ $67 - 20 = 47$
$47 + 30 = 77$ $67 - 30 = 37$

CONCEPT

Addition 48 + 27

Subtraction 73 − 27

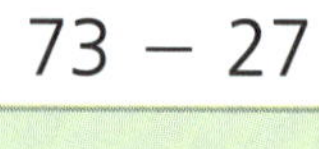
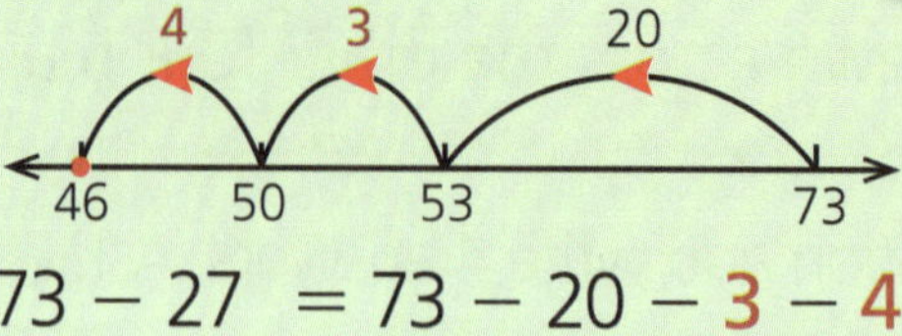

$48 + 27 = 48 + 20 + 2 + 5$
$= 68 + 2 + 5$
$= 70 + 5 = 75$

$73 - 27 = 73 - 20 - 3 - 4$
$= 53 - 3 - 4$
$= 50 - 4 = 46$

Learn the jump strategy.

1 a 42 + 19 ☐ b 35 + 48 ☐ c 39 + 45 ☐

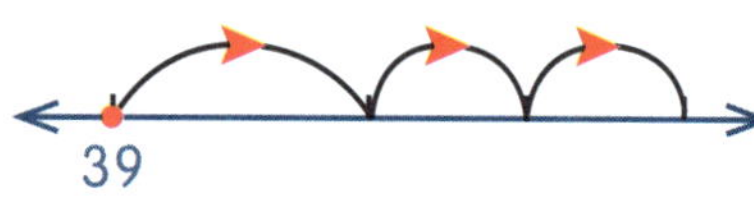

d 27 + 28 ☐ e 73 + 22 ☐ f 85 + 18 ☐

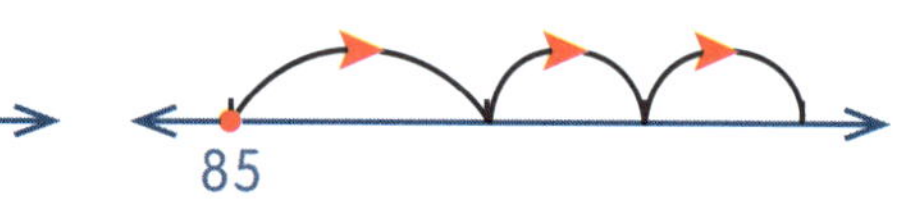

g 47 + 35 ☐ h 86 + 29 ☐

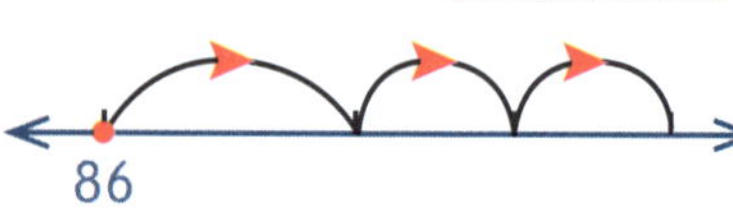

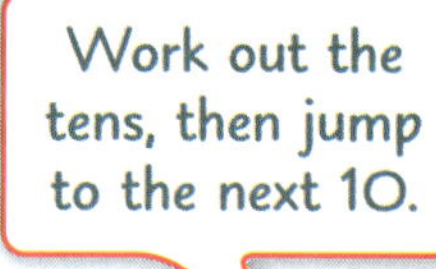

Work out the tens, then jump to the next 10.

2 a 42 − 14 ☐ b 95 − 26 ☐

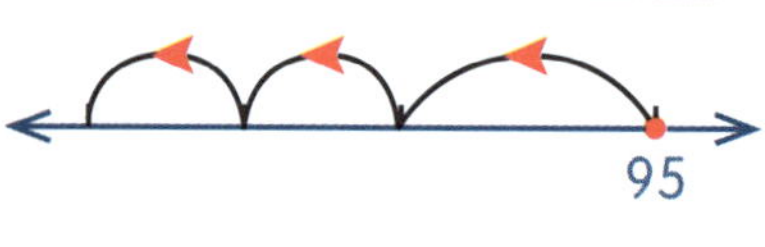

c 52 − 23 ☐ d 73 − 22 ☐ e 85 − 18 ☐

f 66 − 27 ☐ g 88 − 65 ☐ h 94 − 59 ☐

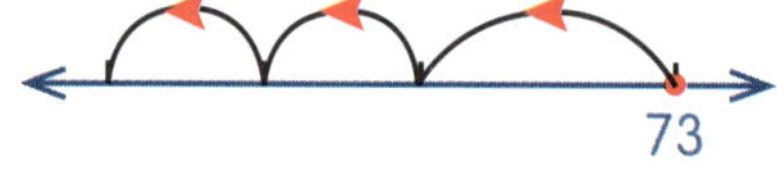
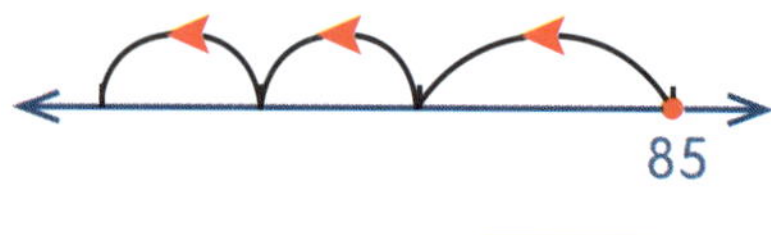

3 a 38 + 25 ☐ b 86 − 29 ☐ c 19 + 42 ☐

Quarters of a group

quarters of 8 rectangles

CONCEPT

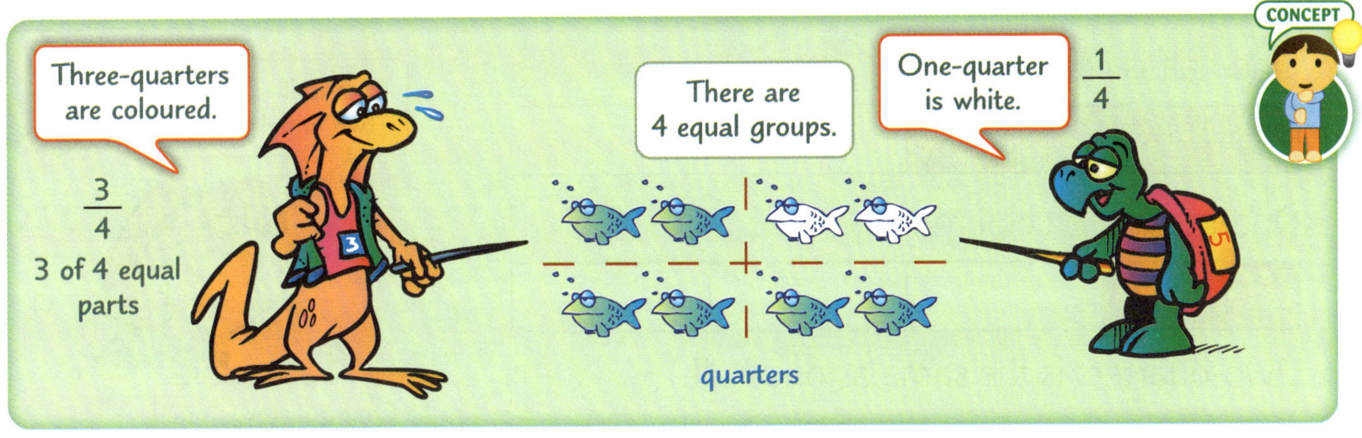

1 Circle the groups that are divided into quarters and colour one-quarter.

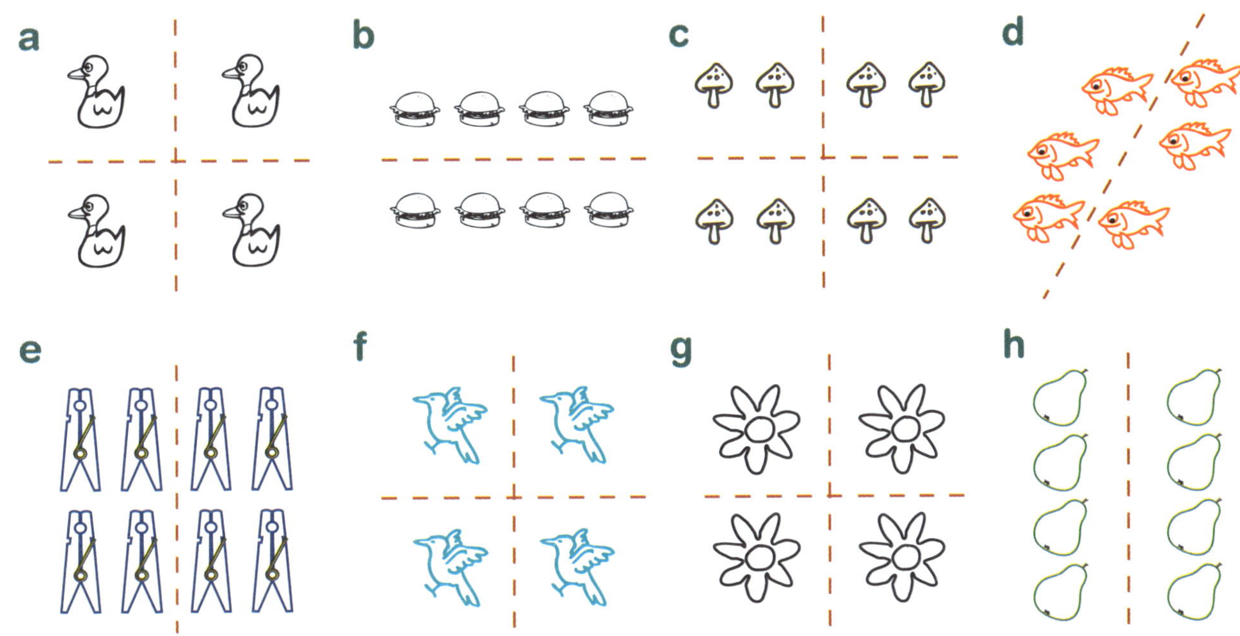

INVESTIGATION

Here we have displayed 12 counters, as quarters of a whole.

Use 8 counters to make a model like this that shows quarters.
Explain how you made your model.

 • *AUSTRALIAN SIGNPOST MATHS 2* • ISBN 9780655708766

28C Halves and quarters

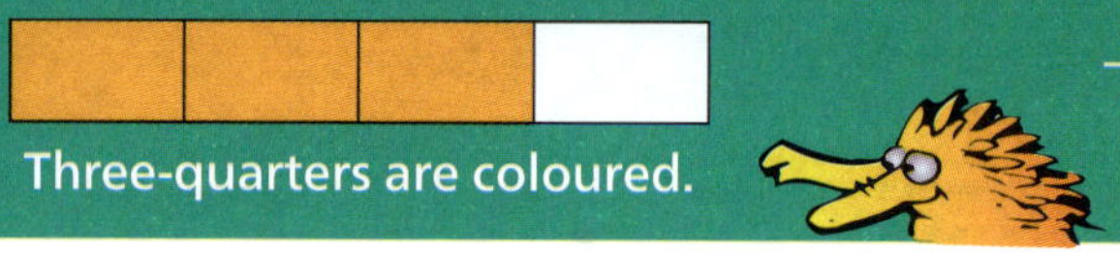

CONCEPT

One-half is coloured.

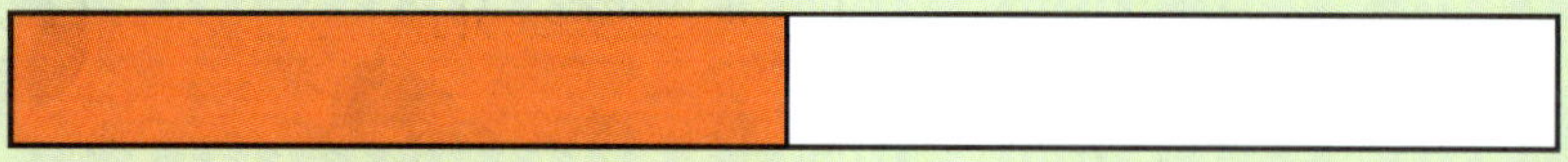

One-quarter is coloured.

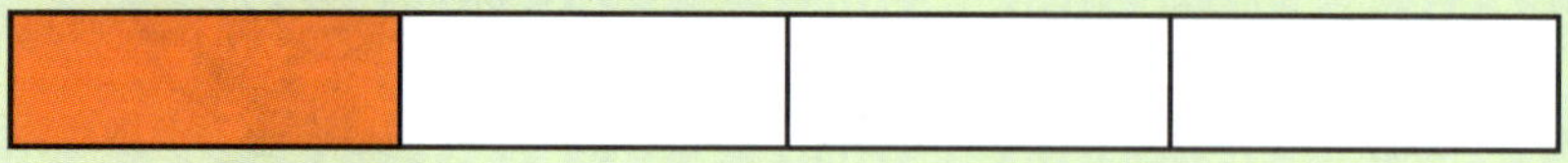

(Two-quarters is the same as one-half.)

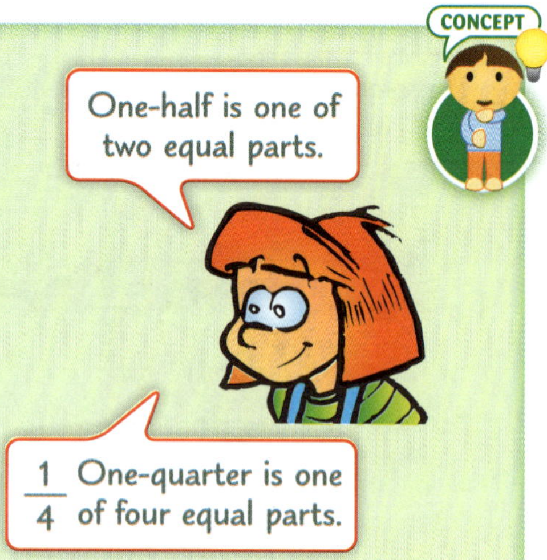

One-half is one of two equal parts.

$\frac{1}{4}$ One-quarter is one of four equal parts.

1 Making halves

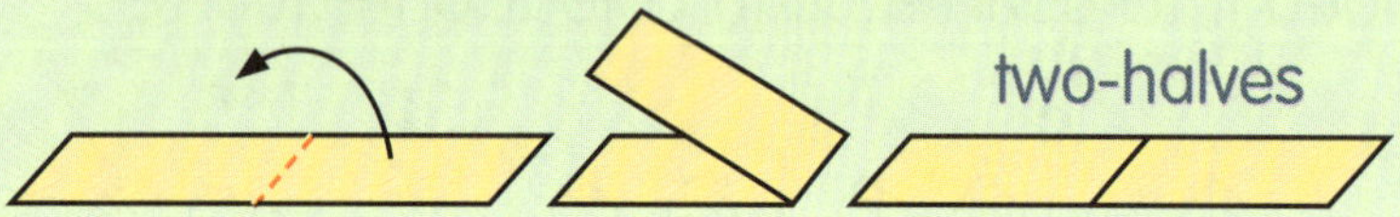

two-halves

We folded the strip of paper into two halves.

2 Making quarters

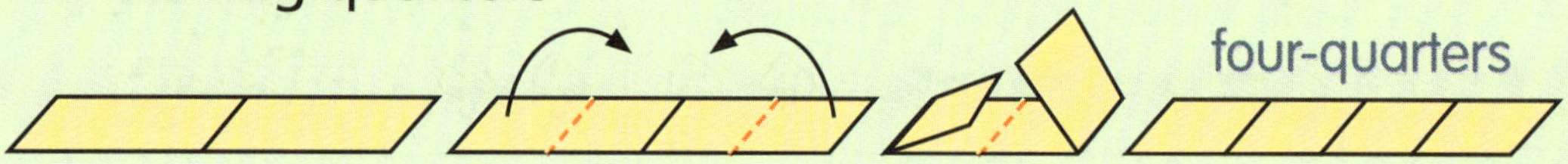

four-quarters

We have folded each half in half.

1. Draw a line to cut each shape in half. Colour half of each shape.

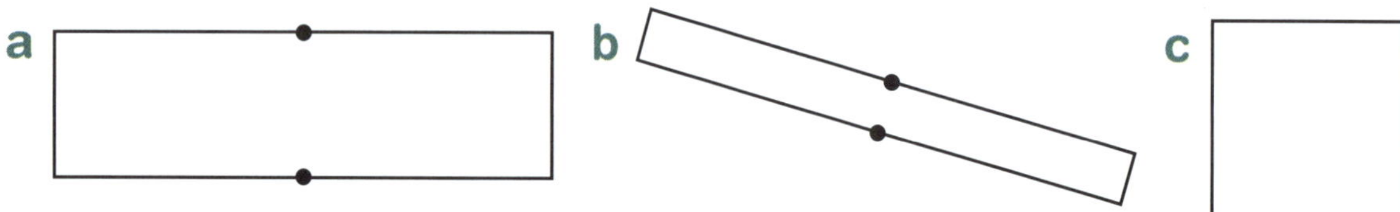

2. Draw lines to cut each shape into quarters. Colour one-quarter of each.

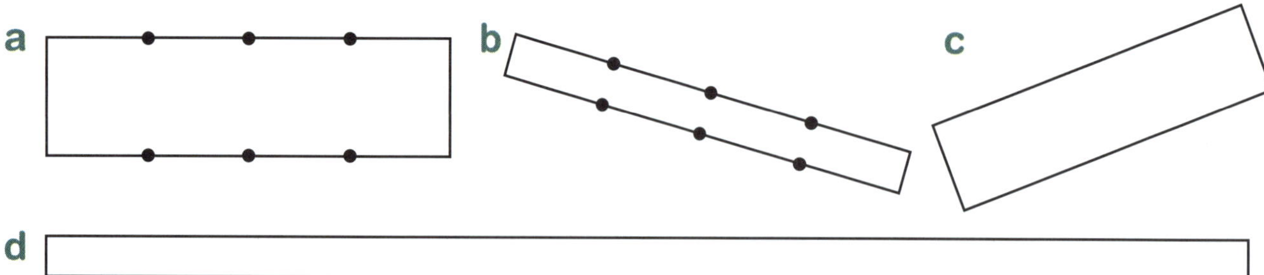

ACTIVITY

Fold lengths of paper into halves and quarters.

Draw lines on the folds. Label each part.

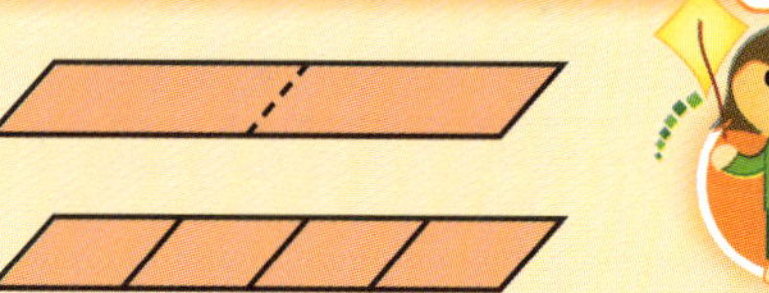

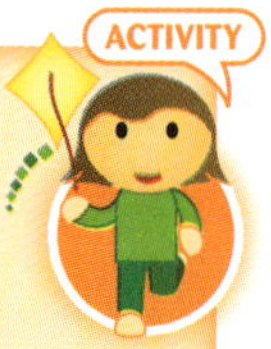

28D Duration / timelines

One hour is 60 minutes.

What Alan does on Saturday

1

7 o'clock	8 o'clock	9 o'clock	10 o'clock	11 o'clock
breakfast	soccer	soccer	reading	craft
12 o'clock	**1 o'clock**	**2 o'clock**	**3 o'clock**	**4 o'clock**
lunch	rest time	swimming	chores	bike riding

It is now lunch. Write what happened:

a 4 hours ago

b 2 hours ago

c at 11 o'clock

d before soccer

Write what happens:

e at 4 o'clock

f just after lunch

g two hours after lunch

h three hours after lunch

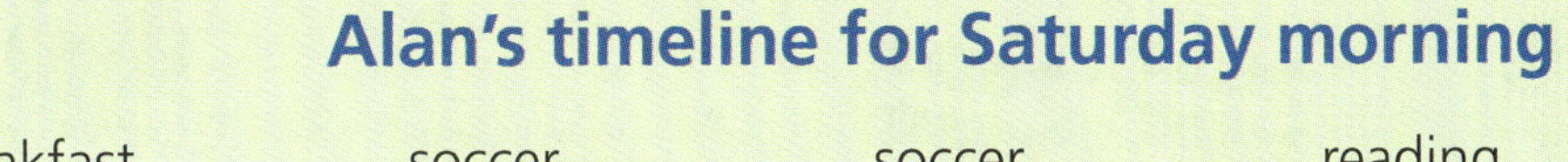

CONCEPT

A **timeline** is a graph of events that happen over time.

Alan's timeline for Saturday morning

breakfast	soccer	soccer	reading	craft
7 o'clock	8 o'clock	9 o'clock	10 o'clock	11 o'clock

2 Make a timeline of what Alan does on Saturday afternoon.

Alan's timeline for Saturday afternoon

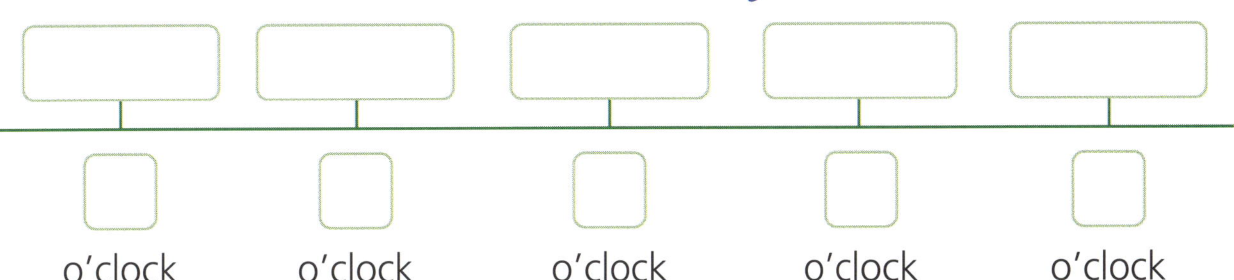

29A Fractions of a group

- The two halves of a collection will have the same number of items.
- To find one-quarter of a collection, we halve and halve again.
- Halving again gives us eighths.

1 Circle half of each group. ($\frac{1}{2}$ is one of two equal parts.)

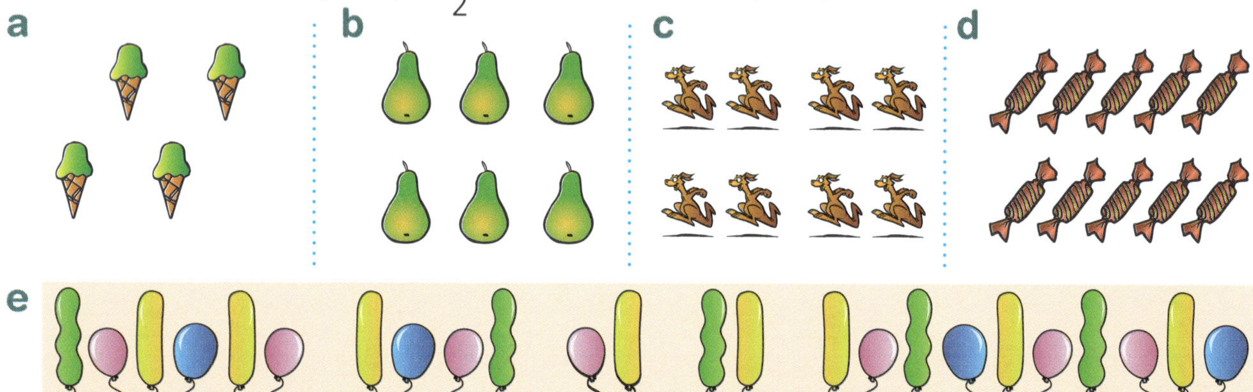

2 Circle one-quarter of each group. ($\frac{1}{4}$ is one of four equal parts.)

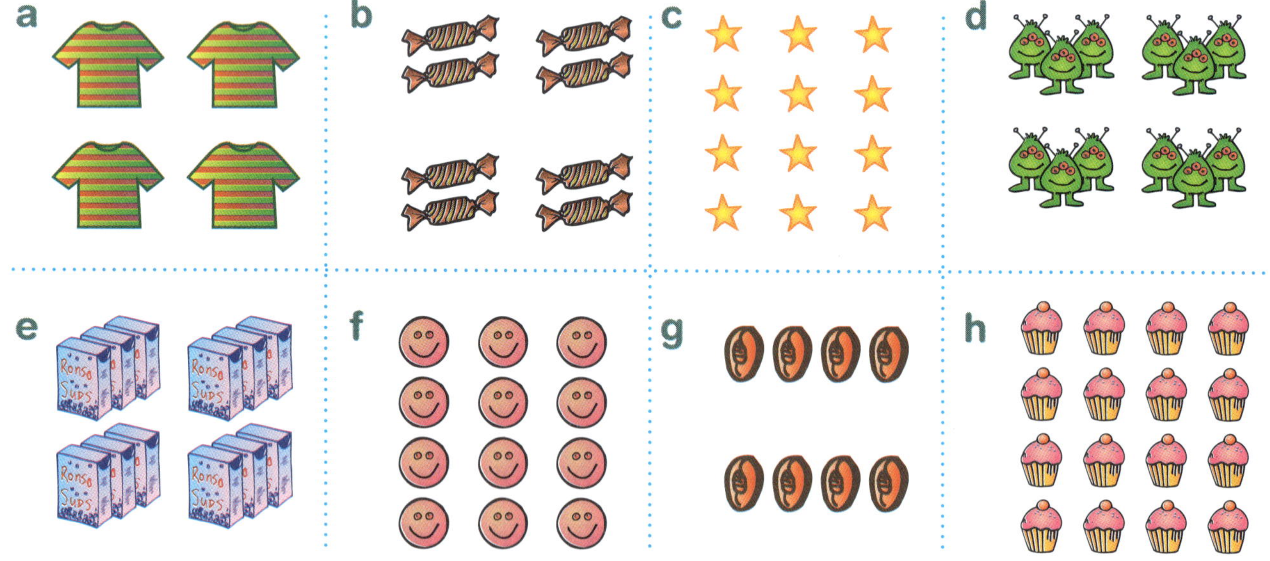

3 Colour one-half of each group. Circle one-quarter. Underline one-eighth.

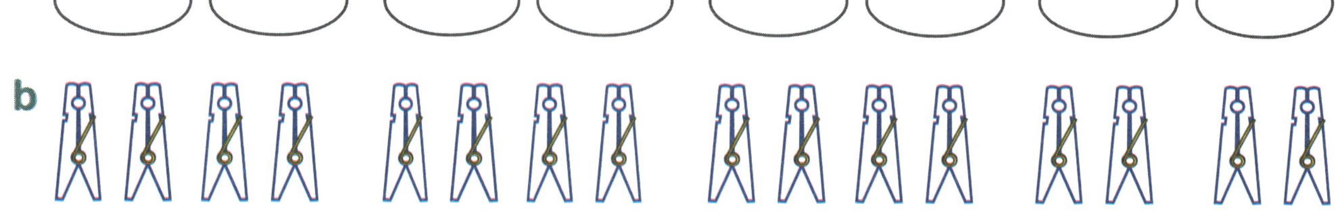

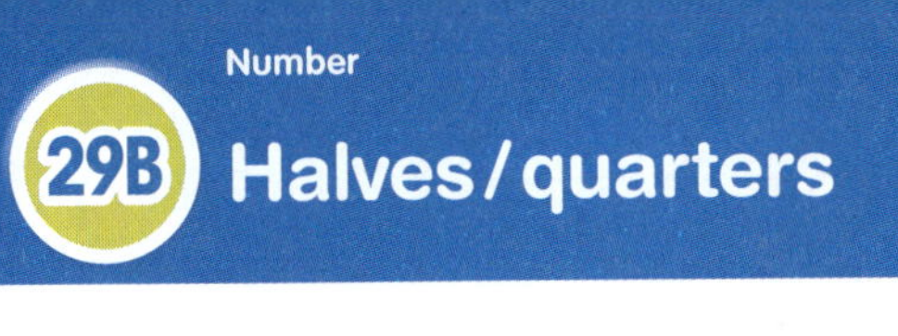

29B Halves/quarters

12			
6		6	
3	3	3	3

whole
halves
quarters

CONCEPT

Jake lined up 8 apples.

8	
4	4

He put a pencil at the halfway point.
He shared half of his apples with Mae. Each half has 4 apples.

1. Line up an even number of items. Use a pencil to mark the halfway point.
   - a Write what you did.
   - b How many in each half? ☐
   - c When you take away the pencil, how many items are there? ☐

CONCEPT

Toby shared 8 books equally among 4 friends. He put the books in a line.

He put a pencil at the halfway point.
He then halved each half, placing pencils at those points too.
There were 2 books in each quarter. Each friend was given 2 books.

8			
2	2	2	2

2. Line up 12 counters. Use 3 pencils to separate them into quarters.
   - a Write what you did.

   - b How many in each quarter? ☐
   - c When you take away the pencils, how many counters are there? ☐

 • *AUSTRALIAN SIGNPOST MATHS 2* • ISBN 9780655708766

29C Duration of time

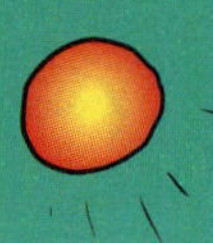

CONCEPT

Summer	Autumn	Winter	Spring
December January February	March April May	June July August	September October November

Memorise the order of the months.

1 How many months is it from the beginning of summer to the:

a end of autumn? ☐ b beginning of autumn? ☐

c end of spring? ☐ d beginning of spring? ☐

July

S	M	T	W	T	F	S
				1	2	3
4	5	6	7	8	9	10
11	12	13	14	15	16	17
18	19	20	21	22	23	24
25	26	27	28	29	30	31

August

S	M	T	W	T	F	S
1	2	3	4	5	6	7
8	9	10	11	12	13	14
15	16	17	18	19	20	21
22	23	24	25	26	27	28
29	30	31				

September

S	M	T	W	T	F	S
			1	2	3	4
5	6	7	8	9	10	11
12	13	14	15	16	17	18
19	20	21	22	23	24	25
26	27	28	29	30		

October

S	M	T	W	T	F	S
					1	2
3	4	5	6	7	8	9
10	11	12	13	14	15	16
17	18	19	20	21	22	23
24	25	26	27	28	29	30
31						

November

S	M	T	W	T	F	S
	1	2	3	4	5	6
7	8	9	10	11	12	13
14	15	16	17	18	19	20
21	22	23	24	25	26	27
28	29	30				

December

S	M	T	W	T	F	S
			1	2	3	4
5	6	7	8	9	10	11
12	13	14	15	16	17	18
19	20	21	22	23	24	25
26	27	28	29	30	31	

2 How many months and days is it from 5th July to:

a 7th September? ☐ months ☐ days

b 25th August? ☐ months ☐ days

c 10th December? ☐ months ☐ days

d end of the year? ☐ months ☐ days

3 How many weeks and days is it from 5th July to:

a 7th September? ☐ weeks ☐ days

b 25th August? ☐ weeks ☐ days

c 10th December? ☐ weeks ☐ days

d end of the year? ☐ weeks ☐ days

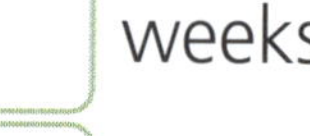

Some First Nations Australians use six seasons. The six major seasons of the Yolngu people in Arnhem Land, Northern Territory are called:

Dhuludur, Barramirri, Mayaltha, Midawarr, Dharratharramirri and Rarrandharr.

 • *AUSTRALIAN SIGNPOST MATHS 2* • ISBN 9780655708766

Graphs

There are many types of graphs.
Some you may not have seen before.

1. Try to match each name below, to a graph.
2. How are B and C the same?

   How are B and C different ?

- dot plot
- column graph
- picture graph
- bar chart
- pie chart

3. Do all of these graphs show the same data?
4. Which graph do you like the most?
5. Which graph was the hardest to understand? Why was this?
6. Enter this data into a spreadsheet to make graphs. (Monday: 5, Tuesday: 8, Wednesday: 7, Thursday: 2)

A

B

C

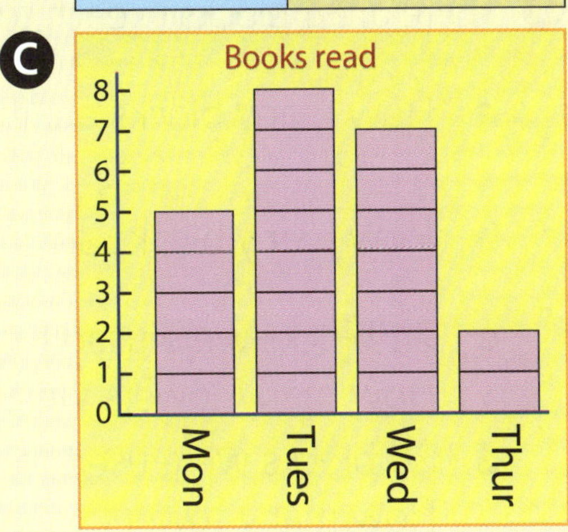

D

E

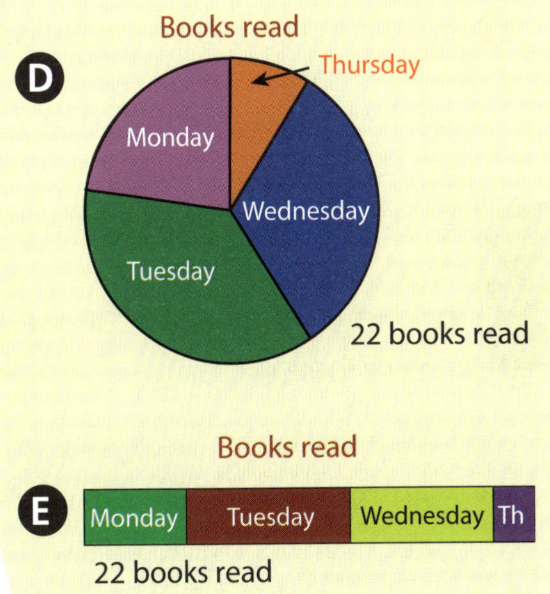

30A Problem solving

CONCEPT

Jan made 8 towers with 4 blocks in each tower.
How many blocks did she use?

4, 8, 12, 16, 20, 24, 28, 32 …

☐ columns of 4

Jan used 32 blocks.

8 columns of 4 = 4 + 4 + 4 + 4 + 4 + 4 + 4 + 4 = ☐

1. There are 4 blocks in each tower. (You can use the skip counting pattern above.)

a	How many blocks are in 3 towers?	☐ columns of 4	There are ☐ blocks.
b	How many blocks are in 4 towers?	☐ columns of 4	There are ☐ blocks.
c	24 blocks were used to build towers. How many towers were built?	How many 4s in 24 blocks?	There are ☐ towers.
d	20 blocks were used to build towers. How many towers were built?	How many 4s in 20 blocks?	There are ☐ towers.

2. Each can holds 3 tennis balls. (You can use the skip counting pattern above.)

a	How many balls are in 7 cans?	☐ groups of 3	There are ☐ balls.
b	How many balls are in 6 cans?	☐ groups of 3	There are ☐ balls.
c	How many cans can we fill with 12 balls?	How many 3s in 12 balls?	There are ☐ cans.

INVESTIGATION

- Jimmy bought 8 cans of 3 tennis balls. He gave 2 balls to each of his friends. How many friends were given balls ? ☐
- Ava bought 5 boxes of 4 cakes. She gave 3 cakes to her sister and 8 cakes to her brother. How many cakes did she have left? ☐

30B Problem solving

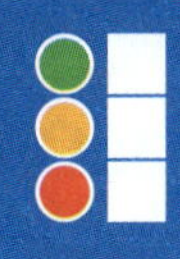

CONCEPT

John made 6 towers with 5 blocks in each tower.
How many blocks did he use?

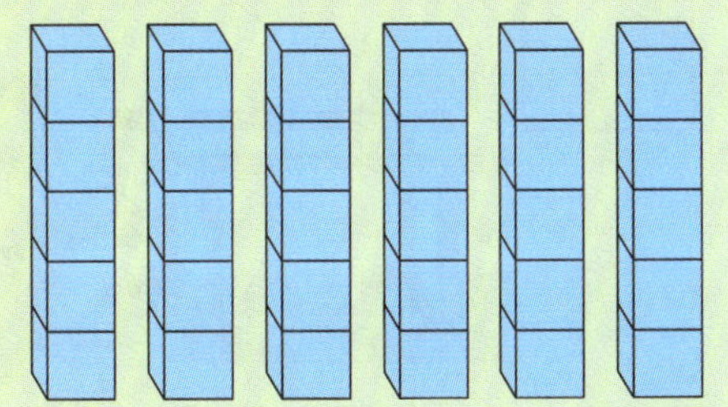

5, 10, 15, 20, 25, 30

John used 30 blocks.

Show working on your own paper.

6 columns of 5 = 5 + 5 + 5 + 5 + 5 + 5 = 6 × 5 = 30

1 **a** How many apples are in 3 bags if 3 apples are in each bag? 3 bags of 3 apples. There are ☐ apples.

b If there are 15 apples and 3 in each bag, how many bags? How many 3s in 15 apples? There are ☐ bags.

c You have 18 apples and put 3 in each bag. How many bags were used? How many 3s in 18 apples? There are ☐ bags.

2 Each tower is made of 5 blocks. (You can use the skip counting pattern above.)

a How many blocks are in 4 towers? ☐ groups of 5 There are ☐ blocks.

b How many blocks are in 6 towers? ☐ groups of 5 There are ☐ blocks.

c How many towers can be built using 20 blocks? How many 5s in 20 blocks? There are ☐ towers.

INVESTIGATION

Draw as many arrays as you can that use 24 tiles.
This array is 12 squares long and 2 squares wide.

Make sure that each array is a rectangle.

Parallel lines

A square has 4 right angles and 2 sets of parallel lines.

CONCEPT

Parallel lines are always the same distance apart.

- They are straight lines.
- They go in the same direction.
- They will never touch.
- Arrows can be used to show parallel lines.

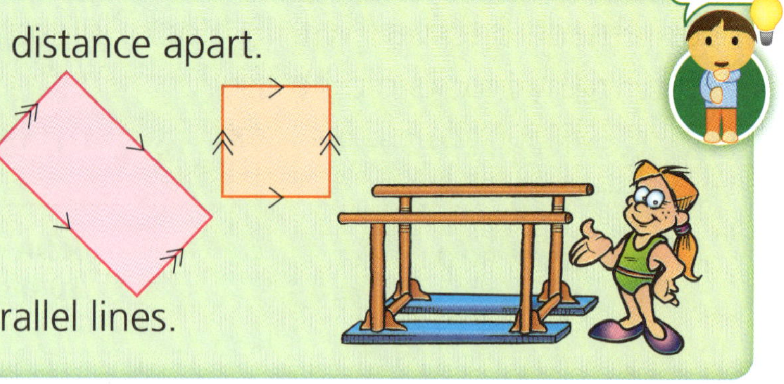

1 Use arrows to show which sides are parallel on these shapes.

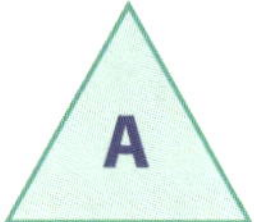
A

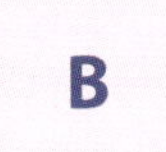
B

C

D

E

F

G

a Which shapes have opposite sides equal?

b Which shapes have curved sides?

c Which shapes have only straight sides?

d Which shape has 3 pairs of parallel lines?

e Which shapes have right angles? (Right angles are square corners.)

2

a List things in this picture that are parallel.

b List things in your classroom that are parallel.

INVESTIGATION

Use digital tools to create regular shapes. Investigate what happens when you manipulate them (e.g. move vertices, rotate, reflect shapes). Label and mark each shape to identify its features.

 • *AUSTRALIAN SIGNPOST MATHS 2* • ISBN 9780655708766

Following instructions

up down right left

1. Little Red Riding Hood followed these instructions. Colour her path red.

Grandma's house | Woodcutter

Start here

Instructions
Move
2 left
1 up
3 left
1 up
1 left
3 up
4 right
2 up
2 left

2. Give directions for the bird to go to the bridge. Colour that path green.
3. Give directions for the woodcutter to move to the wolf. Colour that path blue.
4. Give directions for the wolf to move to the house. Draw a red line along that path.

Make up other trips using the grid.

31A Doubling and halving

Halve 10 then double.

CONCEPT

Jacob kept doubling the number of counters he had.
Then he kept halving the number of counters he had.

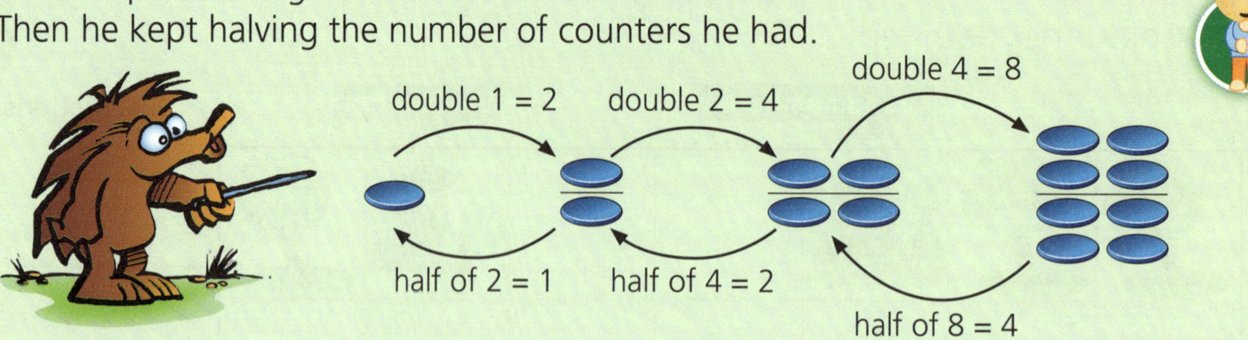

1 Draw pictures to double the number of shapes.
Then cross out half of the answer. Write what you found.

x 2 ÷ 2

a

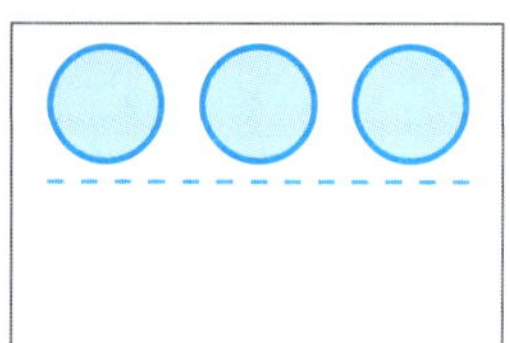

Double 3 = ☐

Half of 6 = ☐

b

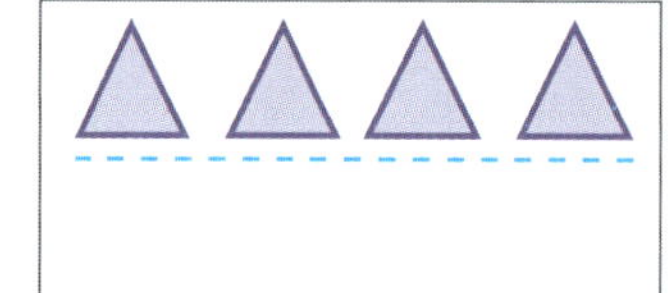

Double 4 = ☐

Half of ☐ = ☐

If you double a number and halve the result, the number …

☐

☐

2 Half my money is shown. Draw the rest and then write the total amount.

a

Total = ☐

b

Total = ☐

3 I doubled my money then spent half of the total. Draw what I did.

a

Double $1 = ☐

Half of the last answer = ☐.

b

Double $2 = ☐

Half of the last answer = ☐.

 • *AUSTRALIAN SIGNPOST MATHS 2* • ISBN 9780655708766

31B Doubling (2 x) and halving (÷ 2)

CONCEPT

Memorise your doubles up to 2 x 10.

2 x 3 = 6   **2 x** doubles the number.

6 ÷ 2 = 3   **÷ 2** halves the number.

1. Join each question to the correct answer using a pencil and ruler. You could practise your doubles and halves by rubbing out your answers and doing them again.

a

	x	
2 x 2		0
2 x 4		2
2 x 0		4
2 x 1		6
2 x 3		8
2 x 7		10
2 x 5		12
2 x 10		14
2 x 9		16
2 x 6		18
2 x 8		20
Scores:		

b

	x	
2 x 3		0
2 x 0		2
2 x 5		4
2 x 1		6
2 x 7		8
2 x 2		10
2 x 8		12
2 x 4		14
2 x 6		16
2 x 10		18
2 x 9		20
Scores:		

c

	x	
2 x 1		0
2 x 3		2
2 x 0		4
2 x 5		6
2 x 2		8
2 x 7		10
2 x 4		12
2 x 6		14
2 x 10		16
2 x 9		18
2 x 8		20
Scores:		

d

	x	
2 x 0		0
2 x 4		2
2 x 2		4
2 x 5		6
2 x 1		8
2 x 7		10
2 x 3		12
2 x 9		14
2 x 6		16
2 x 8		18
2 x 10		20
Scores:		

e

	÷	
4 ÷ 2		0
8 ÷ 2		1
0 ÷ 2		2
2 ÷ 2		3
6 ÷ 2		4
14 ÷ 2		5
10 ÷ 2		6
20 ÷ 2		7
18 ÷ 2		8
12 ÷ 2		9
16 ÷ 2		10
Scores:		

f

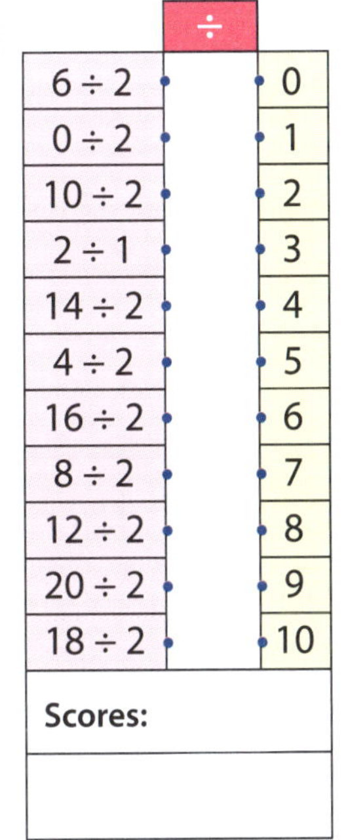

	÷	
6 ÷ 2		0
0 ÷ 2		1
10 ÷ 2		2
2 ÷ 1		3
14 ÷ 2		4
4 ÷ 2		5
16 ÷ 2		6
8 ÷ 2		7
12 ÷ 2		8
20 ÷ 2		9
18 ÷ 2		10
Scores:		

g

	÷	
2 ÷ 2		0
8 ÷ 2		1
0 ÷ 2		2
10 ÷ 2		3
4 ÷ 2		4
6 ÷ 2		5
16 ÷ 2		6
12 ÷ 2		7
20 ÷ 2		8
14 ÷ 2		9
18 ÷ 2		10
Scores:		

h

	÷	
0 ÷ 2		0
8 ÷ 2		1
6 ÷ 2		2
2 ÷ 2		3
4 ÷ 2		4
14 ÷ 2		5
12 ÷ 2		6
16 ÷ 2		7
10 ÷ 2		8
20 ÷ 2		9
18 ÷ 2		10
Scores:		

31C Fractions of a whole

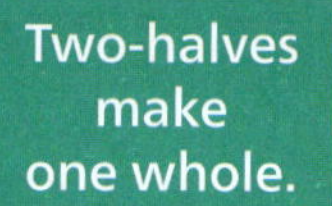

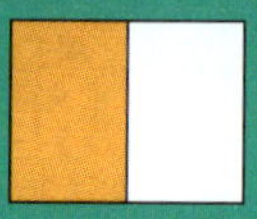

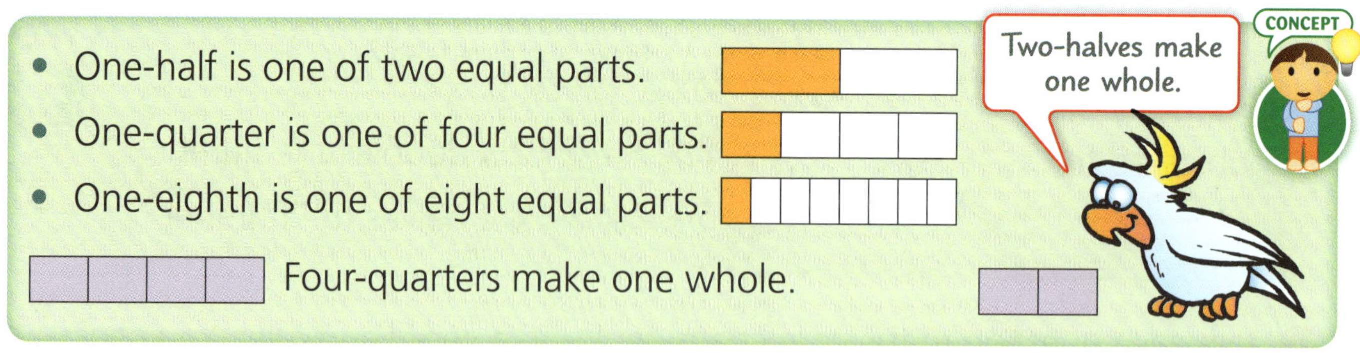

1. What part of the shape is coloured: one-half, one-quarter or one-eighth?

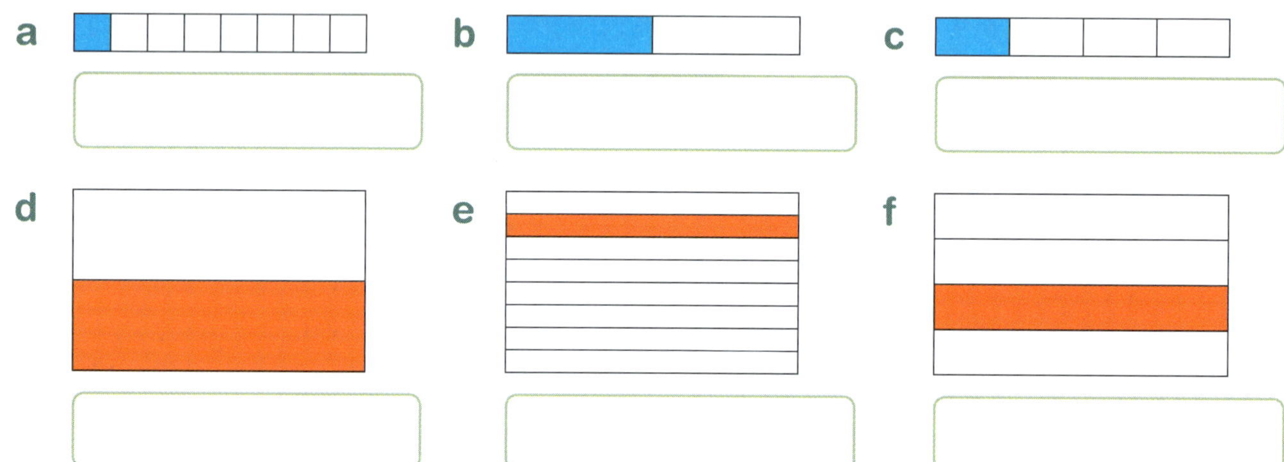

2. Colour part of each shape to match the given fraction.

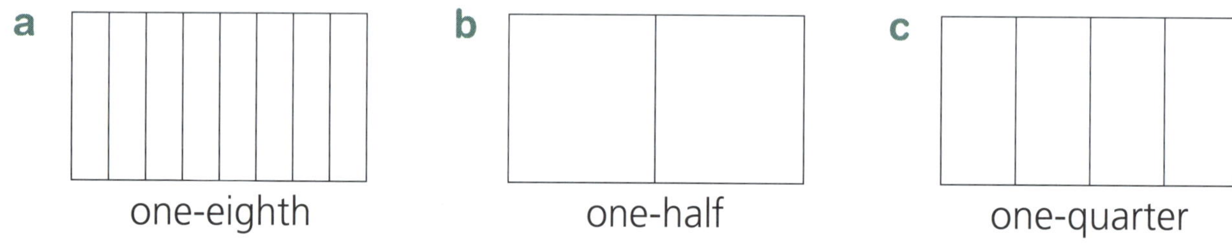

INVESTIGATION

- Draw lines to cut this shape into halves. Then draw lines to cut each half into two equal parts (quarters).
- Draw 2 lines to cut this shape into quarters. Then draw lines to cut each quarter into two equal parts (eighths).

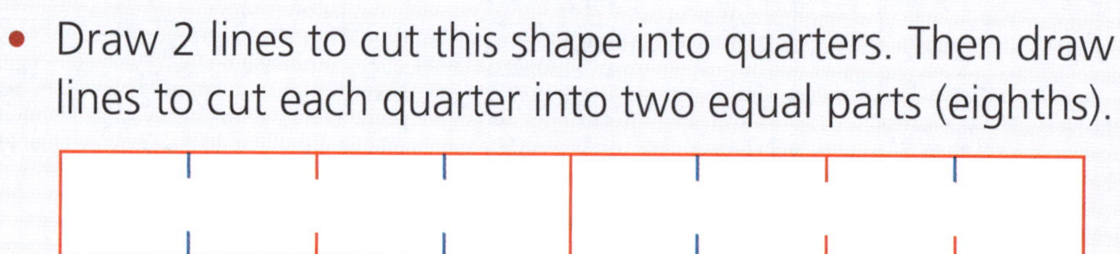

31D Calendars

1 Complete this calendar for a month of the year. Add special events and weekly class activities.

Word bank: Monday, Tuesday, Wednesday, Thursday, Friday

Month: ____________

Sunday			Wednesday			Saturday

2 On this calendar, what is the date:

a of the first event you have added? ____________

b 2 weeks after the first event? ____________

c 2 weeks before the last day of the month? ____________

3 Ask a partner more questions about their calendar.

32A Number patterns

1 Start at 2. Colour every 2nd number green. These are even numbers.

1	2	3	4	5	6	7	8	9	10
11	12	13	14	15	16	17	18	19	20
21	22	23	24	25	26	27	28	29	30

2 Describe the pattern shown on each number line.

a
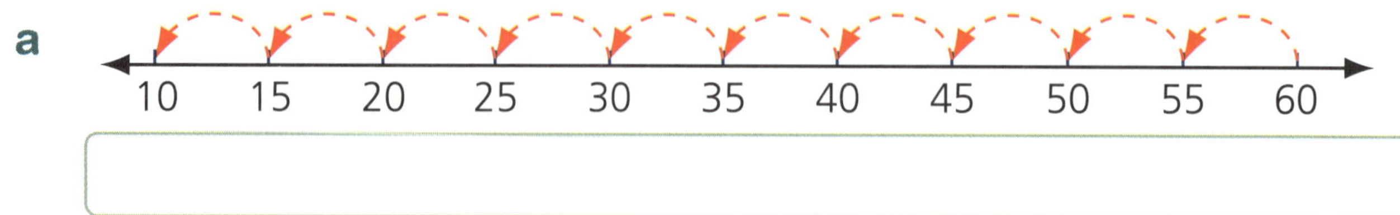

b
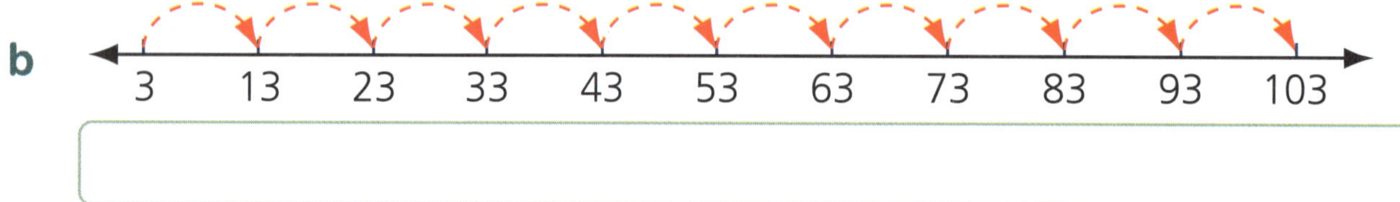

3 Write the missing numbers. Describe the rule for each pattern.

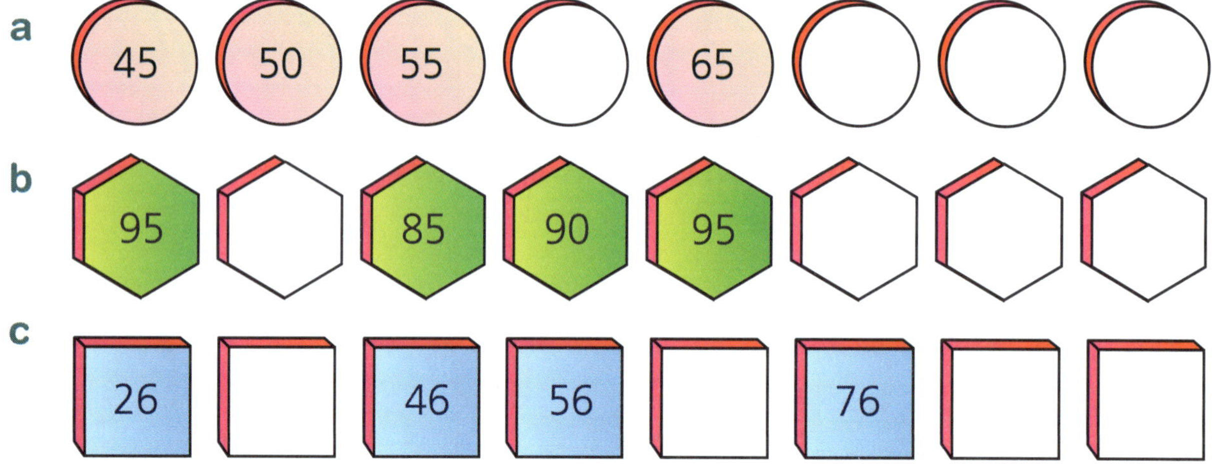

4 Write the next three numbers in each number pattern.

a 64, 54, 44,

b 65, 70, 75,

c 90, 80, 70,

d 37, 47, 57,

e 15, 25, 35,

f 34, 36, 38,

How does a number change as you continue to add ten (56, 66, 76 ...)?

Counting by tens

3, 13, 23, 33 … forwards

96, 86, 76, 66 … backwards

CONCEPT

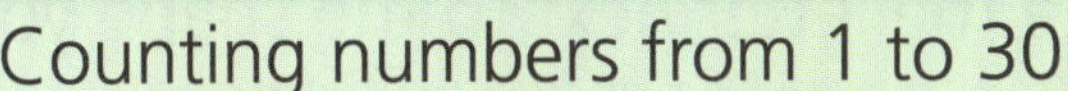

Counting numbers from 1 to 30

1	2	3	4	5	6	7	8	9	10
11	12	13	14	15	16	17	18	19	20
21	22	23	24	25	26	27	28	29	30

Counting numbers from 101 to 130

101	102	103	104	105	106	107	108	109	110
111	112	113	114	115	116	117	118	119	120
121	122	123	124	125	126	127	128	129	130

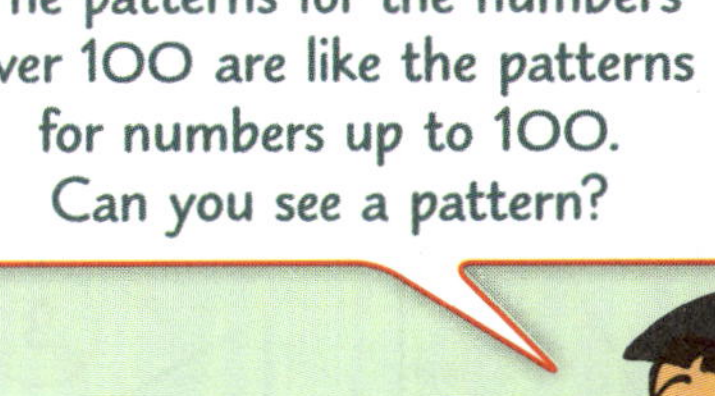

7, 17, 27 …
107, 117, 127 …

307, 317, 327, …
807, 817, 827, …

1 Complete the tens patterns.

a 7, 17, 27, ___, 47, ___, 67, ___

b 48, 58, 68, ___, ___, ___, ___, ___

c 52, 62, 72, ___, ___, ___, ___, ___

d 39, 49, 59, ___, ___, ___, ___, ___

e 21, 31, 41, ___, ___, ___, ___, ___

2 Complete these counting by tens patterns.

a 103, 113, 123, ___, ___

b 609, 619, 629, ___, ___

c 345, 355, 365, ___, ___

d 432, 442, 452, ___, ___

e 128, 118, 108, ___, ___

f 581, 571, 561, ___, ___

g 345, 355, 365, ___, ___

h 432, 442, 452, ___, ___

i 103, 113, 123, ___, ___

j 609, 619, 629, ___, ___

 • *AUSTRALIAN SIGNPOST MATHS 2* • ISBN 9780655708766

32C Quarter turns

a quarter turn clockwise (the way a clock goes)

turn to the left

turn to the right

quarter turn anticlockwise

quarter turn clockwise

A

B

C

D

1. Write the letter next to the shape you get if you move shape (A):
   - **a** a quarter turn clockwise
   - **b** a half turn clockwise
   - **c** a quarter turn anticlockwise
   - **d** a half turn anticlockwise
   - **e** a quarter turn to the right
2. Is a half turn clockwise the same as a half turn anticlockwise?
3. How does triangle (A) change after it is moved through a half turn?
4. The 1st pattern is made using quarter turns. Complete the 2nd pattern.

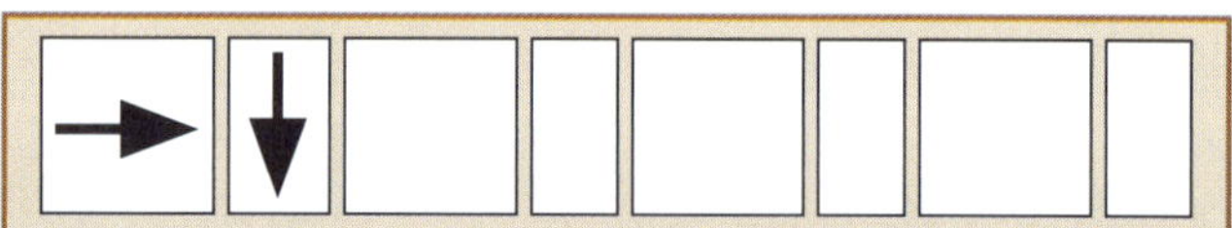

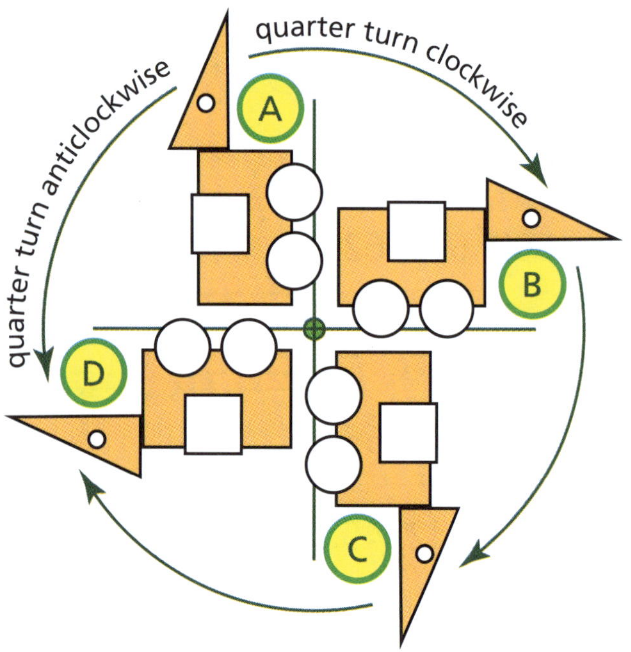

5. Which picture does (B) become if you turn it:
   - **a** a quarter turn clockwise?
   - **b** a half turn clockwise?
   - **c** a quarter turn anticlockwise?
   - **d** a half turn anticlockwise?
6. If you turn (A) through a full turn, which picture does it become?
7. If you turn a shape, does it stay the same shape and size?

Half and quarter turns

turn to the left: anticlockwise

turn to the right: clockwise

1 Write a "H" for the half turns and a "Q" for the quarter turns.

a 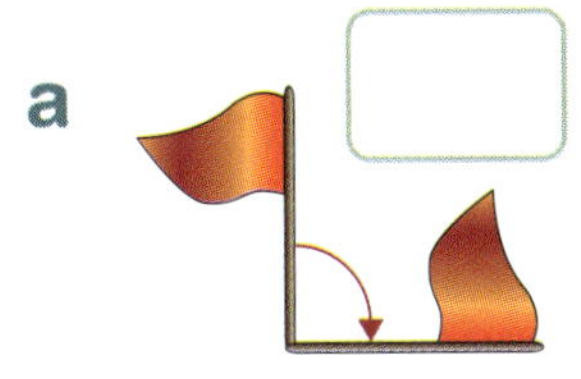

b 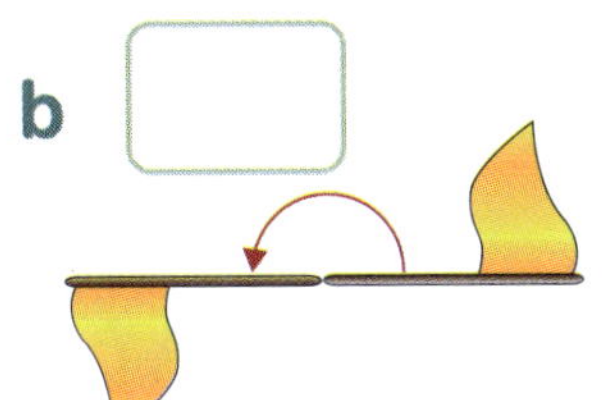

c 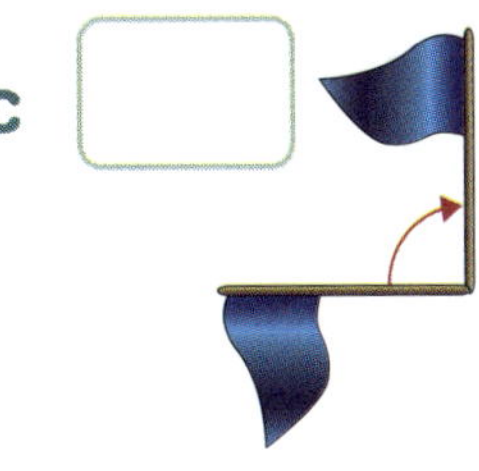

d 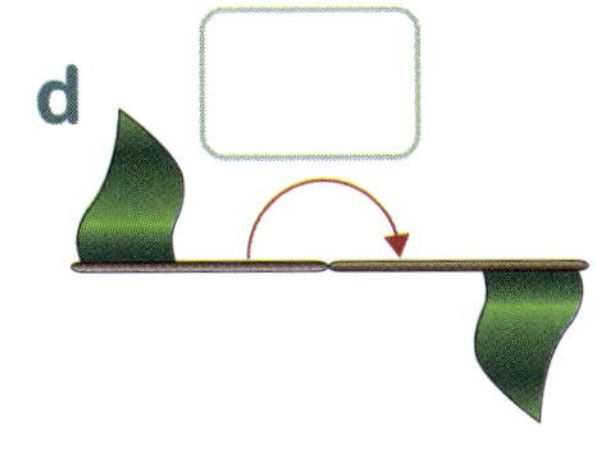

2 Continue the **quarter turn** pattern to finish each design.

a 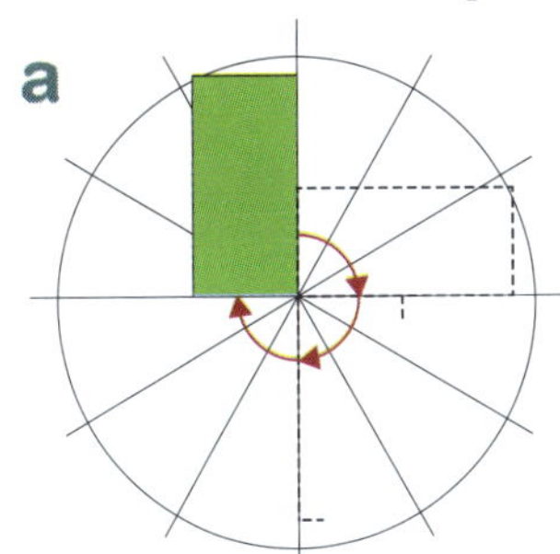

b 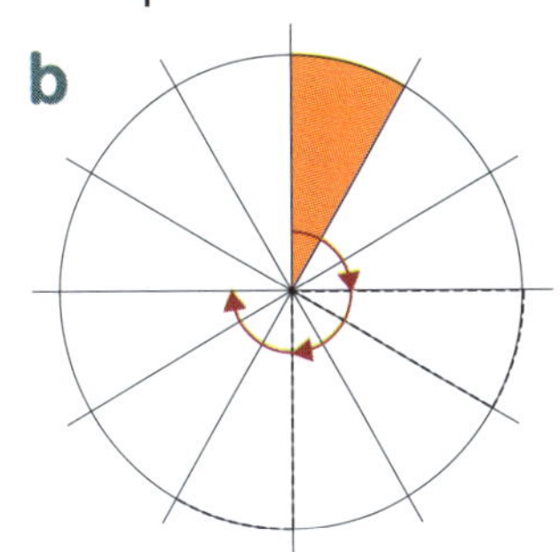

c 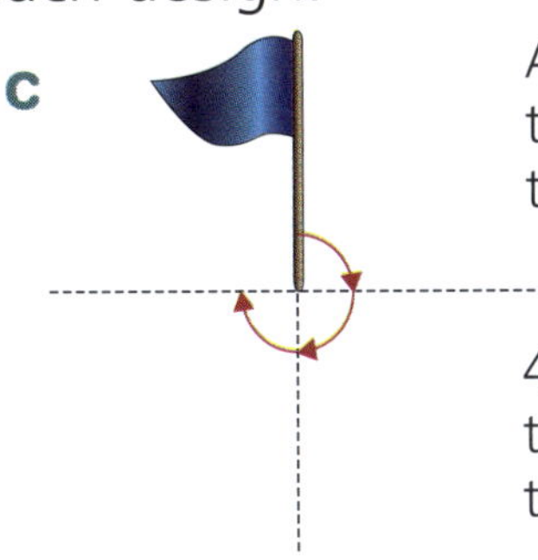

A full turn takes you back to the start.

4 quarter-turns take you back to the start.

3 Continue the **half turn** pattern to finish each design.

a 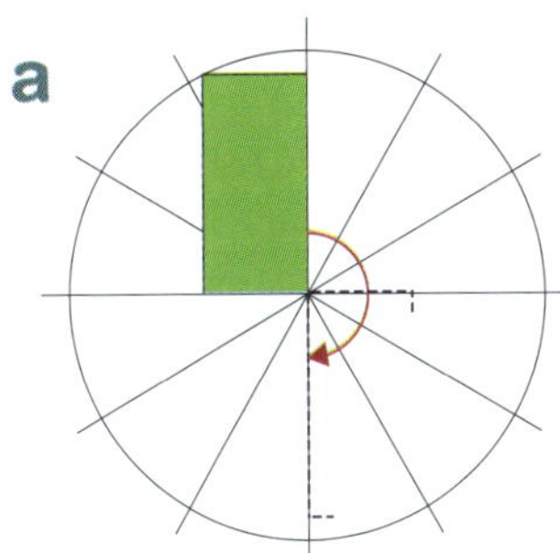

b 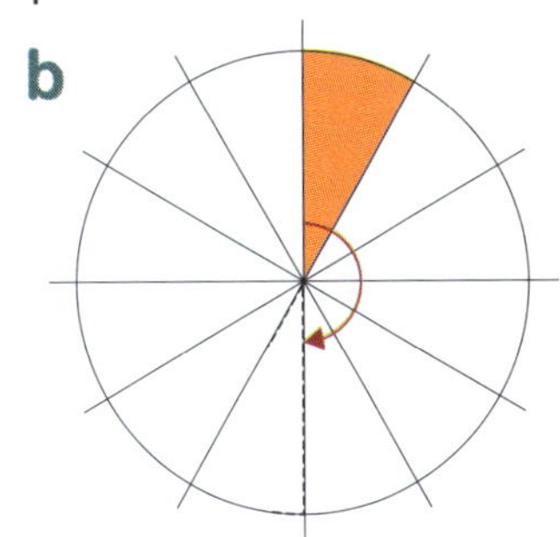

c 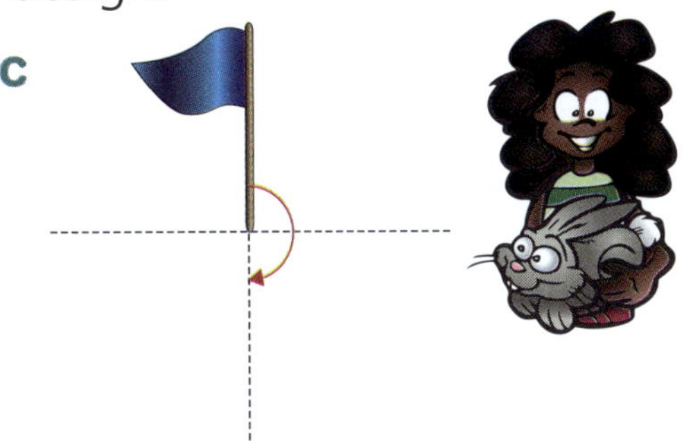

4 Describe each turn in Question 1 as either clockwise or anticlockwise.

a

b

c

d

INVESTIGATION

Show where each minute hand will be after the turn.

Start

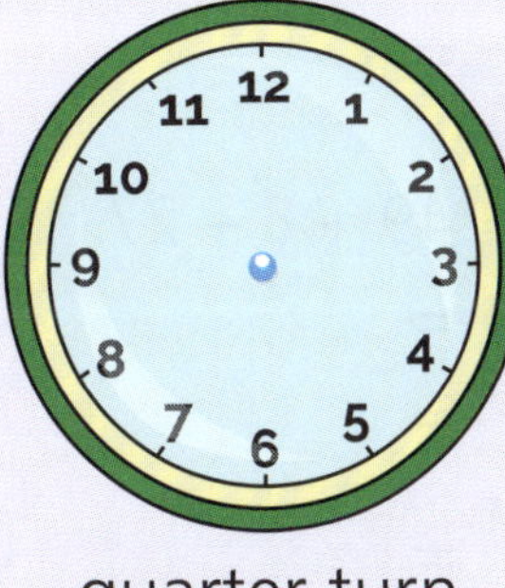

quarter turn clockwise

half turn clockwise

three-quarter turn clockwise

33A Using a strategy

$17 + 6 = (17 + 3) + 3 + 23$
$32 - 8 = (32 - 2) - 6 = 24$

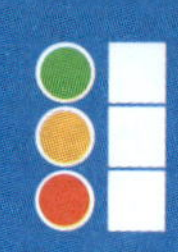

1 Match each question with the most appropriate strategy. Explain why you chose each strategy.

Strategy	Question	Strategy
doubles	36 + 10	near doubles
	57 − 12	
split strategy	22 + 3	jump strategy
	6 + 7	
adding 10	19 − 3	counting on
	42 − 16	
addition facts	17 + 3	counting back

2 Write the best strategies to solve each problem. Discuss why you chose each strategy.

a 64 − 10 = ☐ subtracting 10 or using blocks

b 39 + 4 = ☐ ______

c 9 + 9 = ☐ ______

d 29 + 34 = ☐ ______

e 7 + 8 = ☐ ______

3 Use strategies to complete these questions. Discuss the strategies used.

a **14** + 69
= 69 **+ 1 + 13**
= 70 + 13
= ☐

b 26 **+ 7** + 9
= 26 **+ 4 + 3** + 9
= 30 + 12
= ☐

c 38 **+ 6** + 17
= 38 **+ 2 + 4** + 17
= 40 + 21
= ☐

d 17 **+ 8** + 32
= 17 **+ 3 + 5** + 32
= 20 + 37
= ☐

e **15** + 58
= ....
= ....
= ☐

f 28 **+ 5** + 7
= ....
= ....
= ☐

g 49 **+ 8** + 27
= ....
= ....
= ☐

h 16 **+ 6** + 61
= ....
= ....
= ☐

33B Choosing a strategy

47 − 38 = 49 − 40
+2 +2

a 49 + 14 = ☐

(40 + 10) + (9 + 4)

= 50 + 13

= 63

I used the split strategy.
I added the tens, then the ones.

b 52 − 27 = ☐

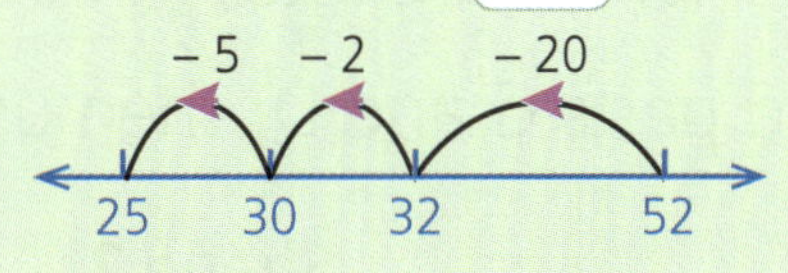

52 − 20 − 2 − 5

= 25

$$\begin{array}{r} 52 \\ -\ 27 \\ \hline 25 \end{array}$$

I used the jump strategy.

 Use the boxes to show how you found each answer.

a 18 + 9 = ☐

b 56 − 10 = ☐

c 36 + 4 = ☐

d 41 − 4 = ☐

e 28 + 16 = ☐

f 72 + 15 = ☐

33C Combine and separate shapes

Opposite sides are equal.

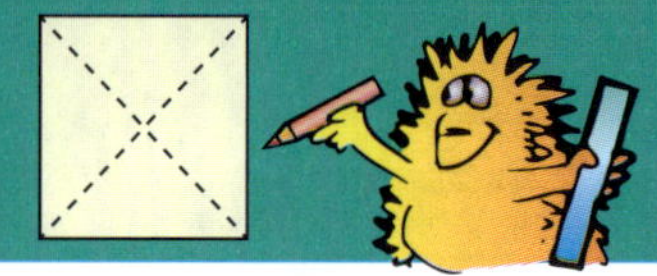

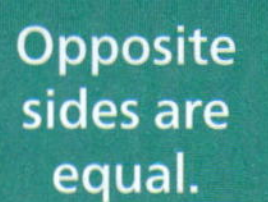

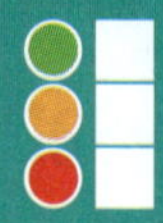

- Mary used a ruler to draw lines from corner to corner on her square paper.
- She then cut her square into 4 triangles and labelled them A, B, C and D.
- She coloured parts C and D, then used the 4 parts to make these shapes.

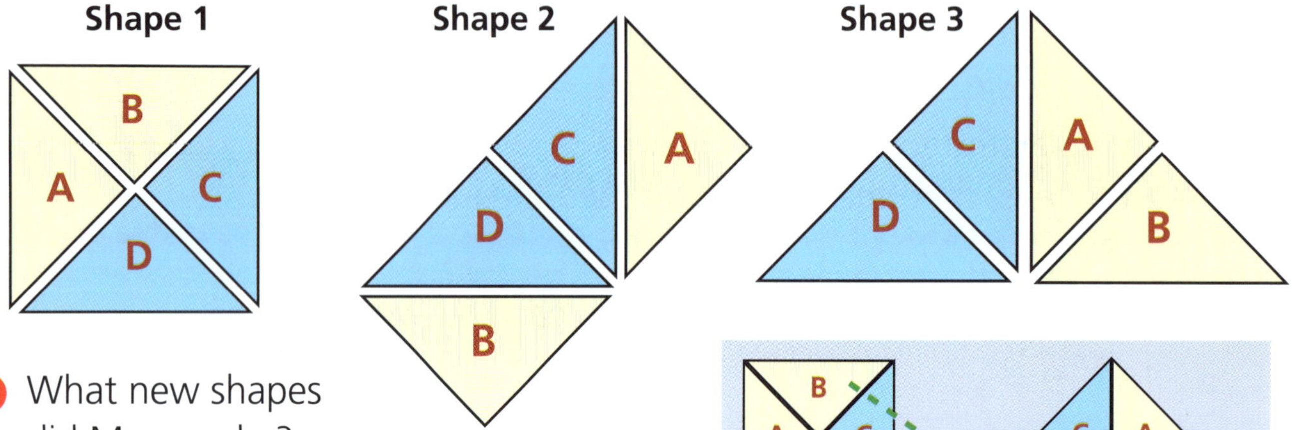

Shape 1
B
A
C
D
Shape 2
C
A
D
B
Shape 3
C
A
D
B

1 What new shapes did Mary make?

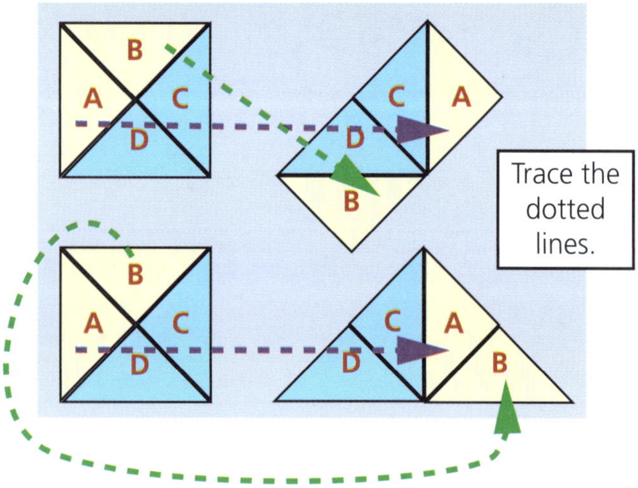

B
A
C
D
C
A
D
B
Trace the dotted lines.
B
A
C
D
C
A
D
B

How many ones blocks are needed to cover her square?

How many ones blocks are needed to cover her rectangle?

Do you think the square and the rectangle have the same area?

Would the triangle have the same area as the other two shapes?

Explain your answer.

ACTIVITY

- Use 1 cm grid paper.
- Use Mary's method to cut a square into 3 triangles. Use your 3 shapes to make a triangle and a rectangle.

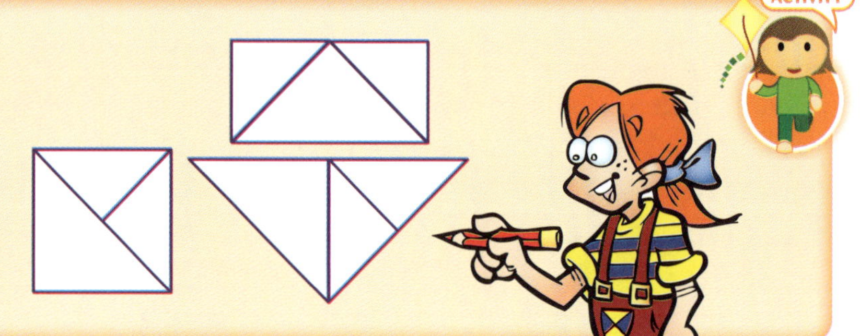

 • *AUSTRALIAN SIGNPOST MATHS 2* • ISBN 9780655708766

3D objects

This cube has eight vertices.

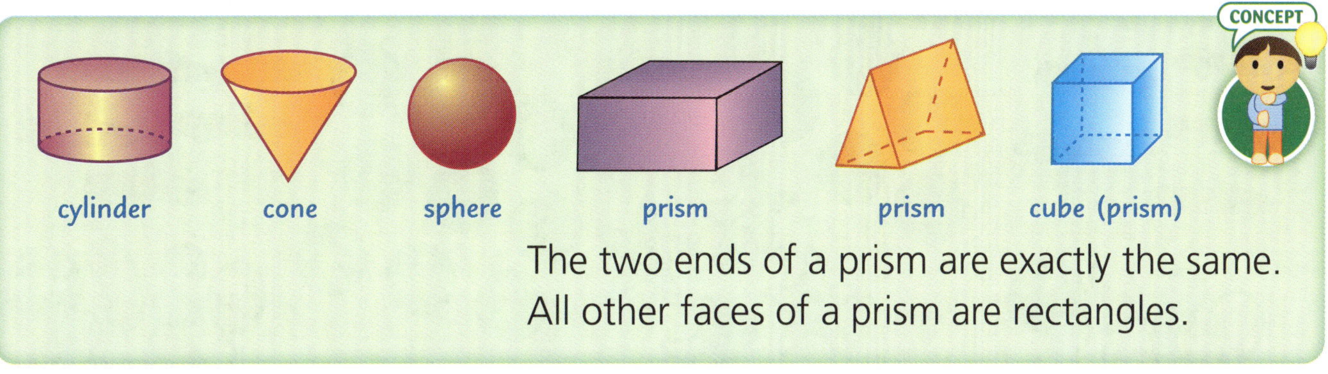

The two ends of a prism are exactly the same.
All other faces of a prism are rectangles.

1. Write the name of each 3D object.

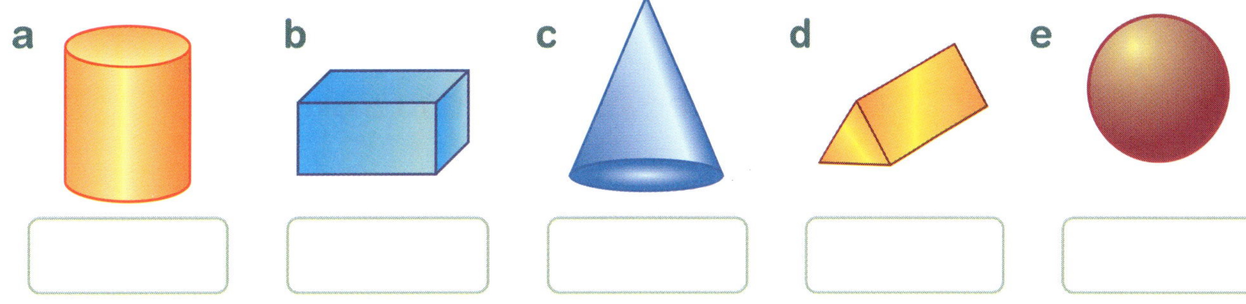

2.

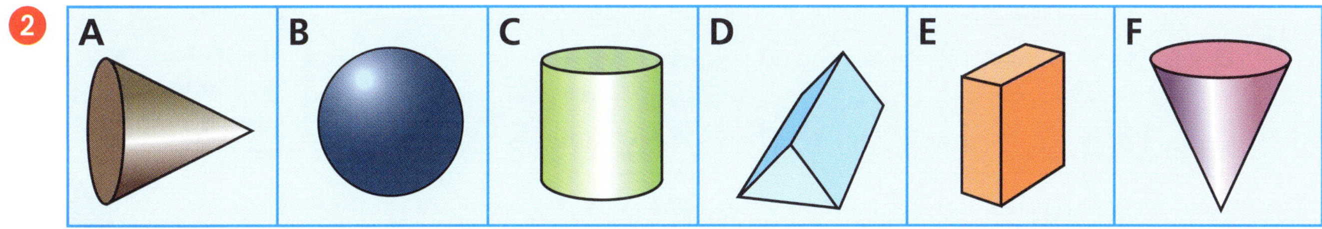

Which 3D objects have:

a curved surfaces?

b only flat surfaces?

c both curved and flat surfaces?

3. A **face** is a flat surface that has only straight sides.

Cube: faces, edges, vertices

Prism: faces, edges, vertices

 • *AUSTRALIAN SIGNPOST MATHS 2* • ISBN 9780655708766

34A How many more?

16 + (3 + 1) = 20
16 + (1 + 3) = 20

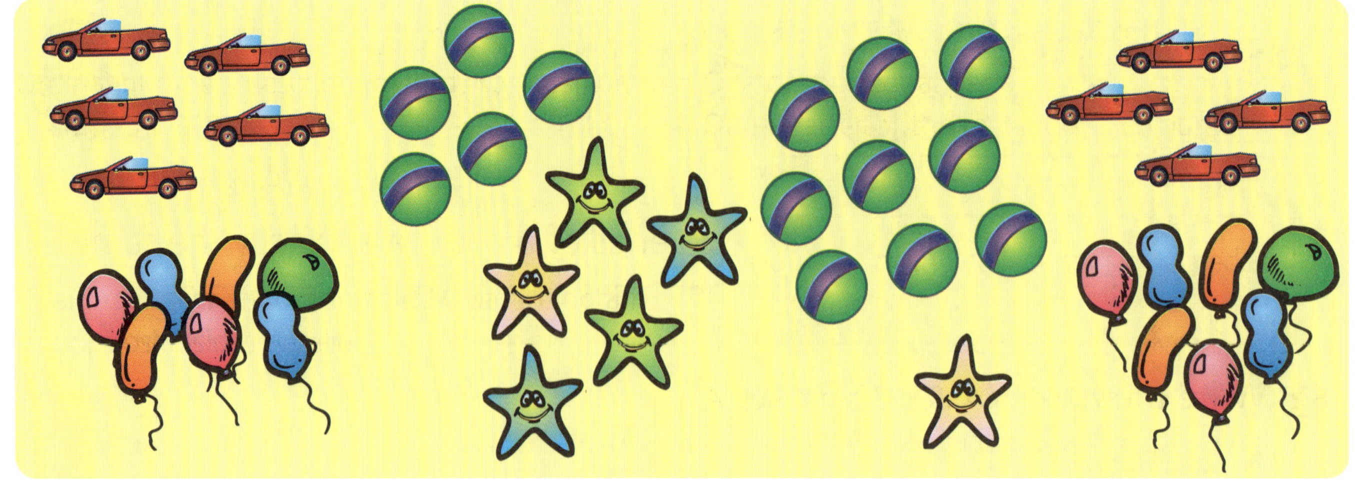

1 In this picture, how many more would I need to make 20:

a cars? 5 + 4 + ☐ = 20
b balloons? ☐ + ☐ + ☐ = 20
c balls? ☐ + ☐ + ☐ = 20
d starfish? ☐ + ☐ + ☐ = 20

2
a 6 + ☐ = 12
b 3 + 8 + ☐ = 16
c 11 + ☐ = 15
d 4 + ☐ + 5 = 13
e ☐ + 9 = 13
f 10 + ☐ + 5 = 19
g 5 + ☐ = 12
h 8 + 9 + ☐ = 20
i ☐ + 8 = 16
j 7 + 3 + ☐ = 20

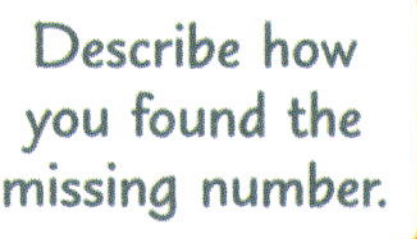

INVESTIGATION

- List all possible answers.

a
6 + ☐ + ☐ = 10
6 + ☐ + ☐ = 10
6 + ☐ + ☐ = 10
6 + ☐ + ☐ = 10
6 + ☐ + ☐ = 10

b
17 + ☐ + ☐ = 20
17 + ☐ + ☐ = 20
17 + ☐ + ☐ = 20
17 + ☐ + ☐ = 20

- Explore possible answers for 10 + ☐ + ☐ = 20.

34B Inverse strategy, subtraction

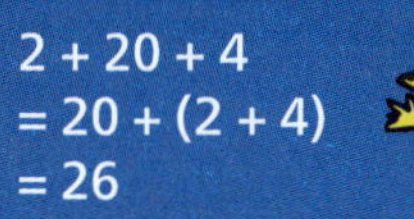

74 – 48

Use a number line to jump from the smaller number to the larger one.

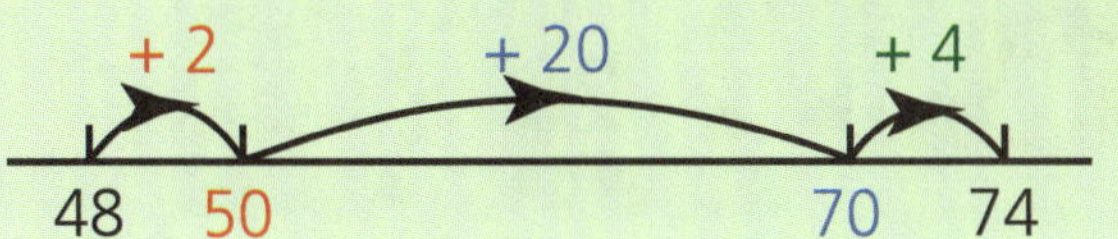

Start at **48**, add 2 to make **50**,
then add 20 to make **70**,
then add 4 to make **74**.

Total the bits added on.

74 – 48
= 2 + 20 + 4
= 26

This is called the shopkeeper's method.

1 Find the total of these numbers.

a 3, 10 and 2 ☐ **b** 6, 30 and 1 ☐ **c** 4, 60 and 3 ☐

2 Use the inverse strategy to complete each question.

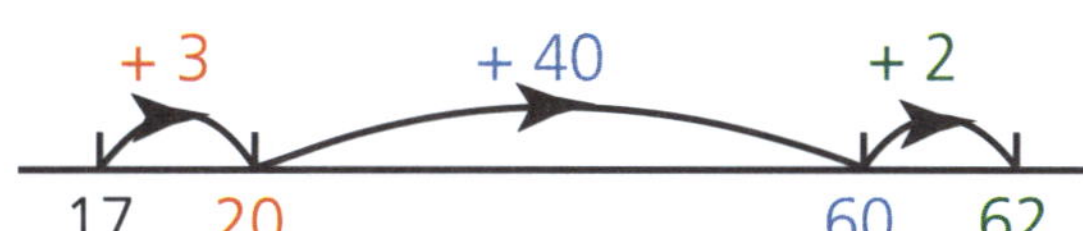

a 62 – 17 Start at **17**, add 3 (20) then add 40 (60) then add 2 (62).

+ 3, + 40, + 2; 17, 20, 60, 62

3 + 40 + 2 = ☐

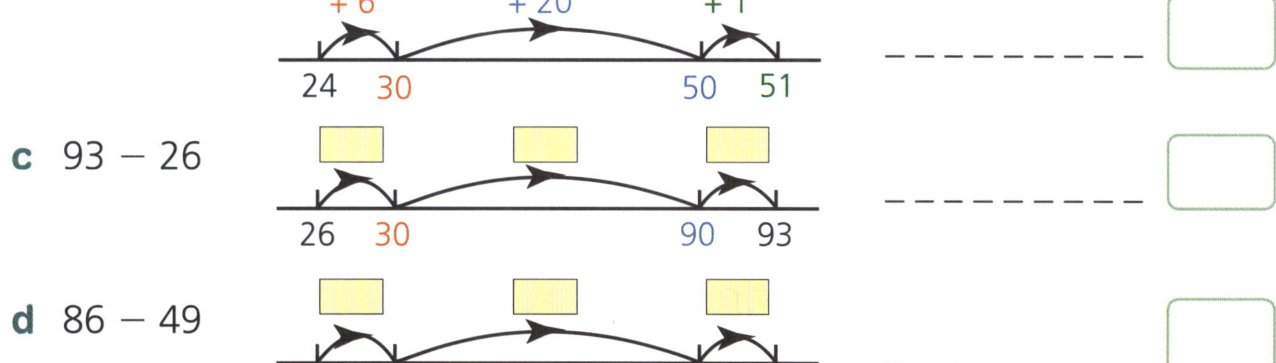

b 51 – 24 Start at **24**, add 6 (30) then add 20 (50) then add 1 (51).

+ 6, + 20, + 1; 24, 30, 50, 51

_ _ _ _ _ _ _ _ _ _ ☐

c 93 – 26

26, 30, 90, 93

_ _ _ _ _ _ _ _ _ _ ☐

d 86 – 49

49, 86

_ _ _ _ _ _ _ _ _ _ ☐

3 Use the inverse strategy to find each answer.

a 64 – 25 Add ____, then add ____, then add ____. _ _ _ _ _ ☐

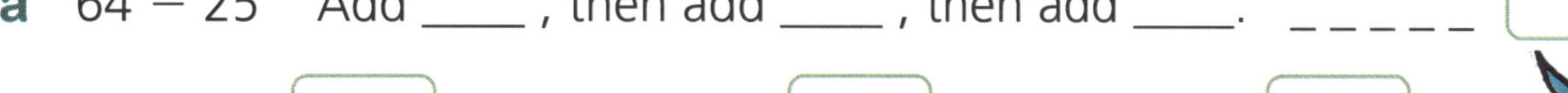

b 85 – 27 ☐ **c** 63 – 29 ☐ **d** 77 – 39 ☐

e 47 – 18 ☐ **f** 82 – 56 ☐ **g** 94 – 67 ☐

Use addition.

 • *AUSTRALIAN SIGNPOST MATHS 2* • ISBN 9780655708766

34C Money

1 Write the total value of each group of banknotes.

a 

b 

c 

d 

2 Circle the larger amount.

a 

b 

c 

3 Write the amounts in order from smallest to largest.

a 

$25

b 

$30

c 

 • *AUSTRALIAN SIGNPOST MATHS 2* • ISBN 9780655708766

Comparing objects

Objects can have length, area, volume and mass.

CONCEPT

An estimate is your best guess.

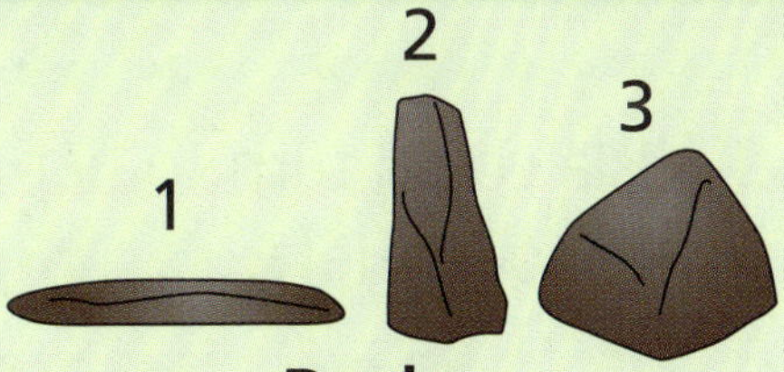

Rocks: 1, 2, 3

You can use ones blocks to measure lengths.

1 Estimate which of these rocks is:

a the tallest ☐ b the shortest ☐ c the heaviest ☐

d the lightest ☐ e the widest ☐ f the narrowest ☐

g the one that takes up the most space (has the largest volume) ☐

h the one that takes up the least space (has the smallest volume) ☐

Containers

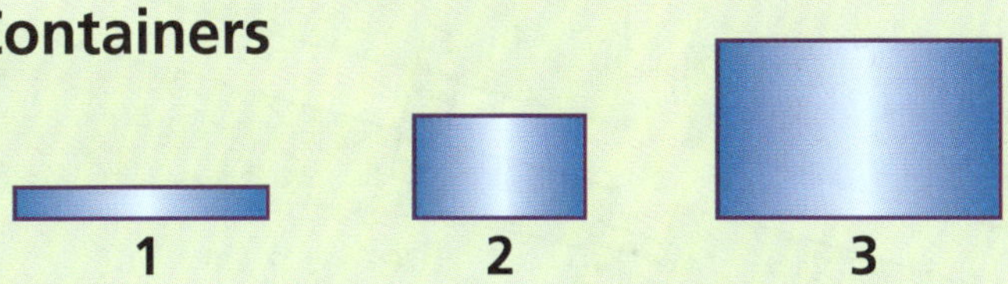

1 2 3

These are filled with water.

2 Estimate which of these containers:

a holds the most water ☐ b is the lightest ☐

c is the widest ☐ d holds the least water ☐

e is the heaviest ☐ f is the narrowest ☐

g has the most outside area ☐

ACTIVITY

3 Find three objects and draw them. Compare them.
Draw lines to match each object with its properties.

tallest | shortest | biggest area | smallest area | heaviest | lightest

Use your hand as a unit of area.

Use balance scales to find the heaviest.

 • *AUSTRALIAN SIGNPOST MATHS 2* • ISBN 9780655708766

35A Giving directions

1 a Use this map and the **words** above to explain how to go from B to F.

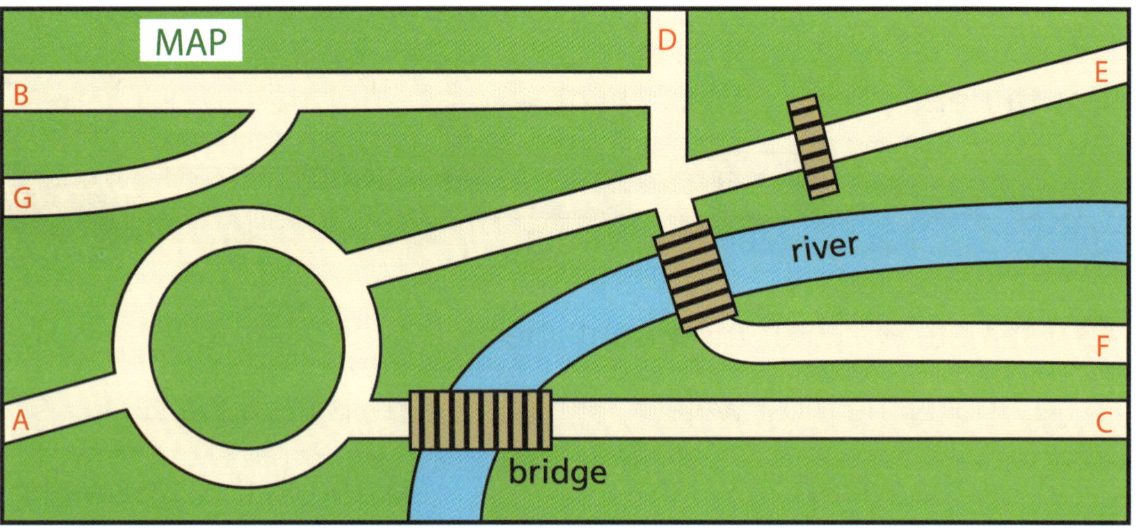

b Give directions to go from A to another letter on the map.

Work with a partner and take turns.

2

a If Jamila goes forwards 3 squares, she reaches ☐.

b What forwards and backwards directions does she need to spell the word "CAKE"? Discuss.

3 Talk about how to get to the principal's office.

35B More shapes (extension)

These shapes are **quadrilaterals**. They have 4 straight sides and 4 vertices. **Parallel lines** go in the same direction. They are always the same distance apart.

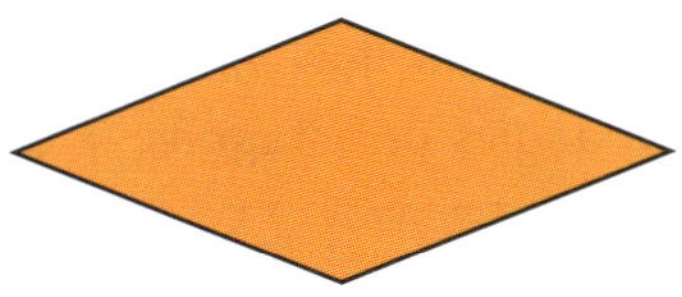

A **rhombus** has all sides equal. A diamond is a rhombus.

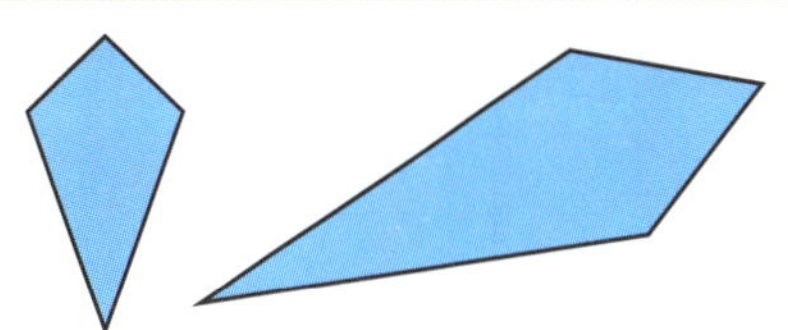

A **kite** has two pairs of equal sides. Toy kites can fly.

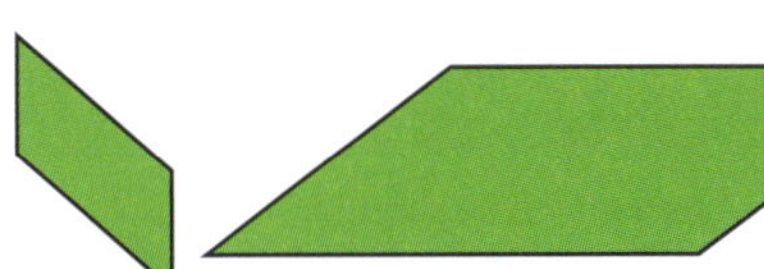

A **parallelogram** has opposite sides equal and parallel.

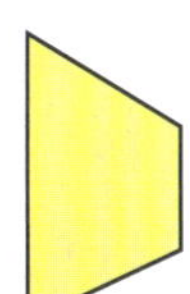
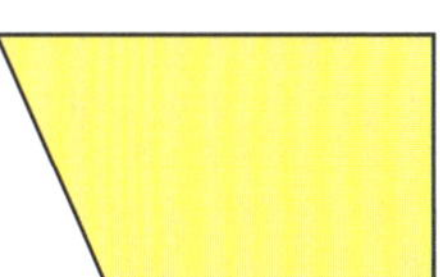

A **trapezium** has one pair of parallel sides.

1 Put a letter on each shape. Write:

R for rhombus K for kite

P for parallelogram T for trapezium.

Squares and rectangles are also quadrilaterals.

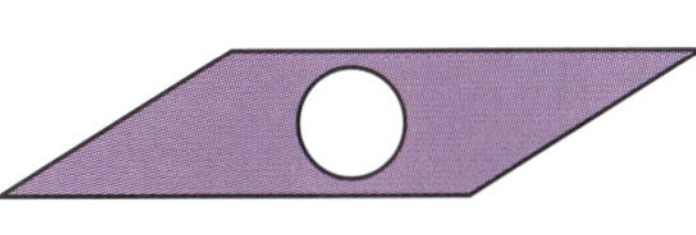
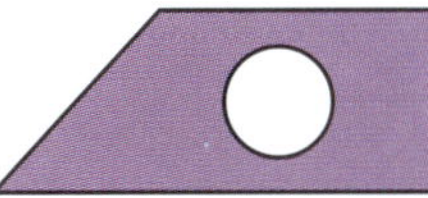
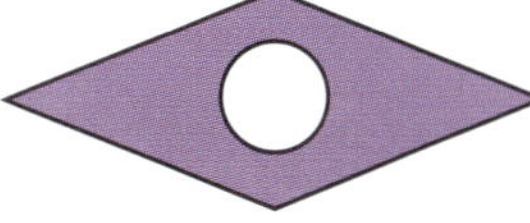
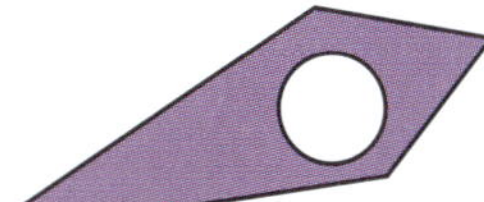

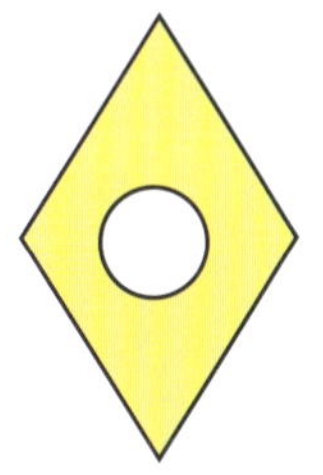
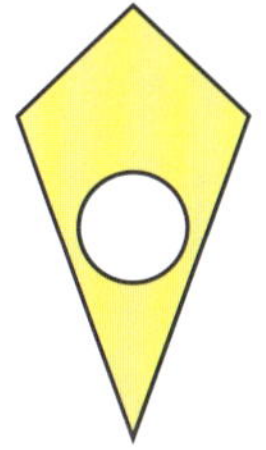
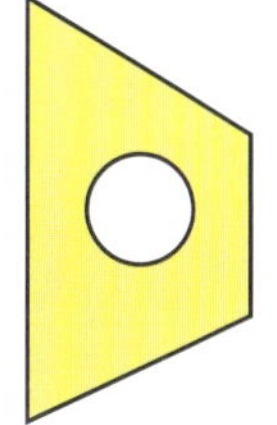
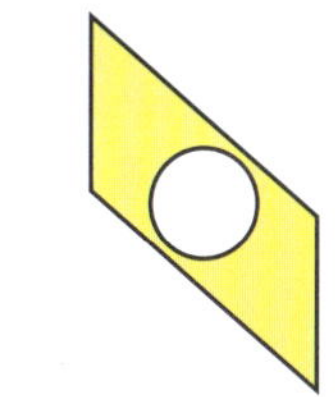

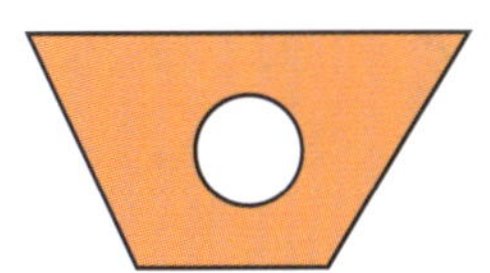
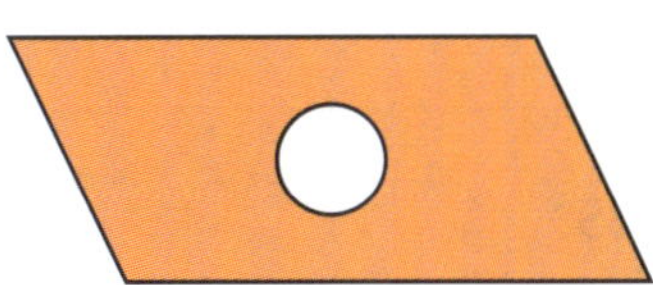
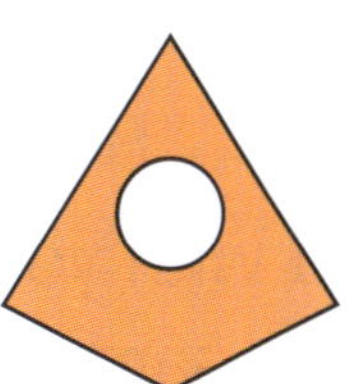
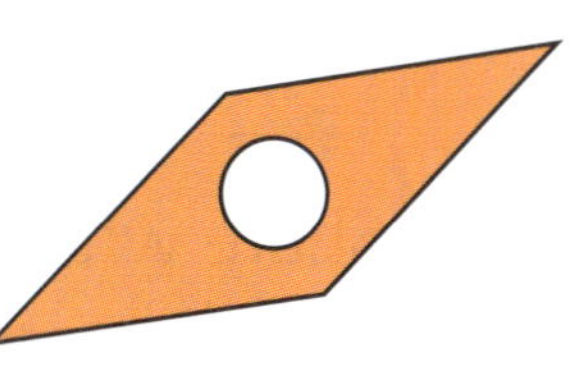

35C Problem solving with addition

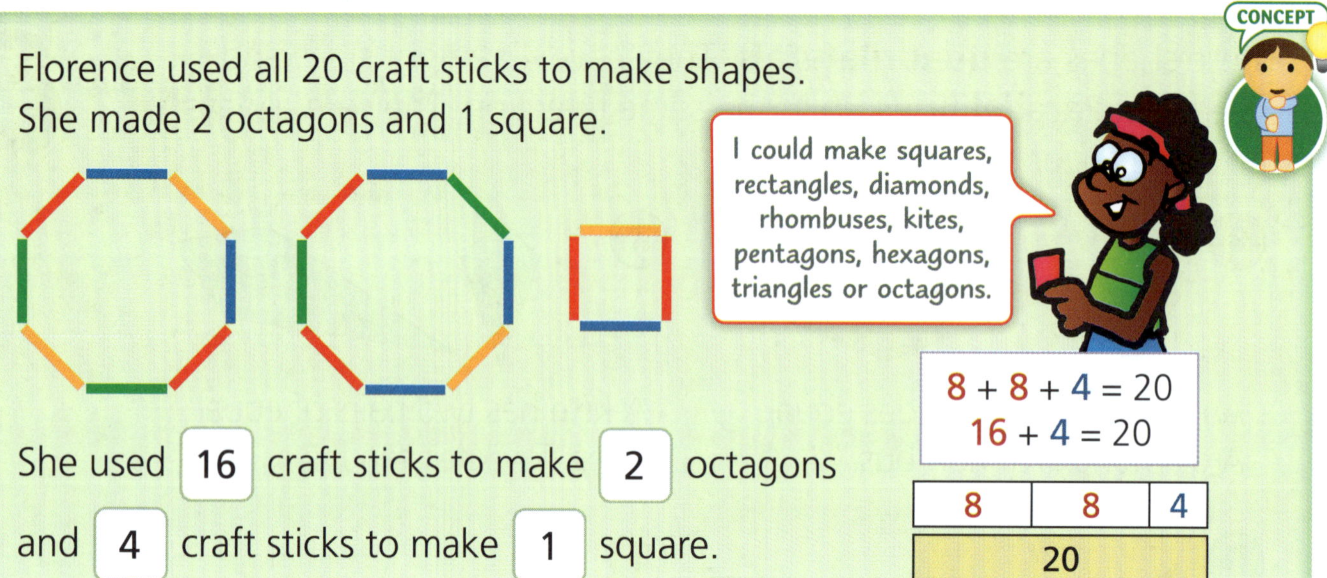

Florence used all 20 craft sticks to make shapes.
She made 2 octagons and 1 square.

She used 16 craft sticks to make 2 octagons and 4 craft sticks to make 1 square.

8 + 8 + 4 = 20
16 + 4 = 20

8	8	4
20		

1 a Use 20 crafts sticks to see what other combinations of shapes you can make. Try to use all of the craft sticks. Draw and write about what you did.

b Share what you did with your class. Did everyone get the same answer?

 • *AUSTRALIAN SIGNPOST MATHS 2* • ISBN 9780655708766

35D Problem solving with groups

INVESTIGATION

Isaac arranged groups of dice to show 12 dots altogether. Each dice had the same number of dots.

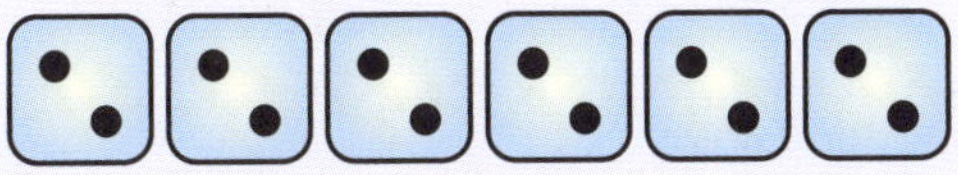

There are a few ways I can do this. I used 2s.

2	2	2	2	2	2
12					

6 dice with 2 dots on each dice makes 12 dots altogether.

1 **a** Show two other ways Isaac could arrange the dice so that 12 dots are shown in each box. Each box must have the same number on each dice.

b Write about what you did in one of your boxes.

2

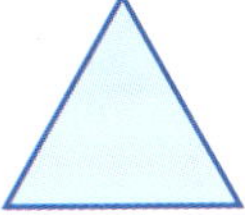   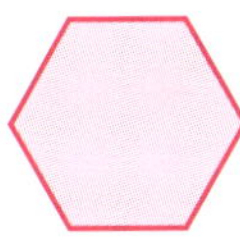 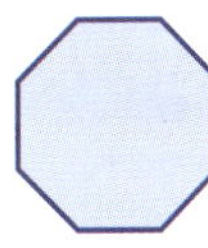

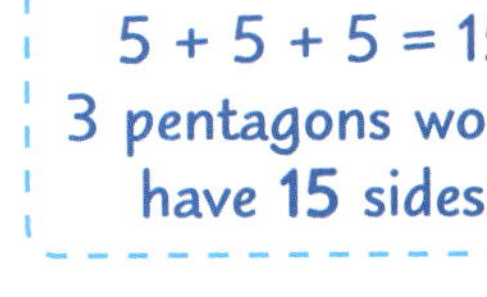

5 + 5 + 5 = 15
3 pentagons would have 15 sides.

Repeat the same shape in each box to match the number of sides given. Write the shape you used.

a 18 **b** 16 **c** 24

 • *AUSTRALIAN SIGNPOST MATHS 2* • ISBN 9780655708766

Identifying and addressing areas of need

An essential part of a teacher's role is identifying and addressing areas of student need.

This includes recognising areas where memory is fading and discovering any concepts that have been missed or misunderstood.

Testing is a great way to identify areas of need, but is only really useful when the results are used to help the student.

It is important to build a strong foundation when teaching new concepts and skills.

It is also important to revise/re-teach areas of weakness you discover so that these areas will not be barriers to the future learning of related concepts.

Progress tests and retests (see adjacent page)

Progress tests 1 to 5 are found in the online Teacher Resource.

After each test, notes and answers are supplied.

Progress test questions are cross-referenced to appropriate Student Book pages.

Progress retests 1 to 5 are found in the online Teacher Resource.

The remediation records pages are used to provide a record of each student's progress.

These are found in the online Teacher Resource.

For each error recorded, the question should be discussed, and using the Student Book cross-reference provided, practice should occur. Retesting should follow using the progress retests.

Summary

1 Test recent work.

2 Enter any mistakes in the Remediation records.

3 Use this record to direct your revision/re-teaching.

4 Retest using the matching retest questions to ensure understanding.

Teaching and learning

Successfully teaching content and skills is a complex process.

A **good textbook** is an important tool alongside **effective teaching and planning**.

Knowledge, understanding and skills must be embedded in the student's mind so that recall continues with time. This will be done using:

(1) instruction (2) practice (3) drill (4) review.

Instruction involves explicit explanation, investigation and the use of good educational resources.

Practice forms neural pathways within the brain.

Drill strengthens neural pathways. The stronger the pathways become, the longer the understanding or knowledge is retained. 'Overlearning' prolongs recall.

Review revitalises weakened neural pathways.

Progress test 1

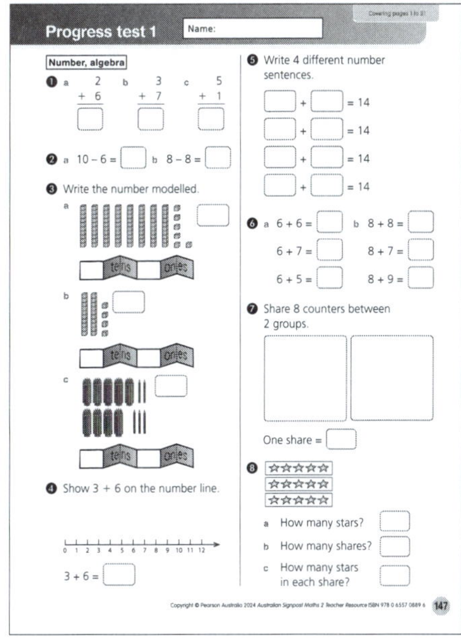
Progress test 1 Name:
Covering pages 1 to 21
Number, algebra
1 a 2 + 6 b 3 + 7 c 5 + 1
2 a 10 − 6 = b 8 − 8 =
3 Write the number modelled.
tens ones
4 Show 3 + 6 on the number line.
3 + 6 =
5 Write 4 different number sentences.
+ = 14
6 a 6 + 6 = b 8 + 8 =
6 + 7 = 8 + 7 =
6 + 5 = 8 + 9 =
7 Share 8 counters between 2 groups.
One share =
8 a How many stars?
b How many shares?
c How many stars in each share?
147

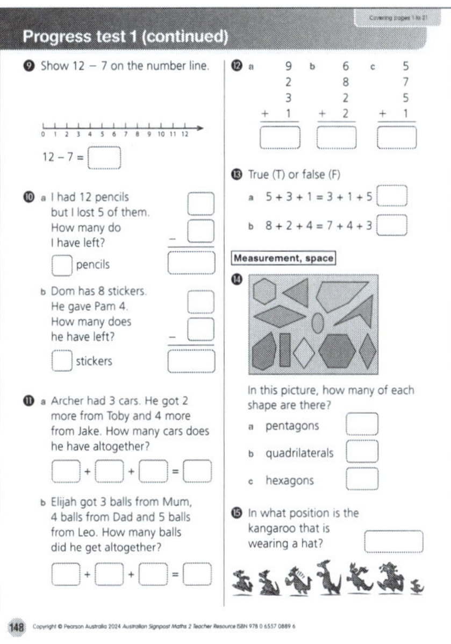
Progress test 1 (continued)
Covering pages 1 to 21
9 Show 12 − 7 on the number line.
12 − 7 =
10 a I had 12 pencils but I lost 5 of them. How many do I have left? pencils
b Dom has 8 stickers. He gave Pam 4. How many does he have left? stickers
11 a Archer had 3 cars. He got 2 more from Toby and 4 more from Jake. How many cars does he have altogether?
b Elijah got 3 balls from Mum, 4 balls from Dad and 5 balls from Leo. How many balls did he get altogether?
12 a 9 + 2 + 3 + 1 b 6 + 8 + 2 + 2 c 5 + 7 + 5 + 1
13 True (T) or false (F)
a 5 + 3 + 1 = 3 + 1 + 5
b 8 + 2 + 4 = 7 + 4 + 3
Measurement, space
14 In this picture, how many of each shape are there?
a pentagons
b quadrilaterals
c hexagons
15 In what position is the kangaroo that is wearing a hat?
148

Progress retest 1

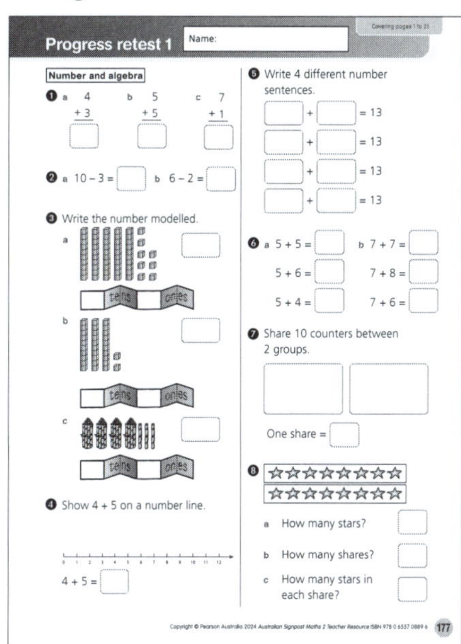
Progress retest 1 Name:
Covering pages 1 to 21
Number and algebra
1 a 4 + 3 b 5 + 5 c 7 + 1
2 a 10 − 3 = b 6 − 2 =
3 Write the number modelled.
tens ones
4 Show 4 + 5 on a number line.
4 + 5 =
5 Write 4 different number sentences.
+ = 13
6 a 5 + 5 = b 7 + 7 =
5 + 6 = 7 + 8 =
5 + 4 = 7 + 6 =
7 Share 10 counters between 2 groups.
One share =
8 a How many stars?
b How many shares?
c How many stars in each share?
177

Notes and answers for Progress test 1

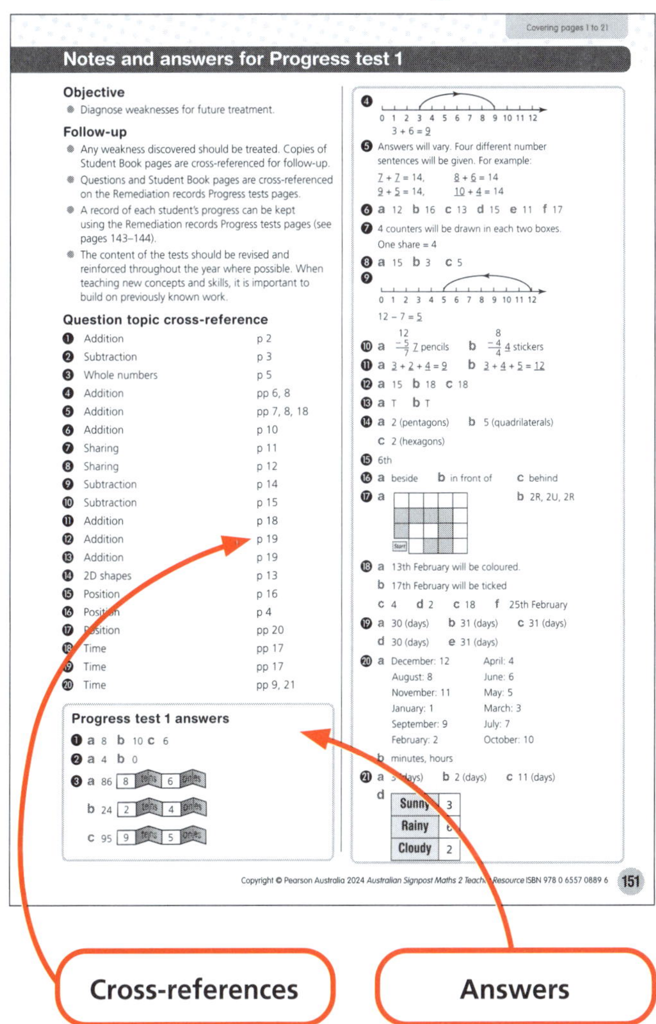
Covering pages 1 to 21
Notes and answers for Progress test 1

Objective
- Diagnose weaknesses for future treatment.

Follow-up
- Any weakness discovered should be treated. Copies of Student Book pages are cross-referenced for follow-up.
- Questions and Student Book pages are cross-referenced on the Remediation records Progress tests pages.
- A record of each student's progress can be kept using the Remediation records Progress tests pages (see pages 143–144).
- The content of the tests should be revised and reinforced throughout the year where possible. When teaching new concepts and skills, it is important to build on previously known work.

Question topic cross-reference

1	Addition	p 2
2	Subtraction	p 3
3	Whole numbers	p 5
4	Addition	pp 6, 8
5	Addition	pp 7, 8, 18
6	Addition	p 10
7	Sharing	p 11
8	Sharing	p 12
9	Subtraction	p 14
10	Subtraction	p 15
11	Addition	p 18
12	Addition	p 19
13	Addition	p 19
14	2D shapes	p 13
15	Position	p 16
16	Position	p 4
17	Position	pp 20
18	Time	pp 17
19	Time	pp 17
20	Time	pp 9, 21

Progress test 1 answers
1 a 8 b 10 c 6
2 a 4 b 0
3 a 86 8 tens 6 ones
b 24 2 tens 4 ones
c 95 9 tens 5 ones
4 3 + 6 = 9
5 Answers will vary. Four different number sentences will be given. For example:
7 + 7 = 14, 8 + 6 = 14
9 + 5 = 14, 10 + 4 = 14
6 a 12 b 16 c 13 d 15 e 11 f 17
7 4 counters will be drawn in each two boxes. One share = 4
8 a 15 b 3 c 5
9 12 − 7 = 5
10 a 7 pencils b 4 stickers
11 a 3 + 2 + 4 = 9 b 3 + 4 + 5 = 12
12 a 15 b 18 c 18
13 a T b T
14 a 2 (pentagons) b 5 (quadrilaterals) c 2 (hexagons)
15 6th
16 a beside b in front of c behind
17 b 2R, 2U, 2R
18 a 13th February will be coloured
b 17th February will be ticked
c 4 d 2 e 18 f 25th February
19 a 30 (days) b 31 (days) c 31 (days) d 30 (days) e 31 (days)
20 a December: 12, August: 8, November: 11, January: 1, September: 9, February: 2, April: 4, June: 6, May: 5, March: 3, July: 7, October: 10
b minutes, hours
21 a 3 (days) b 2 (days) c 11 (days)
d Sunny 3, Rainy 6, Cloudy 2
151

Remediation records: Progress tests

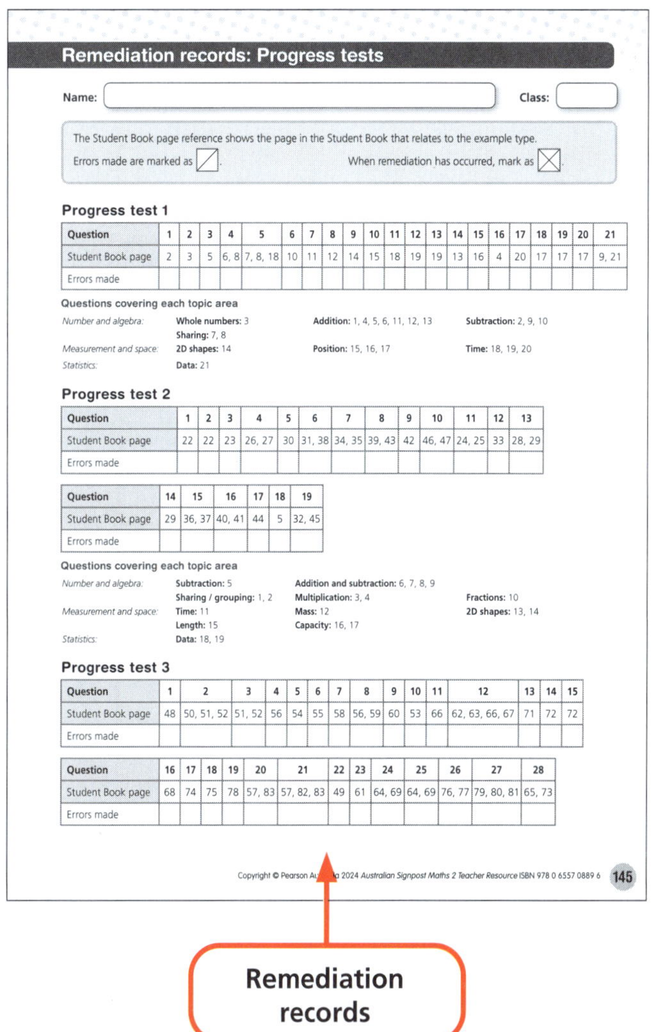
Remediation records: Progress tests

Name: Class:

The Student Book page reference shows the page in the Student Book that relates to the example type.
Errors made are marked as ⧄. When remediation has occurred, mark as ☒.

Progress test 1

Question	1	2	3	4	5	6	7	8	9	10	11	12	13	14	15	16	17	18	19	20	21
Student Book page	2	3	5	6, 8	7, 8, 18	10	11	12	14	15	18	19	19	13	16	4	20	17	17	17	9, 21
Errors made																					

Questions covering each topic area
Number and algebra: Whole numbers: 3; Addition: 1, 4, 5, 6, 11, 12, 13; Subtraction: 2, 9, 10; Sharing: 7, 8
Measurement and space: 2D shapes: 14; Position: 15, 16, 17; Time: 18, 19, 20
Statistics: Data: 21

Progress test 2

Question	1	2	3	4	5	6	7	8	9	10	11	12	13
Student Book page	22	22	23	26, 27	30	31, 38	34, 35	39, 43	42	46, 47	24, 25	33	28, 29
Errors made													

Question	14	15	16	17	18	19
Student Book page	29	36, 37	40, 41	44	5	32, 45
Errors made						

Questions covering each topic area
Number and algebra: Subtraction: 5; Sharing / grouping: 1, 2; Addition and subtraction: 6, 7, 8, 9; Multiplication: 3, 4; Fractions: 10
Measurement and space: Time: 11; Length: 15; Mass: 12; Capacity: 16, 17; 2D shapes: 13, 14
Statistics: Data: 18, 19

Progress test 3

Question	1	2	3	4	5	6	7	8	9	10	11	12	13	14	15
Student Book page	48	50, 51, 52	51, 52	56	54	55	58	56, 59	60	53	66	62, 63, 66, 67	71	72	72
Errors made															

Question	16	17	18	19	20	21	22	23	24	25	26	27	28
Student Book page	68	74	75	78	57, 83	57, 82, 83	49	61	64, 69	64, 69	76, 77	79, 80, 81	65, 73
Errors made													

145

Cross-references

Answers

Remediation records

Addition facts to 20

A	1 + 1 ☐	2 + 4 ☐	5 + 1 ☐	2 + 3 ☐	4 + 5 ☐
B	3 + 4 ☐	0 + 4 ☐	3 + 1 ☐	1 + 6 ☐	2 + 5 ☐
C	0 + 7 ☐	7 + 1 ☐	1 + 3 ☐	2 + 6 ☐	3 + 6 ☐
D	7 + 0 ☐	9 + 3 ☐	2 + 7 ☐	3 + 5 ☐	6 + 5 ☐
E	4 + 1 ☐	8 + 3 ☐	0 + 5 ☐	9 + 0 ☐	9 + 4 ☐
F	2 + 2 ☐	3 + 7 ☐	6 + 3 ☐	6 + 0 ☐	5 + 2 ☐
G	5 + 3 ☐	3 + 2 ☐	2 + 8 ☐	4 + 2 ☐	1 + 7 ☐
H	5 + 5 ☐	8 + 2 ☐	6 + 4 ☐	4 + 4 ☐	7 + 2 ☐
I	4 + 3 ☐	5 + 4 ☐	7 + 3 ☐	6 + 2 ☐	6 + 6 ☐
J	1 + 8 ☐	2 + 1 ☐	6 + 1 ☐	3 + 3 ☐	4 + 6 ☐
K	7 + 7 ☐	9 + 1 ☐	5 + 6 ☐	1 + 4 ☐	9 + 9 ☐
L	8 + 1 ☐	1 + 2 ☐	4 + 8 ☐	6 + 7 ☐	9 + 8 ☐
M	1 + 5 ☐	0 + 9 ☐	8 + 8 ☐	8 + 0 ☐	1 + 9 ☐
N	9 + 2 ☐	8 + 4 ☐	4 + 7 ☐	7 + 9 ☐	9 + 6 ☐
O	7 + 6 ☐	2 + 9 ☐	7 + 4 ☐	3 + 8 ☐	5 + 7 ☐
P	3 + 9 ☐	4 + 0 ☐	9 + 7 ☐	6 + 8 ☐	5 + 9 ☐
Q	8 + 6 ☐	4 + 9 ☐	8 + 7 ☐	5 + 8 ☐	7 + 5 ☐
R	7 + 8 ☐	8 + 9 ☐	8 + 5 ☐	6 + 9 ☐	9 + 5 ☐

Subtraction facts to 10

8 – 3 ☐

Ask:

3 plus what makes 8?

3 + ☐ = 8

9 – 7 ☐

Ask:

7 plus what makes 9?

7 + ☐ = 9

You could also use the number line.

0 1 2 3 4 5 6 7 8 9 10 11 12 13 14 15 16 17 18 19 20

A	7 – 0 ☐	3 – 2 ☐	7 – 1 ☐	6 – 3 ☐	5 – 4 ☐
B	9 – 8 ☐	4 – 3 ☐	4 – 1 ☐	9 – 9 ☐	8 – 0 ☐
C	2 – 1 ☐	6 – 4 ☐	6 – 1 ☐	5 – 3 ☐	9 – 5 ☐
D	7 – 4 ☐	3 – 1 ☐	7 – 6 ☐	7 – 5 ☐	9 – 6 ☐
E	7 – 7 ☐	8 – 1 ☐	6 – 5 ☐	8 – 6 ☐	9 – 8 ☐
F	9 – 7 ☐	8 – 5 ☐	5 – 1 ☐	5 – 5 ☐	9 – 0 ☐
G	4 – 0 ☐	4 – 2 ☐	9 – 3 ☐	6 – 0 ☐	7 – 2 ☐
H	8 – 3 ☐	5 – 2 ☐	6 – 2 ☐	8 – 7 ☐	8 – 2 ☐
I	8 – 4 ☐	9 – 2 ☐	7 – 3 ☐	9 – 4 ☐	6 – 6 ☐
J	10 – 3 ☐	10 – 5 ☐	10 – 2 ☐	10 – 6 ☐	
K	10 – 8 ☐	10 – 7 ☐	10 – 4 ☐	10 – 9 ☐	

 • *AUSTRALIAN SIGNPOST MATHS 2* • ISBN 9780655708766

Subtraction facts to 20

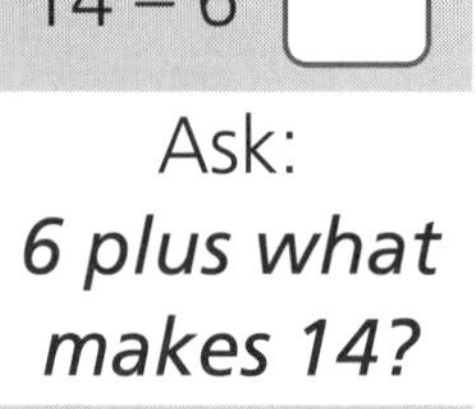

14 – 6 ☐

Ask:
6 plus what makes 14?

6 + ☐ = 14

16 – 9 ☐

Ask:
9 plus what makes 16?

9 + ☐ = 16

You could also use the number line.

0 1 2 3 4 5 6 7 8 9 10 11 12 13 14 15 16 17 18 19 20

A	14 – 7 ☐	12 – 3 ☐	11 – 6 ☐	18 – 9 ☐
B	12 – 8 ☐	13 – 7 ☐	17 – 8 ☐	16 – 8 ☐
C	10 – 9 ☐	10 – 3 ☐	12 – 3 ☐	11 – 5 ☐
D	11 – 3 ☐	13 – 4 ☐	10 – 5 ☐	10 – 8 ☐
E	11 – 2 ☐	12 – 4 ☐	11 – 7 ☐	16 – 9 ☐
F	13 – 6 ☐	11 – 9 ☐	11 – 4 ☐	11 – 8 ☐
G	14 – 6 ☐	13 – 9 ☐	15 – 7 ☐	13 – 8 ☐
H	10 – 7 ☐	16 – 7 ☐	14 – 8 ☐	15 – 9 ☐
I	15 – 6 ☐	10 – 4 ☐	12 – 7 ☐	14 – 9 ☐
J	12 – 9 ☐	14 – 5 ☐	12 – 5 ☐	12 – 6 ☐
K	13 – 5 ☐	10 – 6 ☐	15 – 8 ☐	17 – 9 ☐

 • *AUSTRALIAN SIGNPOST MATHS 2* • ISBN 9780655708766

Skip counting / number chart

Skip count by 2. 2, 4, 6, 8, 10, 12, 14, 16, 18, 20 …

Skip count by 10. 10, 20, 30, 40, 50, 60, 70, 80, 90, 100 …

Skip count by 5. 5, 10, 15, 20, 25, 30, 35, 40, 45, 50 …

Skip count by 4. 4, 8, 12, 16, 20, 24, 28, 32, 36, 40 …

1	2	3	4	5	6	7	8	9	10
11	12	13	14	15	16	17	18	19	20
21	22	23	24	25	26	27	28	29	30
31	32	33	34	35	36	37	38	39	40
41	42	43	44	45	46	47	48	49	50
51	52	53	54	55	56	57	58	59	60
61	62	63	64	65	66	67	68	69	70
71	72	73	74	75	76	77	78	79	80
81	82	83	84	85	86	87	88	89	90
91	92	93	94	95	96	97	98	99	100
101	102	103	104	105	106	107	108	109	110
111	112	113	114	115	116	117	118	119	120
121	122	123	124	125	126	127	128	129	130

Know your addition facts

+	1	2	3	4	5	6	7	8	9	10
1	2	3	4	5	6	7	8	9	10	11
2	3	4	5	6	7	8	9	10	11	12
3	4	5	6	7	8	9	10	11	12	13
4	5	6	7	8	9	10	11	12	13	14
5	6	7	8	9	10	11	12	13	14	15
6	7	8	9	10	11	12	13	14	15	16
7	8	9	10	11	12	13	14	15	16	17
8	9	10	11	12	13	14	15	16	17	18
9	10	11	12	13	14	15	16	17	18	19
10	11	12	13	14	15	16	17	18	19	20

- Learn the addition tables with answers up to 10. (**2 + 5 = 5 + 2 = 7**)
- Learn the addition tables with answers up to 20. (**7 + 6 = 6 + 7 = 13**)
- Learn your doubles and halves.

Numbers	1	2	3	4	5	6	7	8	9	10
Doubles	**2**	**4**	**6**	**8**	**10**	**12**	**14**	**16**	**18**	**20**

4 + 4 = 8 **Double 4 = 8.** **2 x 4 = 8**

Numbers	2	4	**6**	8	10	**12**	14	16	**18**	20
Halves	**1**	**2**	**3**	**4**	**5**	**6**	**7**	**8**	**9**	**10**

Half of 10 = 5. **10 ÷ 2 = 5**

 ISBN 9780655708766

6A Problem solving

Use pictures, number lines or counters to solve these problems.

1. I have egg cartons that hold 6 eggs each.

   a How many egg cartons would I need to hold 24 eggs? ☐

   b How many egg cartons would I need to hold 34 eggs? ☐

2. I am making bracelets for my friends. Each bracelet has 10 beads.

   a How many bracelets can I make if I have 56 beads? ☐

   How many more beads do I need to make the next bracelet? ☐

   b How many bracelets can I make if I have 73 beads? ☐

   How many more beads do I need to make 2 more bracelets? ☐

3. On the Monday before the 11th of May it was three weeks and four days until my birthday. What is the date of my birthday? ☐

May						
Sun	Mon	Tues	Wed	Thurs	Fri	Sat
				1	2	3
4	5	6	7	8	9	10
11	12	13	14	15	16	17
18	19	20	21	22	23	24
25	26	27	28	29	30	31

4. I am 12 years old and my sister is 9 years old. My cousin is five years younger than me. What is the total of our ages? ☐

4. **a** Pa had 28 apples. There were 5 in the first bag, 6 in the second and 12 in the third. How many are in the last bag? ☐

   b Pa gave me half of the apples in the bags that held an even number of apples. How many apples did he give me? ☐

Answers can be found at the end of the Teacher Notes for 35D.

Use pictures, number lines or counters to solve these problems.

1. After I gave three strawberries to my sister, I had 10, and she had 7.
   How many strawberries did I have at the start?
   How many more strawberries did I have than my sister at the start?

2. It costs $14 for an adult to go on the train and $6 less than that for a child. How much would it cost for my three younger brothers, Mum, Dad and I, to go on the train together?

3. a My 6 darts hit this target. My score was 30. What could my 6 scores have been?

   b If my darts only landed on a white circle, what could my 6 scores have been if my total was 40?

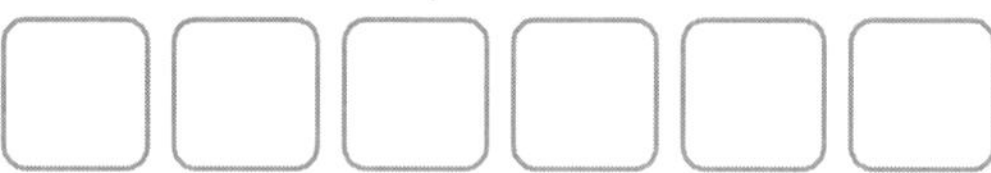

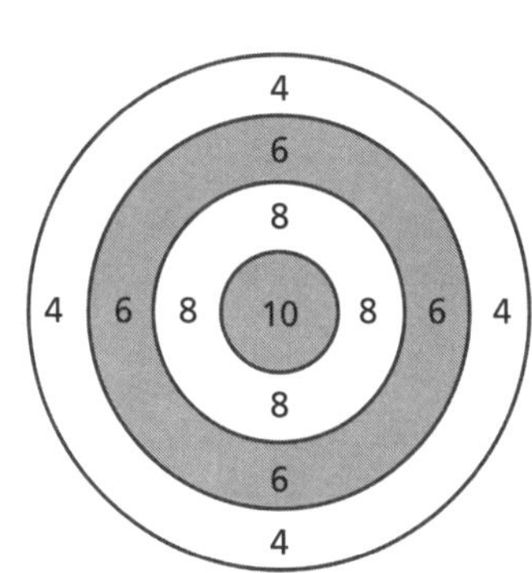

4. These 2D shapes join on their sides to make one large shape with 12 sides.
   Join on more of these shapes to make one large shape that has 16 sides.

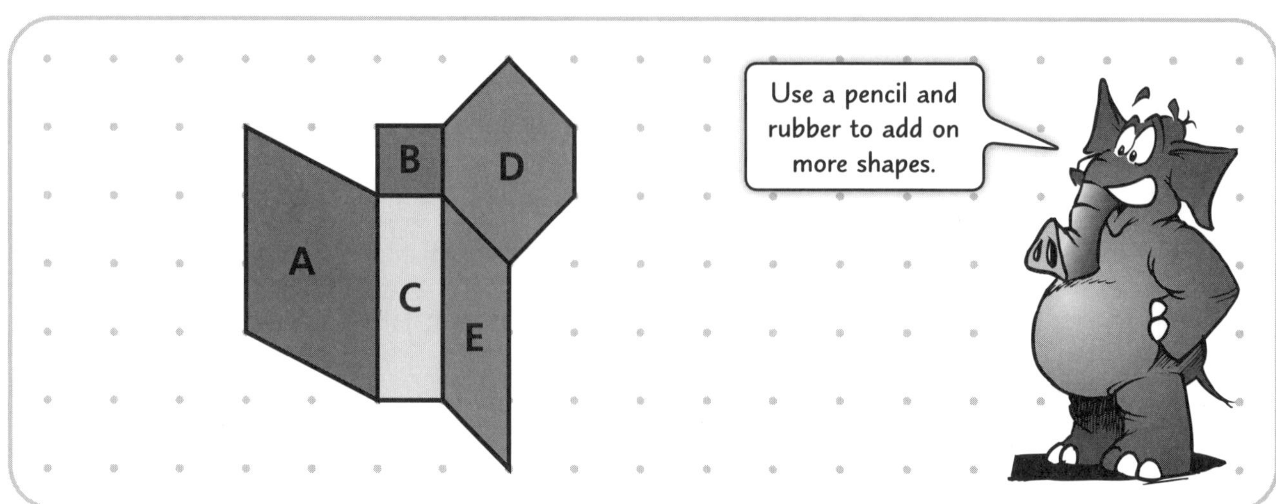

Answers can be found at the end of the Teacher Notes for 35D.

 ISBN 9780655708766